20:20 Project Management

20:20 Project Management

How to deliver on time, on budget and on spec

Tony Marks

KoganPage

LONDON PHILADELPHIA NEW DELHI

First published in Great Britain and the United States in 2012 by Kogan Page Limited

120 Pentonville Road	1518 Walnut Street, Suite 1100	4737/23 Ansari Road
London N1 9JN	Philadelphia PA 19102	Daryaganj
United Kingdom	USA	New Delhi 110002
www.koganpage.com		India

© Tony Marks, 2012

ISBN   978 0 7494 6608 4
E-ISBN 978 0 7494 6609 1

British Library Cataloguing-in-Publication Data

A CIP record for this book is available from the British Library.

Library of Congress Cataloging-in-Publication Data

Marks, Tony.
  20:20 project management : how to deliver on time, on budget and on spec / Tony Marks.
    p. cm.
  Includes index.
  ISBN 978-0-7494-6608-4 – ISBN 978-0-7494-6609-1   1. Project management.   I. Title.
II. Title: Twenty twenty project management.
  HD69.P75M3675 2012
  658.4'04–dc23

                                                                              2012020097

Typeset by Graphicraft Limited, Hong Kong
Print production managed by Jellyfish
Printed and bound by CPI Group (UK) Ltd, Croydon, CR0 4YY

CONTENTS

Acknowledgements   ix
Using this book   x
About the author   xi

Introduction   1

01   Starting your project   29

Introduction   29
The project objectives   29
The business case   32
The project management plan (PMP)   38
The purpose of the project management plan   38
The project management plan (example)   38
Project success and benefits management   46
Benefits vs project success   47
Key performance indicators (KPIs)   53
Avoiding project failure   53
Twenty actions to help ensure project success   56
Project manager's weekly checklist   60
Ten tips for guaranteed failure   62
Financial evaluation in projects   63
Things to consider   68
Conclusion   69
Case study: Starting projects at Subsea 7   70

02   Defining your project   77

Introduction   77
The product breakdown structure (PBS)   78
The work breakdown structure (WBS)   78
The organizational breakdown structure (OBS)   80
The cost breakdown structure (CBS)   80
The responsibility assignment matrix (RAM)   81
Assigning responsibilities to tasks   82
Steps in developing a breakdown structure   82
Common-sense guidelines   83
Requirements management   85
Why do we need requirements management?   86

Project programme planning 87
When to use programmes 87
How to set them up 88
Managing programmes 89
Consolidations 89
Things to consider when defining your project 90
Conclusion 93
Case study: Halliburton and project definition 94

03 Planning your project 97

Introduction 97
Scope management 99
Analysing the network 104
Dependencies 104
Estimating 104
The forward pass 105
Float 108
Critical path 110
Project resources 112
Managing the schedule 116
Things to consider when planning 121
Conclusion 123
Case study: Planning the AMEC way 124

04 Executing your project 129

Introduction 129
Set the measure 129
Cost reporting 130
Information for updating project progress 134
What are the benefits? 138
Change control 150
Project close-out and handover 153
Things to consider when executing a project 155
Conclusion 157
Case study: WGPSN project management framework 157

05 Risk and your project 163

Introduction 163
Risk cultures 164
Stage 1: risk identification 172
Stage 2: risk impact analysis 178
Stage 3: probability analysis 180

Stage 4: risk exposure   181
Stage 5: mitigation strategy   185
Stage 6: risk monitoring and review   187
Things to consider with risk and your project   202
Conclusion   203
Case study: Managing risk the Mott MacDonald way   203

06   Estimating your project   211

Introduction   211
The importance of estimating   211
Estimating techniques   212
Introduction to estimating   212
The importance and practical difficulties of estimating   213
The estimating funnel   213
Classes of estimate   214
Estimating techniques   215
Uncertainty and risk   222
Summary of the basic rules for estimating   223
Common mistakes   224
Things to consider when estimating   224
Conclusion   225
Case study: Estimating the AMEC way   226

07   Project leadership   233

Introduction   233
Leadership vs management   234
Leading in a project environment   235
Visionary   246
Articulation of the vision   247
Preparing the vision   247
Tools and approaches   248
Motivation   248
Conflict management   252
Conflict resolution summary   258
Case study: Leadership at Southwest Airlines   259

08   Teams and your project   261

Introduction   261
Team requirements   262
Team development   271
Developing the project team   274
Team chemistry   276

Things to consider   283
Conclusion   285
Case study: W L Gore   285
Team health check   286

Glossary of terms   289
Index   303

ACKNOWLEDGEMENTS

This book is the culmination of nearly 30 years of project management in practice, with 12 of those years consulting and teaching in some of the world's leading organizations. Inevitably this means that much of the theory and experience contained in this book have come from learning from other people's successes and failures. Much has also been drawn from the professional bodies that have helped collate best practice in project management. These people are too numerous to mention but there are a number of people who have made specific and valued contributions to this book.

First and foremost I would like to thank Graham Chapman, with whom I co-founded 20|20 Business Group eight years ago. A lifelong friend and colleague, Graham has contributed most towards the content of this book. I know of no better project management facilitator and Graham has travelled the world teaching best practice to a wide range of organizations, especially in the energy sector. His knowledge of project management, and especially project teams and leadership, has been invaluable in helping with this book. Amongst my colleagues at 20|20, Dave Gilbert, Jim Littlefair and Pete Walters have helped to edit the text, and Tomas Havlik has painstakingly helped ready the manuscripts for publication.

The case studies are an invaluable part of this book, providing the reader with examples of the practical application of theory, tools and techniques. I would like to thank Iain Sutherland of Talisman Energy (Canada), Craig MacFarlane from Subsea 7 (Norway), Bob Davidson from Halliburton (UK and USA), Shane Forth and Neil Atkinson from AMEC (UK), Alan Baxter and Orlando Ovalles from Wood Group PSN (Global), Dave Phillips and Doug Wilson from Mott MacDonald (Global) for their significant contributions. All of these contributors have busy project roles and have taken time out to help with this book.

I would also like to thank Mick Cope of Wizoz for encouraging me for too many years to write this book and Liz Gooster, editor-at-large with Kogan Page for encouraging me to stick to my project plan! I delivered on spec, on budget and – nearly – on time. But those are the compromises of project management in the real world.

Finally I would like to thank my wife, Alison, who has supported me throughout my life in project management.

USING THIS BOOK

This book is organized for the reader's convenience to follow a project life cycle. This is for two purposes:

- Whilst the reader may read the book from cover to cover before embarking on a project initially, it is envisaged that each chapter can then be read and absorbed in more detail before a particular phase of the project life cycle commences.
- The author recognizes that some project managers may have taken over a project part of the way through the project life cycle. It is therefore useful to be able, for reference, to go directly to the relevant chapter(s).

The book is also organized into two main sections:

- Chapters that follow the project life cycle (Starting your project, Defining your project, Planning your project, Executing your project).
- Chapters that are relevant or useful throughout the project life cycle (Risk and your project, Estimating your project, Project leadership, Teams and your project, and the Glossary of terms).

Each chapter is also divided into subsections as follows:

- Introduction;
- Best practice;
- Things to consider;
- Conclusion;
- Case study.

Finally, there is a continuously updated online resource available at **www.2020projectmanagement.com** to provide further case studies, white papers, project management templates, discussion forums, useful links and details of useful supporting services.

ABOUT THE AUTHOR

Tony Marks is the Chief Executive of 20:20 Business Insight, the UK's largest specialist Project Management Training and Consultancy company, with offices in Scotland, England, the United States and the Czech Republic and partners in Scandinavia, West Africa and the Middle East. He has 30 years' experience in project management – delivering high value projects, consulting and teaching in a wide range of sectors including utilities, nuclear, oil and gas, engineering, construction, IT and telecoms.

Tony is accredited by all three professional bodies including The Project Management Institute (PMI)'s 'Project Management Professional' credential, The Association for Project Management (APM)'s 'APM Professional', and The APM Group's 'Prince 2 Practitioner'. He is also a Fellow of The Association for Project Management (The UK body of an international association covering 55 countries), a Fellow of The Chartered Management Institute, a Fellow of The Institute for Leadership Management, and a member of The Project Management Institute. Tony also holds an MBA majoring in Project Management Systems and Administration.

Tony is a lecturer and examiner for The University of Aberdeen on their MSc in Project Management course. He has written the *Project Management Handbook* for NHS Capital Projects and edited Project Management Handbooks for a number of commercial companies. He lives in Scotland but travels extensively.

Introduction

> *Operations keeps the lights on, strategy provides a light at the end of the tunnel, but project management is the train engine that moves the organization forward.* JOY GUMZ

This chapter sets the scene regarding some of the fundamentals to a successful project, some of which will be discussed in greater detail in later chapters.

The following sections of this chapter discuss the basics of projects, project management and the project management process.

Projects come in many guises from major engineering projects such as shipbuilding, aerospace and oil and gas production to small changes to existing company processes. However wide-ranging in size, projects will all have the same common attributes.

Project management and projects are defined by the UK's Association for Project Management as:

> the process by which projects are defined, planned, monitored, controlled and delivered such that the agreed benefits are realized. Projects are unique transient endeavours undertaken to achieve a desired outcome. Projects bring about change and project management is recognized as the most efficient way of managing such change.

Projects almost always have the following characteristics:

1 clear objective(s);
2 constraints of cost, quality and time;
3 a fixed timescale;
4 a fixed budget;
5 a team of people;
6 little practice or rehearsal;
7 change and uncertainty;
8 uniqueness.

Even if similar projects have been conducted several times they will still follow the characteristics defined above and the uniqueness of a project may come from one of the following:

1 a new team of people;

2 a new customer/client;

3 a different budget;

4 new technology;

5 a different timescale;

6 a different objective;

7 a different location;

8 different working conditions.

What is the purpose of a project?

The purpose of a project is to produce a unique product or service that will deliver some benefit or purpose.

Projects can be categorized into two main areas: those that serve a business purpose and those that serve a social purpose. The main aim of a business project would be to deliver a benefit in terms of increased profitability, efficiency or turnover. The aim of a social project would be to deliver a benefit in terms of relaxation or enjoyment but often with the added benefit of a financial reward.

The following are examples of some typical projects.

TABLE 0.1 Project types

Business projects	Social projects
• Marketing strategy project • Conduct training programme • Introduction of a new range of products • Improvement programme to increase quality of a product or service	• House improvements • New car • Organizing a social function • Further education

Project management

Project management can be defined in several different ways but is probably best summed up as the 'process by which a project is brought to a successful conclusion'. Or as the 'discipline of managing projects successfully'.

Another common definition says that project management is:

to foresee as many dangers as possible, and to plan, organize and control activities in such a way that risks are avoided or countered leading to a final result that satisfies the requirements of the project sponsor without using more money and resources than those which were included in the budget.

A project is considered successful when it meets the criteria stated at its outset.

Using a structured methodology for project management

In an environment where there are no standardized procedures for project management, projects are undertaken in an unpredictable manner, with potentially different techniques and ways of working – all leading to inefficiencies within an organization. Project management methods are employed in order to incorporate best practice procedures, providing a consistent, reusable set of guidelines for those people involved in working on projects.

Project management processes can be developed in house for larger organizations, or they can be adopted through organizations such as the International Project Management Association (IPMA) – which has national associations in most countries, the Project Management Institute (PMI) which has chapters in most countries, or open methods such as PRINCE2, which is owned and maintained by the Cabinet Office in the UK for use in both the private and public sector.

The benefits of using a standard method are:

- Provision of a consistent approach to all projects within an organization.
- A scalable approach that can be used on both large and small projects.
- It increases the chances of successfully achieving objectives.
- It develops an environment to allow continuous development in project management processes.
- It develops common understanding of the various project roles and responsibilities (including stakeholders).

Project management methods may be based around a project life cycle (see later section) and will include:

- process descriptions for each phase of the cycle;
- inputs and outputs for each process;
- documentation guidelines and templates;
- guidelines covering the structure of the project organization, accountability, responsibility and communications;
- role definitions for all those involved in a project;
- a set of procedures to be used throughout the life cycle.

Procedures will set out the steps to be followed in order to perform project management processes. Organizations new to project management may only have a small number of procedures; the number is likely to grow as their experience and expertise grow. Development of these procedures can fall under the remit of a Project Management Office (PMO).

Which methodology?

Earlier in this chapter we identified three different professional bodies for project management – the IPMA, the PMI and the Cabinet Office's PRINCE2 methodology. Some organizations adopt a set standard globally. Some adopt the most popular for their region (typically IPMA in Europe and PMI outside Europe) and some adopt the most popular for their sector (PRINCE2 is prevalent in government, finance and information technology sectors). For this reason you will find no advice in this book on the correct methodology to follow. Instead, you will find the author's selection of the most useful tools and techniques and a project life cycle around which they can be based. This does not detract from the author's acceptance that these methodologies have much to offer. However, they need to be assessed against the specific needs of the organization and the project. No methodology is perfect, each having strengths and weaknesses and providing a well-defined route map for successful project management.

The International Project Management Association

The International Project Management Association (IPMA) is based in Switzerland and can be found at **www.ipma.ch**. As a body it consists of around 50 (and growing) national associations. Each of these national associations maintains a national competency baseline (NCB) which is based on and aligned to the IPMA's international competency baseline (ICB) to ensure that competency requirements of project managers across the association are broadly common. Some of the larger national associations include the UK's

Association for Project Management (APM), France's AFITEP, Norway's NAPM and, whilst the IPMA is primarily a Europe-centric organization, national associations exist as far afield as Australia and the United States. The IPMA membership is maintained through its national associations and each has an accreditation framework aligned to a common IPMA standard – the benchmark qualifications being IPMA Levels D, B, C & A.

The IPMA international competence baseline (ICB) underpins a 'syllabus' based on a high-level 'body of knowledge' for project managers. It tends to state the skills and behaviours required whilst being less specific and process based than the other methodologies. This suits many organizations which then build on this framework their own specific detail.

The Project Management Institute

The Project Management Institute (PMI) has several hundred thousand individual members who are linked to their national 'chapters' but the organization is much more centralized than the IPMA. The PMI has many hundreds of chapters which provide an opportunity to meet locally.

The PMI's 'Body of Knowledge' is much more detailed than the IPMA ICB and is built around a series of process groups and knowledge areas. This process-based approach is more in depth and prescriptive and suits those that are seeking a clear step-by-step and detailed approach.

The PMI offers a wide range of resources via its website at **www.pmi.org** and its benchmark qualification of Project Management Professional (PMP) is recognized globally. Whilst the PMP qualification is based on a similar knowledge level as the IPMA's Level D qualification, it does require candidates to register a minimum numbers of hours of actual experience at each stage of a project life cycle.

PRINCE2

PRINCE2 is probably the most prescriptive of all the internationally recognized methodologies. Originating from a methodology for the information technology sector called PROMPT, PRINCE (and then PRINCE2) has been a favourite governmental standard for many years – originating in the United Kingdom but now used internationally where it has followed its early sectors of government, public sector, finance and information technology. PRINCE2 is a complete methodology based on detailed processes and templates.

PRINCE2 has a reputation for being highly prescriptive and cumbersome. However, it is much maligned as it does provide guidance for mandatory and optional elements. The problem tends to come from a dogmatic implementation of the full methodology by some organizations.

Usefully, much of the PRINCE2 resource base is available in the public domain via websites such as **http://www.cabinetoffice.gov.uk/** and the complete methodology is available at a low cost.

The benchmark qualifications are the PRINCE2 Foundation and PRINCE2 Practitioner knowledge-based qualifications.

Which methodology?

The truth is that it depends. Over the years the three main internationally recognized methodologies have become much more aligned and the main differences are now terminology based or how broad or prescriptive a methodology is required as a starting point. But a starting point they should be.

Each offers a benchmark for assessing knowledge, but need to be considered against the type and scale of projects being managed within an organization.

Compromises of cost, time and quality

The greatest challenge of project management is the integration and control of the three principal interrelated components of each single project.

FIGURE 0.1 The triangle of compromises

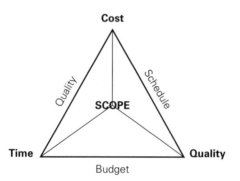

The cost, time, quality triangle implies a tension between the three components such that if any one of the components was to be changed, then it would have an impact on one, or both, of the others. Thus in order to meet the cost objective there may need to be a sacrifice of time or quality. Or in order to meet a quality constraint a sacrifice of either time or cost may be needed. Scope sits in the centre of the triangle as any changes to time, cost and quality will have an impact on the scope and any changes to the scope will have an impact on the time, cost and quality of the project.

It can also be seen in the above triangle if the scope is changed in any way it could have an effect on one or more of the three main drivers.

However, it is important to add that safety is paramount in all projects and, unlike time, cost and quality should not be compromised.

The project context

To ensure a successful project it is important to understand and appreciate the project context. This is sometimes referred to as the project environment and refers to the influences that will affect the project both internally and externally. This in turn will dictate how a project will be managed. Failure to take into account the environment within which the project is undertaken will mean that the scope of the project will not be properly defined.

The main influences can be highlighted and identified using the PESTLE model.

Political

What political influences are impacting on the organization's ability to deliver? What is the political climate? What political stakeholders need to be considered? What influences are there politically within the project organization, the client and subcontractors? Are there regulatory bodies that will be involved or asserting an influence on the project?

Environmental

Are there any environmental issues that will influence the project's success, eg where will the project be carried out, offshore, onshore, will there be a potential of environmental damage or even enhancement of delivery or an environmental benefit?

Social

In terms of cultural or family values. The project may bring a benefit to the local community in terms of an enhancement to their environment. It could also be a negative, whereby jobs are lost due to the running of the project.

Technological

Does the equipment we require to carry out the project exist? Are there sufficient communications or IT to carry out the project?

Legislation

What legal status will the project operate under, will it be subjected to differing legal entities, is it cross cultural? What legal system will the contractual terms be drawn up in and how will that influence the project operation? Are there any specific legal drivers that will need to be adhered to, eg HSE, EC directives, etc?

Economic

This will include exchange rates, employment, inflation, licences, energy savings and reductions, safety issues, ie accidents/damage, etc, effects on health and welfare, improved productivity, positive changes in land use and land values, etc, effects on pollution and waste.

This model is sometimes also known as STEEPLE: sociological, technological, economic, ethical, political, legal, environmental.

By understanding the project context the project can be managed in the most appropriate way and the influences considered and addressed, eg a project that is very political and environmentally influenced and visible would need a different management approach than a project that was being run internally by an organization with few external influences.

The project life cycle (PLC)

Every project has certain phases of development. A clear understanding of these phases permits managers and executives to control the project more efficiently.

By definition, a project has a beginning and an end and passes through several phases of development known as life cycle phases. These phases are varied depending on the industry involved but all follow the same basic steps. The five main phases of the project life cycle we will be using in this book are defined below.

FIGURE 0.2   A generic project life cycle

TABLE 0.2   Generic life cycle definitions

Start-up	This phase is where the project objectives are defined and the conceptual aspects of the project agreed. This may be the phase where a problem is identified and potential solutions suggested.
Definition	Once the project objectives are clearly defined then the appraisal of the solutions is conducted in terms of risks, financial commitment and benefits. The scope of work is now defined in detail.
Planning	The planning phase is where the project is broken down into manageable areas of work and planned in terms of time, cost and resources. This is a continuous process and will extend throughout the execution phase of the project.
Execution	The fourth phase of the project life cycle is the execution phase, where the work is implemented, controlled and monitored.
Close-out	The final phase of the project life cycle is close-out and demobilization, where resources are reassigned, the project is handed over and the post-project review is carried out.

Other project life cycles

It is important to realize that the project life cycle for each project may differ, in both the number of phases it may have and the detail within each of these phases.

The project life cycle below is a typical life cycle used in the development and marketing of a new pharmaceutical drug.

FIGURE 0.3   Pharmaceuticals life cycle

Discovery > Scoping > Business Case > Development > Testing and Validation > Launch

Typically the duration of a project like this will between seven and 25 years with the testing and validation phase alone taking several years depending on how many clinical trials are conducted. Typical costs are $800 million to $1 billion.

The project life cycle below could represent the phases for the implementation of a new business process.

FIGURE 0.4   New business process life cycle

This project may only take several months but would still follow a structured life cycle.

It is important to ensure the project life cycle used on your project is appropriate to the work to be carried out and split into distinct and manageable phases.

Project management processes

As discussed, all projects will have distinct phases within their project life cycle. The project manager will need to apply appropriate project management processes as the project progresses throughout its life cycle to ensure project success.

The Project Management Institute (PMI) recommend five main project management processes areas or groups organized as shown here.

FIGURE 0.5   PMI process groups

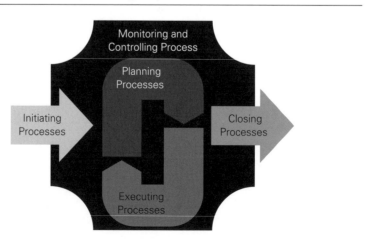

Each of the five process groups interacts and overlaps (ie planning continues alongside execution processes and activities). Equally, close-out activities and processes can commence while execution processes and activities are being carried out.

The diagram overleaf visually depicts the process overlap and the interaction and amount of overlap are indicated in the diagram below.

FIGURE 0.6   PMI process overlaps

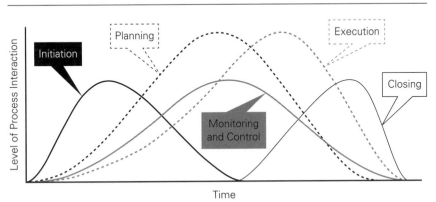

The above diagram indicates substantial overlap amounts throughout project management activities, highlighting the importance of recognizing project life cycle (distinct delivery phases) and project management process (interactive and overlapping project management process) differences.

Figure 0.7 on the following page shows how the relationship between the project management processes and the project life cycle exists.

The project management processes can be applied to each phase of the project ensuring each phase is initiated, planned, executed, monitored and controlled and closed out.

The value of project management

Project management will allow you to break the project down into separate phases, ensuring that each phase is given appropriate time and consideration. A common failing within projects is the desire to get to the execution phase as quickly as possible. By applying project management processes to each phase you increase the chance of your project succeeding, as any changes or adjustments to the project will be made at the outset, where it is easier and more cost effective to make changes.

Figure 0.8 compares the potential to add value – or influence the project – against the varying cost of change – against a timeline (the project life cycle). It is an important reminder that changes made earlier are far cheaper

FIGURE 0.7 PMI processes vs life cycle

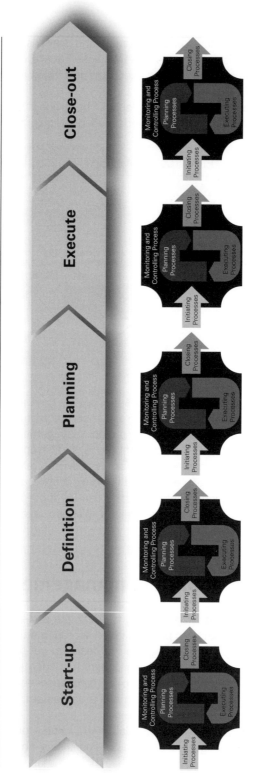

FIGURE 0.8 Value vs cost curves

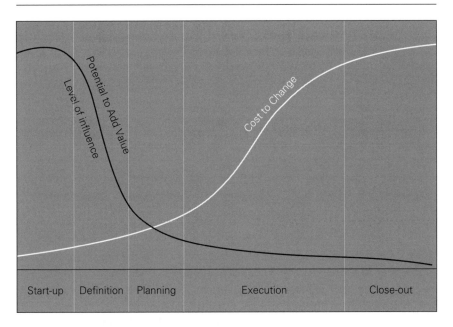

Start-up | Definition | Planning | Execution | Close-out

than changes made late. It also emphasizes that a project manager can best influence the chances of success in their project at the early stages, rather than later when the project plan is fixed.

It also serves to highlight where project management should be focused and that is in the early stages of the project. Although all areas are covered in this book, most of the tools and techniques focus on the early stages of the project.

Many organizations become very good at 'firefighting' project management problems yet this is not something they should be proud of – it tends instead to be a symptom that they place insufficient emphasis on the early stages of a project life cycle, as we will see in this book.

Gate procedure

The stage gate process/procedure incorporates best practice from a variety of sources and is a tried and tested method for delivering projects on time within budget and to the expected quality targets. It defines the way in which projects are managed and implemented and consists of a number of stages with 'gates' or hold points between each stage. If we use the life cycle we discussed previously we can see some of the typical gates that may be set up through the project life.

FIGURE 0.9   Typical stage gate activities

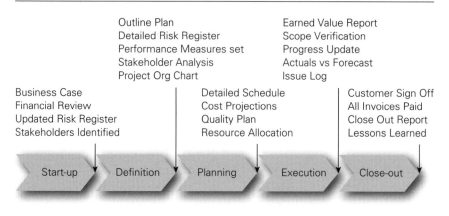

At each stage, approval is generally required from outside the project team before proceeding to the next stage. The process requires documentary evidence at each stage together with an indication of who is able to approve the project to enable it to proceed through the gate to the next stage.

The stage gate process is a generic process which can be applied to any size of project regardless of the industrial or commercial sector. However, the level of detail required on the documentary evidence will be governed by the nature, monetary value and complexity of the project.

Organizational structures

All organizations are structured differently due to the way that they operate and according to their culture. The structure of an organization will affect the way in which projects are managed and this will be determined by the types and differences of organizational structures such as:

- flat;
- tall;
- hierarchal;
- matrix;
- centralized and decentralized.

The key features of an organization

All organizations irrespective of whether they are in the industrial, commercial or public sector typically consist of the following features:

- *Objectives* – Describe the specific direction of the organization to enable them to establish, support and resource requirements to enable projects to be completed to clients' specifications and standards.
- *Rules and regulations* – Some of these may be written down such as the expected levels of behaviour for all of the employees of the organization (eg staff handbook), whilst others may not be written down but should be recognized (eg the relationship between the boss and their staff).
- *Patterns and structures* – All organizations have established procedures for undertaking the work which will be determined by the relevant organizational structure.
- *Posts and offices* – The people who have various responsibilities and tasks to perform in order to meet the objectives of the organization. These are most commonly depicted in an organizational chart.
- *Chain of command* – The organizational chart will also highlight the official chain of command (eg who is responsible to whom within the organizational structure).
- *Authority* – Within the chain of command, there are also varying levels of influence that are vested in the people who have been given the responsibility to occupy these positions within the organizational structure. The levels of authority and responsibility would normally be clearly defined in individual job descriptions.
- *Records* – All organizations need to have systematic and well organized records. In a project context there will be documentary evidence at all stages of the project life cycle.

The term 'organizational structure' refers to the way that it arranges people and jobs so that the work can be performed and its objectives can be met. When a work group or project team is small and face-to-face communication is frequent, a formal structure may not be necessary. However, in larger organizations or where there are a number of people engaged on a project, there will need to be clearly defined roles and responsibilities and an established process for the delegation of specific tasks.

In an organization of any size or complexity the role and responsibilities of its staff are typically defined by what they do, who they report to and for those with more authority and responsibility which staff reports to them. These relationships would be illustrated in an organizational chart. The most appropriate organizational structure will depend on many factors such as the range of business activities or projects it undertakes, the size of the organization in terms of number of staff and the geographical dispersion of the whole organization.

Types of organizational structure

The most common types of organizational structure have 'spans of control'. This refers to the number of staff that are directly responsible to one person. The number of people that one person can supervise needs to be carefully considered. The chain of command and the span of control create a pyramid shape of the organization's structure.

The extent of the chain and the nature of the span of control will determine whether the organization has a 'flat' or 'tall' structure. Where the spans of control are broader and there are fewer levels of authority, an organization is deemed to have a 'flat' structure, as outlined below.

Flat structure

FIGURE 0.10   A flat organizational structure

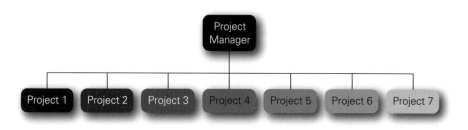

In contrast, where there are narrow spans of control and more layers of authority an organization is deemed to have a 'tall' structure, as shown below.

Tall structure

FIGURE 0.11   A tall organizational structure

There is no single ideal combination of chain of command and span of control for any particular organization. However, the fewer number of levels tends to improve the decision-making and communication processes, but limits the opportunities for promotion, whereas increasing the number of levels could increase the opportunities for promotion and may slow down the decision-making and communication processes, but offers a greater degree of control as decisions are passed up through the organizational structure.

Hierarchal structure

Throughout the 20th century hierarchy was the traditional method of developing an organization. Prior to the widespread use of information and communication technologies, hierarchal organizations were managed by detailed systems and procedures.

An example of a hierarchal organization structure is shown below.

FIGURE 0.12 A hierarchical organizational structure

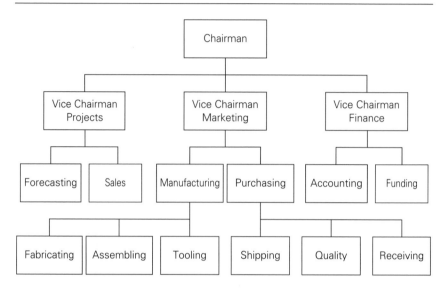

These types of organizations are tightly structured and there are manuals and systems that govern everything that is undertaken by the organization. A working example of this type of organization is that created by Henry Ford.

Matrix structures

In more recent times many organizations now have matrix structures, particularly where there is an emphasis on project work. A project team is responsible for managing a particular project and may consist of a number of individuals who have the responsibility for specific aspects of the project such as planning, scheduling, cost estimating, procurement, etc. It will be noted that these are elements of project control.

One advantage of a matrix structure is that it facilitates the use of specialized staff who may divide their time among a number of projects. In addition, maintaining functional departments promotes functional expertise, whilst working in project groups with expertise from other functions helps create the cross-fertilization of ideas and strategies.

However, the main disadvantage of the matrix structure is the dual reporting structure, as shown in the following example.

FIGURE 0.13 A matrix organizational structure

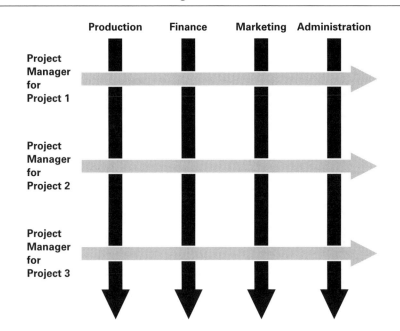

It can be seen from this example that the project manager brings together people from across the various functional areas with their relevant levels of expertise. Whilst the project manager has the responsibility for their own project, the people within the functional area will still have their own management reporting structure.

Centralized structures

In centralized structures, major responsibilities within sections or units remain at the centre of the organization, whereas in decentralized structures many specific responsibilities are delegated away from the centre of the organization, as shown below.

FIGURE 0.14   A centralized organizational structure

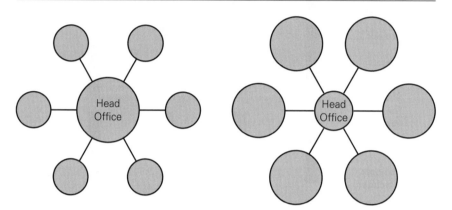

Centralized vs decentralized

In a project context organizations may choose to centralize certain key functions such as accounts and sales and decentralize day-to-day activities such as procurement and planning/scheduling.

Challenges of using project management

An organization will face numerous challenges when using project management.

The various challenges will increase/decrease in severity dependent upon an organization's set-up. On one end of the spectrum is a functional organization, an organization that runs very few projects and is not ideally set up to deal with the specific rigours of project management. On the other end of the spectrum is the projectized organization which makes a living by doing projects. In the centre is the matrix organization which combines elements of both functional and projectized organizations.

TABLE 0.3 The challenges of Project Management

Time, cost and quality	The fundamental challenge faced by all organizations that wish to use project management is ensuring that their projects deliver the agreed objectives within time, cost and to the agreed quality. These factors must be balanced in relation to the overall scope of the project.
Resources	Projects rely on the effective employment of finite resources, whether these are people, equipment or facilities – in other words, anything required to complete a project activity – and these will cost money. The organization faces the challenge of ensuring that they make the most of these finite resources.
People	They are probably the most important resource on any project and the challenge that an organization has to meet when using project management relies on the efficient utilization of those people. This is another area where the severity of the challenge will depend upon the organization's attitude to projects (functional, matrix or projectized). It is, however, vital that the right people are used, that they receive the correct training and that they are clear on the objectives of the project.
Technical	Due to the unique nature of projects there will frequently be the need to employ new technology. The challenge will be dealing with this new technology: do we have the staff who can use it, will they need training, does the technology we require even exist or will we have to make it ourselves?
Legal	An organization will have to deal with law and legislation when embarking on a project. Project work frequently involves working abroad and always includes the use of contracts. The organization must therefore determine which legal system they will employ for their project, if they are working abroad. Depending on the nature of the organization's operations there will be certain industry-specific legislation that must be followed.
Environment	A project does not exist in a vacuum; in order to deliver successful projects an organization must be aware of those factors (both internal and external) that will have an impact on the project.

Benefits of using project management

By applying project management to your project you will be able to utilize project management processes which will allow you to manage the attendant uncertainty that a unique endeavour will bring.

Project management will offer a clear understanding of what needs to be done to deliver the change that the project will bring about. This will include the project's success criteria as set out in the project management plan; also through the use of a product breakdown structure (PBS) all of the project products (deliverables) will be identified. From this a work breakdown structure (WBS) can be created that details all of the work that will be required on the project to complete the deliverables.

Through project management you can apply a structured methodology which can then be applied to projects across an organization. Using a repeatable structure will ensure that staff involved in your organization's projects will have a clear understanding of the roles and responsibilities involved, thus increasing the chances of project success.

Project management allows you to put in place monitoring processes which can be used throughout the project. These monitoring processes will let you know how your project is progressing, whether you are overspending or have fallen behind on schedule, whether the quality of your deliverables are failing to meet the standards set in your quality plan. Again when you think about the unique nature of projects it is vital that you have a process in place that permits you to see at any point in the project if things are going as planned, and if they are not, giving you the ability to make corrections.

Things to consider

Don't jump the gun

It is all too tempting to be focused on 'making things happen' and 'getting into delivery mode' but the truth is that poor preparation leads to poor performance. Planning the start-up, definition and planning phases requires as much focus as the execution phase. Those that spend sufficient time in the early phases will reap the benefits during project execution. The 'Add value' and 'Cost of change' curves on the project life cycle diagram illustrate this perfectly.

Use a methodology and life cycle

Whether the IPMA, PMI, PRINCE2 or a home-grown methodology is selected, the important thing is to have one and to follow it methodically within the organization. Following best practice and using a consistent terminology, tools and techniques are the key to project success.

Remember to separate the interactive aspects of project management processes used from that of the distinct phases of the project life cycle.

Use the most appropriate organizational structure

This chapter describes a number of different organizational structures. Using the right one can mean the difference between success and failure. Changing an organizational structure can be difficult, but managing a project where you do not have control of the necessary resources can be setting yourself up for failure.

The importance of project governance

Most of this chapter discusses governance issues – from organizational roles and responsibilities through to stage gates for control. The case studies section of this book gives a good example of project management governance in practice.

Conclusion

This chapter has sought to set the scene for the management of your project. The next chapters take the reader through each stage of a project life cycle – offering guidance, case studies and important considerations.

This book is designed as a reference tool as well as an approach to successful project management. Please feel free to use the elements that help – every piece of advice heeded might save the project ... or the project manager!

In the next chapter we will start to use a basic project as a simulation where the application of the theories discussed can be seen to be used and applied.

CASE STUDY Introducing project governance at Talisman Energy

About Talisman

Talisman Energy is a global, diversified upstream oil and gas company, headquartered in Canada.

Talisman Energy generate long-term shareholder value by delivering oil and gas projects with world-class execution.

To support this goal, they have established the project delivery system (PDS). PDS provides a consistent, disciplined process to project development, ensuring we do the right projects and in the right manner.

This process facilitates the structured development of business opportunities from discovery well through to 'first oil'. PDS is designed to provide:

- a common language and process to guide project development;

- integrated, multidisciplinary teamwork to deal with today's complex projects;

- a common understanding of minimum expectations and best practices;

- a standardized governance model for project preparation and approvals.

Together these characteristics help to improve business delivery. PDS provides a decision-making process that emphasizes both doing the right project and doing projects right to maximize value for the company. It ensures we make effective use of different disciplines. It reinforces good planning and forecasting, as well as a realistic assessment of risks. It eliminates surprises and increases project predictability.

Talisman's Project Delivery System (PDS) has three core elements:

- *Stage gate process*: PDS is based on a stage gate process of phased project development and commitments.

- *People to deliver PDS*: Successful project development depends on our ability to harness the talents and skills of many people in our organization.

- *Governance*: PDS provides a comprehensive governance framework so that the right oversight is provided throughout the project life cycle.

FIGURE 0.15   Talisman PDS elements

PDS involves a phased project development process supported by a Development Team and governance structure. The three elements of PDS work together so that we can carry out the right projects in the right way, maximizing value for Talisman.

When do we use PDS?

PDS defines how to carry out projects at Talisman and is the required approach for planning and executing our major capital projects. All Talisman-operated projects involving more than US$50 million (gross) are required to comply with the PDS Global Standard. These are large projects where risk exposure can be significant. In addition, all non-operated projects greater than US$100 million (net to Talisman) should follow a process consistent with PDS.

The stage gate process

PDS is based on a five-stage gate system of phased project development. At the end of each stage, staff are required to answer key questions about a project's development:

- *Appraise* (Is there a technically and commercially viable business case?)

- *Select* (Have we selected the best alternative?)

- *Define* (Is the project sufficiently defined for sanction?)

- *Execute* (Is the project ready for operation?)

- *Operate* (Does the operating asset meet original sanction objectives?)

Why implement PDS?

- *Project teams* get clear expectations on what to do and what not to do, templates and guidelines to help them with project delivery, a central point of reference for guidance.

- *Management* gets consistent level of detail, consistent information presentation, consistent quality, more efficient decision making, and ability to intervene when required. A standardized approach to delivering projects.

- *Talisman* gets improved project delivery and predictability, which lead to improved results.

The PDS process

The Project Development team produce the initial PDS road map. The road map provides a simple, visual summary of the work to be performed in each stage of the project, from initiation through start-up and handover to Operations. It highlights the key elements of the stage gate process from project initiation through start-up and handover to Operations. (This is reviewed and updated during each stage gate.)

FIGURE 0.16 Talisman PDS process

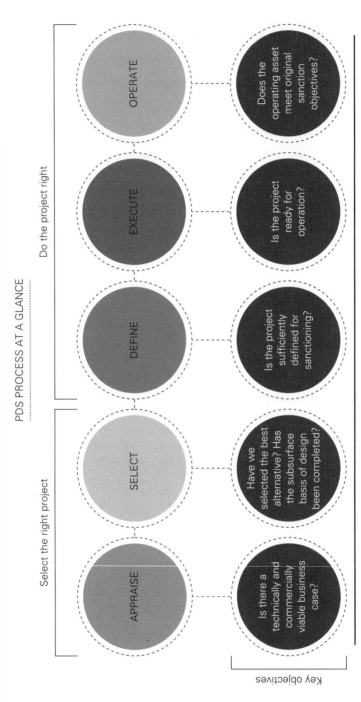

PDS PROCESS AT A GLANCE

Select the right project

Do the project right

APPRAISE — SELECT — DEFINE — EXECUTE — OPERATE

Is there a technically and commercially viable business case?

Have we selected the best alternative? Has the subsurface basis of design been completed?

Is the project sufficiently defined for sanctioning?

Is the project ready for operation?

Does the operating asset meet original sanction objectives?

Key objectives

The stage gate process is a step-by-step process to evaluate and develop business opportunities. In Appraise and Select, our time and efforts are focused on selecting the right project that provides the best overall benefit to Talisman. In Define, Execute and Operate, we focus on doing the project right, steadily increasing our investments in dollars and resources in project development.

FIGURE 0.17 Talisman processes vs life cycle

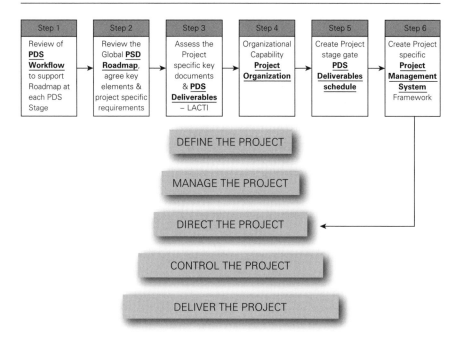

Step 1	Step 2	Step 3	Step 4	Step 5	Step 6
Review of **PDS Workflow** to support Roadmap at each PDS Stage	Review the Global **PSD Roadmap**, agree key elements & project specific requirements	Assess the Project specific key documents & **PDS Deliverables** – LACTI	Organizational Capability **Project Organization**	Create Project stage gate **PDS Deliverables** schedule	Create Project specific **Project Management System** Framework

DEFINE THE PROJECT

MANAGE THE PROJECT

DIRECT THE PROJECT

CONTROL THE PROJECT

DELIVER THE PROJECT

Project assurance reviews

During each PDS stage of the project, it is necessary to carry out independent assurance reviews, usually with peer groups, before proceeding to the gate review. These provide an independent look at project development activities and results, with emphasis on lessons learned, benchmarking and value-improving practices.

Depending on the PDS stage, separate assurance reviews are conducted for subsurface, drilling and completions, HSSE/OA, facilities, cost and schedule, and finance/commercial/marketing. This input helps ensure that project planning and development meet expected performance quality and best practices. It also provides information on which proper decisions can be based.

Before a project can move to the next stage, it must complete two reviews: a gate readiness review followed by a gate review. These reviews are critical in the PDS process for promoting quality recommendations and project decisions.

Performance management

Project dashboards: These provide regular progress reports to the gatekeeper and operating committee, measuring a project's performance against the work plan and budget set at the beginning of the stage. Executive dashboards are prepared quarterly and reviewed by executive management.

Lessons learned: Each development team is mandated to share lessons learned on the company's online project management network (PMN) throughout a project's life cycle.

This provides Talisman's project development teams with an opportunity to share learning and experience throughout the organization. At the beginning of each stage, the team consults the PMN to identify previous lessons learned applicable to their project. A register of lessons learned is prepared and each lesson is assigned for implementation.

Look-back reviews: These review performance management at a strategic level and are undertaken after a project's first year of operation. They provide a detailed appraisal of the project, comparing actual performance against the original sanction document. The results of these reviews are stored on the company's online PMN portal for use by other Talisman project development teams.

Starting your project

01

Introduction

In the business world, the rear-view mirror is always clearer than the windshield. **WARREN BUFFET**

As we have seen in the Introduction, the importance of clarifying the project objectives is of paramount importance. It is imperative during the earlier stages of the project life cycle to enable evaluation and appraisal of similar solutions in order to highlight the most appropriate solution for the project.

As part of the definition process, it is essential that the project success criteria are understood and that all the project stakeholders have been considered.

Success criteria are those things which are tangible and can be measured. Success criteria will commonly be linked to the cost, time and quality triangle. For example, your project could have a budget of £1 million; if your project is completed at or under this figure then it can be deemed a success. The same would apply to the project timescale. The project has duration of 12 months; if it is completed in 12 months then the project can be determined a success.

The project objectives

It is essential before any project appraisal is carried out that the project objectives are clearly defined and understood by all concerned parties. The following project areas must be clearly defined and agreed.

Clarifying the project needs

The initiation or start-up stage of a project is usually undertaken to address a problem or need. The evolution of needs from something quite vague to something tangible can be a challenge but is very important.

It is essential the project objectives are clearly defined and understood by all concerned parties at an early stage in the project life cycle.

Some typical outline objectives may be stated as the following:

- The product must carry out a certain function at a predefined rate.
- The product must operate in a specific environment.
- The product must have a working life of so many years.
- The product's budget must not exceed a certain cost.
- The project must meet certain specifications and standards.
- The product must achieve reliability requirements.
- The product must be energy efficient.
- The product must meet statuary health and safety regulations.
- The ergonomics must be consistent with the latest accepted practices.
- Ease of maintenance and repair must be incorporated into the design.
- A predetermined system redundancy level and interchangeable parts must be achieved.
- Operational requirements must achieve predetermined manpower levels and automation.
- The product must be manufactured with a predefined value of local content.
- The product must provide future expansion opportunities.
- The product must be operational by a predefined date.

Many of these items may be mutually exclusive, which means there will be a trade-off. For example, it is generally not possible to achieve both a minimum construction cost for a machine and minimum maintenance cost. Items of conflict require discussion and resolution during the project start-up stage, with all decisions recorded forming the design brief philosophy.

Defining project objectives

Basic project requirements need to be formalized at an early stage and converted into a clear and concise set of objectives.

The following areas must be clearly defined and agreed to with all the project stakeholders, minimizing the risk of uncertainty.

Objectives are very clear statements of output needs, eg 'To reduce rejects from production line A by 30 per cent by the end of the year'.

Effective objectives are more comprehensive and should be SMART (Table 1.1).

As stated above, it is essential the project objectives are achievable and realistic. The project will in turn fall within the successful measures shown in Figure 1.1.

TABLE 1.1   SMART definition

Specific:	Express objectives in terms of the specific results you believe need to be achieved, not in terms of the activities needed to achieve them; ie outputs not inputs. Avoid ambiguity.
Measurable:	Identify measures you believe will be used to judge project success. Make them as quantifiable and specific as possible, eg time / quantity / quality / cost. Use customer-related measures as well as internal measures.
Agreed / **A**chievable:	All relevant project stakeholders should have the opportunity to discuss and buy-in to the objective, rather than simply having it imposed on them. Ensure the objective is achievable taking into account the environment the project is operating within.
Realistic:	Take past performance into account when assessing how realistic the objective is. Ensure it is achievable, provided the resources available and the demands of other priorities.
Time bound:	If the overall time period is long, include an achievement date inclusive of interim milestones and review points. Agree an appropriate timeframe, relative to the complexity of the task.

FIGURE 1.1   The triangle of compromises

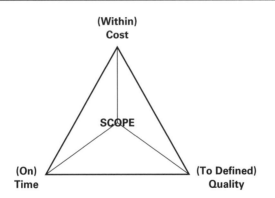

Project viability check

The client may also need assistance checking the viability of the proposal. Will the product be fit for purpose in both technical and commercial terms? Has the client kept away from wish lists and pipe dreams? These questions will form the basis of the client's feasibility study to which the contractor, as a practising specialist, can have a valuable input.

- Consider the effect location has on the project. Can the logistical requirements during the project and subsequent operation be met through existing roads and ports? Large infrastructure projects (power stations) often have to widen roads for their abnormal loads.
- Consider how the environment will affect the product, for example, a hotel in a hot country will require air conditioning for a five-star rating.
- Consider how the product will affect the environment – will the product deplete the ozone layer, or increase the greenhouse effect?
- Calculate the optimum size of the end product. Economies of size are not always a straight-line extrapolation but pass through plateaus of optimum production.
- Are the aesthetics and style commensurate with current fashions?
- Define the target market. Who will buy the product? These questions can be quantified by market research.
- Assess the market supply and demand curve. What is the demand for the product now and forecast demand in the future?
- Assess the competition from other players in the market. How will an increase in your rate of production affect market share?

At the outset of the project it may not be possible to answer all these questions. The unanswered questions will, however, indicate areas that need more research to gain a better understanding of the project and reduce risk.

The business case

Purpose of the business case

The purpose of the business case is to document the justification for the undertaking of a project usually based on the estimated cost of development and implementation against the risks and the anticipated business benefits and savings to be gained. The total business change must be considered, which may be much wider than just the project development costs.

The concept of the business case may exist under other names, eg project brief, project charter, high-level project plan. Irrespective of the name the purpose is to present justification for project start-up and initiation.

Why use business case analysis?

Business case development is a step that companies often use for project selection. It analyses how fulfilling the business case for the project will implement the corporate strategy and sustain the competitive advantage of the company.

The business case can further be developed with the addition of more details. You can convert the business case to action steps and major milestones in order to develop a plan that will guide your venture through the entire project life cycle, including that of the project outcome.

The business case is a key input to the project management plan (discussed later) and is usually owned and created by the project sponsor. Following project close or completion a post-project evaluation (PPE) will usually be held – usually some months after project completion – to measure the project's benefits against those set out in the business case.

The project life cycle

The life of a project generally starts as an initial idea, a customer enquiry or a company need. As discussed in the last chapter the project, if carried out, will progress through several stages until its completion. The business case should be a major part of the conception phase but equally follow the project through its life, being referenced and updated as is necessary. If at any time the project strays from the original business case justification or additional information is gained that threatens the success of the project then consideration should be given to abandoning the project or at least revisiting the business case.

We discussed project life cycles in detail in the last chapter.

FIGURE 1.2   A generic project life cycle

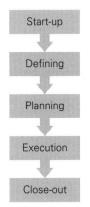

Business and project objectives

It is important to consider both the business benefits and the project benefits. As we have discussed in previous sections the definition of the project benefits is of paramount importance and should be looked at from not only the company's point of view but also from the view of all the stakeholders.

It is also extremely important that the project objectives and goals relate to the business goals, eg the project goal may be to introduce a new IT-based financial system. However, the business goal may be to allow an automated financial interface with customers and suppliers.

It is therefore very important that the goals and objectives are quantified and related back to the business case. In this example one project objective would be to ensure that all customers and suppliers are consulted regarding their systems and ability to interface, prior to the purchase and implementation of a new system.

Business case composition

Most organizations will have a standard approach to composing a business case. However, key elements usually include:

- reasons;
- options (a brief description of the different options considered and option recommended);
- benefits expected (expressed in measurable terms against today's situation);
- risks (summary of the key risks of the project);
- cost (extracted from the project plan);
- timescales (summary of the project plan);
- investment appraisal.

Project benefits

As part of the business case the expected project benefits (see above) should be clearly documented to provide measures for success. There may be obvious benefits such as employment, financial return, etc. However, some of the less obvious benefits should also be highlighted. These may include:

- increased reliability of a product;
- increased market share;
- company exposure and publicity;
- cost savings;
- reduced maintenance costs;

- environmental advantage;
- employee benefits;
- ease of use;
- shareholder satisfaction;
- less cost to produce;
- customer satisfaction.

Ownership of the business case

The business case is a key document for the project manager – it is both the justification for their activities and a benchmark by which the project benefits will be measured. The business case is also a key document of the project portfolio management process and, as such, is the document used by the organization's project investment committee. However, the primary owner of the business case is the project sponsor. The sponsor is responsible for ensuring the continued viability of the project and that the benefits defined in the business case are realized after project completion.

Project simulation

The following pages contain an example business case for the simulation project we will use through the subsequent chapters.

Business case – PM office relocation

Reason

Due to an increase in project delivery within your organization the project workforce has gradually increased. Initially the project office was able to cope with the increased project staff but more recently staff have been housed in several separate locations throughout the office complex. More recently temporary accommodation has been established in the yard of the main office block to accommodate the Penguin project team although it is now at capacity and some personnel have been situated within the functional teams.

This has caused several issues within the project and it is believed that project delivery has suffered as a consequence. Some of the key issues are listed below:

- poor communication between team members;
- disruption in functional teams due to project staff using their office space;
- poor motivation in some project staff due to the unpleasant working conditions;

- staff attrition rates increased since offices have become overcrowded;
- customers expressed concerns over disjointed teams;
- key information being lost due to teams being in different locations;
- lack of team integration;
- safety concerns with project staff crossing the yard.

Objectives

The main objective is to relocate all the company's project personnel to an already empty adjacent building which is up for lease. This will not only house the project teams but it is the intention to establish a project management office which will serve all projects. In addition a client's suite will also be established allowing project clients to work closely with the project team. The key deliverables are:

- Establish a long-term lease in the adjacent building.
- Relocate all project teams to open plan projects office.
- Ensure CAT 5 wiring is installed throughout the office suite.
- Purchase and install up-to-date PCs and peripherals.
- Set-up a project management office (PMO) to serve all projects.
- Establish an area for clients and project sponsors to work from.

Benefits

A number of benefits will be realized by the relocation of the project office, the main being more efficient delivery of all projects resulting in a greater profitability to the company and repeat business from key clients. Some of the additional benefits are listed below:

- better communications between teams resulting in more efficient project delivery;
- cost reductions in telephone communication and travelling;
- more efficient execution of project activities due to establishing a PMO;
- safety risks reduced by excluding yard visits;
- more motivated staff;
- attrition reduced;
- shared resources more easily accessed from within the projects;
- closer working relationship with project sponsors and clients;
- clients appreciate our commitment to running project more efficiently.

Risks

Some of the key risks associated with this project are listed below although a full risk analysis should be conducted in the initiation stage of the project.

- disruption to existing projects in the relocation;
- no buy-in from senior management;
- unable to secure the lease at a reasonable cost;
- unable to find staff to man the PMO;
- communications still suffering due to functions being in separate location;
- connectivity problems to company intranet due to new IT.

Financial appraisal

The approximate costs for relocation and operating for one year are as follows:

TABLE 1.2   Simulation project: costs

	Unit Price ($)	Total ($)
Lease of new office space (10-year lease)	100,000/mth	1,200,000
Estimate for utilities for 1 year	50,000/mth	600,000
IT equipment including peripherals (100 staff)	2000	200,000
Cat 5 wiring including installation		100,000
Furniture including partitions and desks		60,000
Project management time (days) @ $1000/day	50	50,000
Lost time due to move (hrs) @ $2000/hr	20	40,000
Subtotal		**2,250,000**
Contingency @ 8%		**180,000**
Total		**2,430,000**

The project management plan (PMP)

All the professional bodies offer guidelines on the level and type of information that should be defined in the early stages of the project in the form of a project management plan. Such a document should be used as a reference throughout the project to ensure that the management of the project is carried out consistently and in line with policy and procedures. The document also serves a very useful purpose in aiding decision making throughout the project as it provides a constant focus on how the project should be conducted.

The project management plan is also often referred to as a project execution plan, project charter or project initiation documentation.

The purpose of the project management plan

The purpose of such a document is to provide a comprehensive baseline of what has to be achieved by the project, how it is to be achieved, who will be involved, how it will be reported and measured and how information will be communicated. It should be used as a reference for any decision that is made on the project and for clarification of unclear areas.

The PMP should be prepared primarily by the project manager although interface with the project sponsor, client, stakeholders, users etc will be required. Often the business case will be used as the starting point for the PMP. Furthermore, the project manager should own the PMP and it should be developed with the project team.

The PMP should be available to all project members as it can provide essential project information and can be used to introduce project members to the project.

Although it is essential that the PMP is developed as part of the project initiation and definition, it should be a living document that evolves as the project progresses and is updated with the latest relevant information as required.

The following pages illustrate the type of information that may be relevant to include in such a document.

The project management plan (example)

Purpose

The purpose of the project management plan is to provide the project manager with the authority to apply organizational resources to the project's activities.

It will establish the project's purpose and demonstrate that the project team and the customer are committed to the project. It will focus on the customer and project expectations and will identify the project management principles that will be implemented to manage the project from start to finish.

In terms of the audience for the project management plan, it should be available to anyone who is involved in the project eg the customer, the project team and stakeholders in general. The project management plan is probably the main communication document for the project.

Suggested contents of the project management plan

Executive summary

This section should include a few paragraphs describing, at a high level, the key elements of the project that are detailed throughout the project plan.

Strategic/organizational alignment

It must be determined which organizational objectives will be supported by undertaking the project. It is often not enough for a project to simply deliver a profit. The company as a whole will have objectives that they wish to achieve and projects will be selected based on their ability to support the achievement of these objectives.

This section will also include the results of the project's stakeholder analysis; who are the people or organizations impacted by or interested in the project. It will also help to clearly identify who are the users, suppliers and the customers.

Project scope definition

In this section of the project management plan the purpose of the project will be stated along with the projects objectives. These objectives should be clear and it is important that they are SMART.

There should also be definition as to the scope of the project as well as the major deliverables. Not only will this include the products to be produced by the project (in scope) but also those products which are not part of the project scope (out of scope). This is important as it ensures that everyone involved in the project is clear as to their responsibilities.

The main structures that are utilized to determine the scope of the project are the product breakdown structure (PBS) and the work breakdown structure (WBS). The PBS will define the products that the project must deliver and the WBS will detail the work involved in delivering the products. These are described later in the 'Defining your project' chapter.

Be as clear as possible in defining the project deliverables. Clear and obtainable deliverables set the direction of the project and eliminate confusion about what work is performed and what products/services are delivered.

Quality specifications will also be included in this section, describing the product or service performance criteria from a customer perspective.

There will also be the inclusion of project assumptions, which will clarify grey areas in the project scope. Assumptions are made to fill knowledge gaps; they may later prove to be incorrect and can have a significant impact on the project. Only those assumptions that have a reasonable chance of occurring should be listed.

Feasibility assessment and contingency plans

This section should evaluate the economic, technical, operational, and organizational feasibility of the project; identify and assess project risks; and provide contingency plans to address high-impact risk factors.

Constraints

In this section there will be a requirement to list any known constraints imposed by the environment or by management. Typical constraints may include fixed budget; limited resources; imposed interim and/or end dates; predetermined software systems and packages; and other predetermined solutions.

Human resource requirements

Define the project team organization, roles and responsibility requirements. Provide a description of major participants including the various internal and external organizations.

Human resources include your team members, client, sponsor and end-users, and any on-site vendors with whom you may consult for direction in completing your project. Be sure to list contact information for and the kinds of information/expertise to be provided by each of these human resources.

TABLE 1.3   Human Resources requirements

Role	Responsibility	Time commitment	Duration	Source (internal, external)

This will include the need to identify training requirements and begin the development of the project training plan.

The training needs will include, technical training relevant to the project domain, team training, project management training and training in the procedures to be used on the project.

Material/equipment requirements

This section should define the space, hardware/software, and other resources needed to complete your project successfully. Space resources will include a designated team, meeting and work site, including any on-site office space your client may provide.

Hardware/software resources include those provided by you as a team and those provided by your client.

Make it crystal clear who will provide what. For example, does the client assume that you have the necessary software tools to complete your project, or will your client provide them? Other resources include any documentation of the existing system, vendor technical literature, systems manuals, etc that you will need to consult.

Project schedule and milestones

The contents of this section will define the milestones and activity schedule of the project, integrating three key elements: deliverables, due date or duration and critical dependencies (this section contains text and diagrams/charts).

In the text section, there will be a brief discussion of the project schedule (eg, time line for major phases) and a definition of the project milestones and baselines. Here you should also identify any critical task or resource dependencies that may significantly impact your ability to adhere to the planned schedule (eg, if the client must provide certain IT resources or access to end users in order for you to complete a task).

In your initial project Gantt chart (described later) you will identify and schedule – in detail! – all early project activities and resources related to analysis and design and – more broadly – later activities such as construction, testing, and installation. You will identify and schedule these later activities in detail as you develop a clearer sense of your project deliverables (ie after you have minutely defined system requirements).

Note: If your project is such that you can clearly define requirements at this time, then include these requirements in your project overview section and outline *all* activities in detail in your initial project Gantt chart. It is strongly encouraged that a CPM network model (what MS Project calls a PERT diagram) is created in addition to your Gantt chart so that task dependencies are made explicit.

Your Gantt chart should include at minimum the following information:

- activity ID and name;
- brief activity description (can be provided in a separate table in your project schedule section);

- start and completion dates;
- team member(s) assigned;
- resources required (can be provided in the separate table noted above; resources include those listed in the project Resource section above and should also indicate the approximate number of hours each team member will need to devote to this activity);
- schedule analysis.

Be sure to schedule team meetings and client reviews. That is, plan not only the activities required to deliver your *product* but also those activities required to manage your *process*.

Budget/cost estimate

Estimates are typically prepared for:

- the duration of the project;
- the human resource requirements in terms of numbers and types of skills required on the team;
- the cost of performing the work defined in the project plan;
- the material and equipment resources in terms of quantity and duration.

As the project traverses through the various project management phases, more information will be known and unpredictability will be reduced. Therefore, at the end of each phase and after each milestone, the cost–benefit analysis is updated and the information communicated as needed.

Good estimates require:

- time and focus;
- historical information or previous experience;
- multiple, consistent estimating methods;
- knowledge of the work.

Costs are divided into three types:

- *capital items*: associated with the procurement of assets that are capitalized such as hardware and software;
- *expense items*: associated with operating expenses, material, travel, training, supplies, books, copying, printing, etc;
- *labour*: associated with the total time team members work on a project based on an hourly rate for each skill set or the actual salary of the team members.

Risk management

This section will detail the process to be employed on the project in order to manage risk. It will also contain the outputs of the process in regards to the risk events identified by the use of the process. Please see the Risk chapter for further information on this process which will be followed at every stage of the project life cycle.

Project issues

This section will define the process to be used to manage issues identified on the project. It is worth noting that issues are things that have happened which are outside the authority of the project manager and need to be escalated in order to achieve a resolution.

Change management

This section will describe the change management process to be utilized on the project. The PMP acts as a baseline for the project and any changes made to base-lined items must go through formal change control.

Communication management

In this part of the PMP there will be a description of the system of communications and the project performance documentation that will be provided to the various stakeholders.

- Define procedures for interacting with your client. How will they contact you?
- Who on your team is the primary contact (ie team leader/manager)?
- How will you contact your client? How do you gain access to interview end users?
- How often will you provide written and/or oral reviews?
- Does your client have a specific format for project status reports?
- Who makes the go/no-go decisions, including changes in project scope or requirements?
- Does your client expect you to adhere to any particular development methodology or standards?
- How will the final review (user acceptance review) be conducted?
- Be sure to schedule well in advance a mid-point and a final review time and date with your sponsor and end-user representatives.

In summary, your purpose in this section is to outline the structure of your client interaction, whether by phone, e-mail, in person, or in formal reports. See sample communications plan below.

Sample communications management plan

The purpose of this document is to identify and manage the communications required to successfully complete the project.

TABLE 1.4 A communications management plan

ID	Title	Description / Content	Audience	Medium	Frequency
01	Milestone report	Major milestones	Project team Dept manager Key stakeholders Project sponsor	E-mail	Weekly
02	Project plan	Deliverable, dates	Project team	E-mail	Ad hoc – see 01
03	Meeting minutes	Decisions, action items	Project team	E-mail	As held
04	Brief status meeting	Progress reporting, issues, action items	Project team	Informal verbal	Weekly
05	Issues	Issues	Select members of project team, at times full team	Teleconference	Ad hoc – few hours' notice
06	Progress	Progress	Project team	Teleconference	Weekly
07	Customer correspondence	Any activity/question	Business development manager	E-mail/verbal	Ad hoc/weekly status

Related products and deliverables

In this section you will document known project dependencies with other groups within or outside of the organization to ensure the project is not exposed by other business processes.

Approvals

This section will be used to capture approval signatures from project stakeholders. The table below is an example of a simple approval form.

TABLE 1.5   Project agreement approval form

Project Agreement Approval Form		
Project Name: I have reviewed the information contained in the Project Plan dated _____ , and agree to the baseline commitments specified in it.		
_____ Name, Project Manager	_____ Signature	_____ Date
_____ Name, Project Sponsor	_____ Signature	_____ Date
_____ Name, Title	_____ Signature	_____ Date
_____ Name, Title	_____ Signature	_____ Date
_____ Name, Title	_____ Signature	_____ Date
_____ Name, Title	_____ Signature	_____ Date

Attachments

Included in this section will be pointers to pertinent documents such as the business case, notes and related documents; the team charter should also be included as a separate document along with the project plan. You would also include a project binder which will include all of the supporting materials to your project plan.

Project success and benefits management

Project management is not a new discipline. Indeed techniques such as critical path analysis have been applied to projects for decades; risk management is really part of human intuition; realizing that people in a team need to bond for success is not a new concept. Yet still projects fail – in some organizations, and even in some industries, with alarming frequency.

The IT industry, for example, seems to receive a particularly bad press when it comes to project failure. This may be an exaggeration of the state of that particular industry, but some of the statistics speak for themselves:

- A recent survey showed that 66 per cent of projects overran time and 55 per cent exceeded budget.
- A UK survey showed that 56 per cent of companies in the UK believed that runaway IT projects occurred frequently, and 62 per cent of these companies had experienced this within the last five years.
- In another survey in the USA, it was found that 84 per cent of IT projects failed to deliver.

There are many reasons why projects fail to meet their objectives – sometimes these reasons are completely out of the control of the project team, but the most common reasons, which are discussed below, provide a common theme to all projects and, in almost all circumstances, can at least be minimized, if not prevented.

What is a successful project?

Whether a project is 'successful' or not can often depend on your viewpoint. Here are some common comments that get made and some commentary to consider.

The project was successful because it made a significant profit.

This project is therefore a financial success. There is no indication as to whether there were any sacrifices made to achieve that result. For example, the quality may have suffered by using cheaper and poorer materials than originally specified.

The project was successful because the client got far more quality than they expected.

The first question with this project is, did this extra quality cost us unnecessary time and money to achieve? Secondly, did the client actually want this additional level of quality, for example this may have an impact on his future maintenance and running costs?

The project was a success because we finished it one month early.

Although there is a definite benefit in completing not only on time, but early, we need to determine why the project was early. It may have been completed so early because extra resources were brought in at significant additional cost just to beat the end date.

The project took longer but we were able to incorporate newer technology in the project.

Like the 'extra quality' situation, was the change in technology necessary, did it bring significant benefits and is it really what the client wants?

As we have already discussed the traditional measures of success are as follows and it is important that each area is not considered in isolation.

Benefits vs project success

The sponsor or client may view the success of a project based on the achievement of the overall objective specified in their business case. This will generally be a result of the successful delivery of the project itself. However, successful delivery of the project may not always guarantee delivery of the overall benefits.

For example, a house builder may have a project objective of building 20 houses on a new residential site. The project may be delivered successfully within the time, cost and quality constraints agreed. The client is looking for a benefit of selling these on to potential house buyers, at a profit. However, if the housing market was to change and house prices dropped or the reputation of the area was to deteriorate, the benefits that were initially expected may not materialize although the project was delivered successfully.

Project success and benefits therefore need to be considered together to ensure that as far as possible the project deliverables also deliver benefits to all the stakeholders.

FIGURE 1.3   Project benefits vs success

At handover, it will be known whether the project has achieved its success criteria. Success is the responsibility of the project manager.

Benefits may not be realized until after close-out and handover. Ownership of benefits realization rest with the sponsor.

Benefits can be measured quantitatively, such as financial, market share, staff satisfaction, new markets, and brand position.

At the close-out of the project it should be known whether the project has achieved the success criteria. However, benefits may not be realized until after the project is closed and handed over.

The success criteria must be agreed with all stakeholders at the definition of the project and quantitative measures put in place via KPIs (key performance indicators) and be tracked throughout the life of the project.

Stakeholders

Stakeholders are any group or individuals who have an interest in or are impacted by the project and can be divided into two main areas, primary stakeholders and secondary stakeholders.

FIGURE 1.4   Stakeholder areas

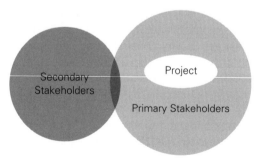

Primary stakeholders are those directly involved with the project and the scope that the project entails. Some typical primary stakeholders are listed below along with the type of questions that should be considered regarding them.

TABLE 1.6 Primary stakeholder questions

Primary stakeholders	Some questions to be answered
Project manager	Why are you doing this job and what do you want as your outcome?
Project team	What does the project team want from the project? Is it more than employment and wages; are there development and career issues?
Company and company management	Why is the company taking on the job? Is it a strategic decision? What is expected as an outcome? Margin? Further work?
Customer (entity paying the bill)	Why is this customer undertaking the project? What is the most important element of the job? Amongst the myriad of requirements, which are the most important? Are there political dimensions to this activity? What sort of organization is behind this? What are the sensitivities of the customer?
End user	There may be several groups of these and expectations may be quite different between groups and also between end users and the customer. This can be very difficult to explore but the PM ignores end users at his peril. Conflicts must be resolved.
Suppliers and sub contractors	Do they expect more work after this? How important is this job to them? Are they supplying standard equipment?
Integrated project teams (joint teams with customer, supplier and end users)	What are the expectations from this organizational structure? eg cost savings, reduced risk etc.

Secondary stakeholders are part of the environment of the project, ie they have an influence on the project but are not directly part of it. Some typical secondary stakeholders are listed below. It is important that they are considered and their primary drivers are identified.

TABLE 1.7   Secondary stakeholder questions

Secondary stakeholder	Seek understanding on:
Government bodies	Legislative requirements
Political groups, pressure groups	Attitudes towards project. Influences.
National and international influences	Identify
Locals likely to be affected by the project	Identify and assess pros and cons

Stakeholder analysis

The purpose of the needs analysis is to determine the needs and expectations of all the stakeholders. Project stakeholders are organizations or people (both internal and external) who are either actively involved in the project, or whose interests are affected by the project being implemented. It is the project manager's responsibility to identify all the stakeholders and determine their needs and expectations. These needs and expectations should then be managed, influenced and balanced, to ensure project success. The project manager should create an environment where the stakeholders are encouraged to contribute their skills and knowledge, which may be useful to the success of the project.

Consider the following headings:

- *Originator*: the person who suggested the project.
- *Owner*: the person whose strategic plan created the need for the project.
- *Sponsor*: the company or client who will authorize expenditure on the project – this could be an internal client.
- *Project champion*: the person who makes the project happen. Often a person with influence in high places.

- *User*: the person who will use the product on behalf of the owner when the project is completed.
- *Customers*: the people who will receive and pay for the benefit from the facility. For example we are all customers for electricity, telephones and commercial travel facilities. Customers may prefer a wide range of fashionable products – this would encourage short production runs and quick turn-round times.
- *Project team*: the team members who plan, organize, implement and control the work of the contractor to deliver the product within the constraints of time, cost and quality (also consider the effect on their families).
- *Senior management*: within your company who you need to support your project (mentoring).
- *Functional managers*: within your company who will be supplying the workforce for your project (matrix structure).
- *Boss*: your boss, the person you report to, can play an important role in establishing your working environment, the support you receive and your career prospects within the organization.
- *Colleagues*: although they may not be working on your project, indirectly they can supply useful information and offer moral peer support, or conversely peer pressure.
- *Contractors*: the external companies or people offering specialist expertise to supplement the company's resources.
- *Suppliers and vendors*: the external companies or people who supply materials and equipment. They have a wealth of experience which should be tapped.
- *Supporters*: the parties who provide goods and services to enable the facility to be built, for example the suppliers of telephones, electricity, postal service and even the corner shop. Financial support through the banking system could also be included here.
- *Legal requirements*: rules and regulations both nationally and internationally that must be complied with.

There are other stakeholders (usually external) who may not be directly involved with the project, but can influence the outcome:

- regulatory authorities – health and safety;
- trade unions;
- special interest groups (environmentalists) who represent the society at large;
- lobby groups;
- government agencies and media outlet;
- individual citizens.

Some stakeholders are interested in the outcome of the project, while others are only interested in the project while it is being implemented. Stakeholders can be further classified into those who are *positively* affected and those that are *negatively* affected by this project. Where possible, identify the key decision makers (those with power) and focus your attention on their needs. Any differences between the stakeholders should be resolved in favour of the client and customers, but not necessarily at the expense of other stakeholders.

FIGURE 1.5   Stakeholder grid

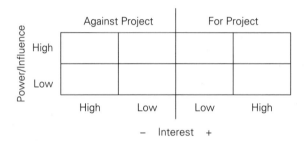

Stakeholder grid

Some stakeholders will support the project, while others will oppose the project. It is important to address those who oppose the project and discuss their fears and objections, because it is these stakeholders that could derail your project, particularly if they have power. Some of their concerns may be valid and with some flexibility could be accommodated. At the end of the day you may not be able to please all your stakeholders and in this conflict environment you will need to establish the priority of your stakeholders' needs and make your decisions accordingly.

By using the above grid you will be able to assess the balance of stakeholders for and against the project and which are of the greatest risk or the greatest supporters of the project. If there are any stakeholders sitting in a position of high power with a high negative interest this must be addressed to try and move them to a position of positive interest.

The process of stakeholder management should be as follows:

- *Identify* – Identify the stakeholders and assess where they fall in the above grid.
- *Analyse* – Analyse their need, objections, and concerns.
- *Communication* – Establish what and how you are going to communicate with them.
- *Management* – Continually review, manage and communicate with each stakeholder.

Key performance indicators (KPIs)

Many things are measurable. That does not make them key to the organization's success. In selecting key performance indicators, it is critical to limit them to those factors that are essential to the organization reaching its goals. It is also important to keep the number of key performance indicators small just to keep everyone's attention focused on achieving the same KPIs.

That is not to say, for instance, that a company will have only three or four total KPIs in the company. Rather there will be three or four key performance indicators for the company and all the units within them will have three, four or five KPIs that support the overall company goals and can be 'rolled up' into them.

If a company key performance indicator is 'increased customer satisfaction', that KPI will be focused differently in different departments.

The manufacturing department may have a KPI of 'Number of units rejected by Quality Inspection', while the sales department has a KPI of 'Minutes a customer is on hold before a sales rep answers'. Success by the sales and manufacturing departments in meeting their respective departmental key performance indicators will help the company meet its overall KPI.

KPIs in project management

Key performance indicators can be used as a performance management tool, but also as a carrot. KPIs give everyone in the organization a clear picture of what is important, or what they need to make happen. They can also be used to manage performance, if you make sure that everything the people in your organization do is focused on meeting or exceeding those key performance indicators. You can also use the KPIs to help individual and team motivation. This can be achieved by posting KPIs on the walls of conference rooms, on the company intranet, some of them can even be put on the company website, showing what the target for each KPI is and showing the progress toward that target for each of them. People will be motivated to reach those KPI targets and can see how their projects are contributing towards them.

Avoiding project failure

Many studies have been done to identify exactly why projects fail. The majority of these studies come to the same general conclusion that the root of the failure lay not in the classic project management areas, such as project plans, but much earlier in the project life cycle when the project was being defined and appraised. Lack of clarity and proper analysis at this stage meant that no matter how good the planning and control systems in the project were the project objectives were fundamentally flawed.

Another key area that led to project failures was related to people issues – teams that did not function well and did not collectively aim for the project goals.

Below are listed the main factors affecting a project's likely success which are common to most surveys, along with a description of what measures can be put in place to eliminate them, or reduce their impact.

Objectives

Poorly defined, unclear and ambiguous project objectives
Solution: Use a project management plan, or terms of reference, to clearly lay out all objectives and deliverables. (Life cycle stage: Defining your project)

Objectives are incomplete
Solution: Have the project objectives agreed with the client or sponsor. Question any assumptions and ask for clarification. (Life cycle stage: Defining your project)

Objectives are unrealistic
Solution: Involve the project manager, or intended project manager, at the definition stage of the project so that front line experience can be brought to bear upon the process. Also, ensure that risk analysis is carried out prior to committing to the project to determine overall feasibility. (Life cycle stage: Defining your project)

Commitment

Lack of executive support resulting in the project having low priority within the organization
Solution: Use a project sponsor or project champion within upper management who feels a sense of ownership for the project, ensuring it will receive the required executive attention. (Life cycle stage: Defining your project) Also, ensure that project information is visible and high profile during the project. (Life cycle stage: Planning your project, Executing your project)

Lack of client involvement leading to loss of focus
Solution: Agree objectives with client; and ensure that the client is kept abreast of the project at all times. It may be appropriate to include the client on certain risk analysis sessions. (Life cycle stage: Definition, appraising, planning, execution)

Poorly defined authority structures leading to confusion and delayed or unauthorized decision making
Solution: Define roles and responsibilities for all team members. Produce a responsibility/authority chart for the entire project indicating who can make what decisions and to what level. (Life cycle stage: Defining your project)

Planning

Not anticipating undesirable events

Solution: Implement a simple but effective risk analysis and management strategy for the project, to which everyone is invited to contribute. Such a scheme should be active throughout the project life cycle and its results should constantly feed the Planning your project and Executing your project phases to aid in contingency planning and decision making. (Life cycle stage: Defining your project, Planning your project, Executing your project)

Poorly detailed plans

Solution: Create a work breakdown structure at the beginning of the project which defines the project down to an appropriate task level. Avoid having activities in plans which are of a very long duration relative to all other activities in the plan. (Life cycle stage: Planning your project)

Inaccurate plans which do not reflect the actual project status

Solution: Use software planning tools with care – do not let the constraining features of a software tool drive the project. Ensure that actual project progress is applied to project plans to reforecast dates and costs. Ensure that any progress data is accurate and not assumptions. (Life cycle stage: Planning your project, Executing your project)

Control

Constantly changing objectives or project scope

Solution: Implement a change control regime in the project whereby any action that may result in alteration to project plans or objectives are properly appraised and agreed before implementation. Avoid implementing change requests from the client without explaining the potential impact on the project and ensure the client agrees, perhaps through the use of a variation order. (Life cycle stage: Executing your project)

Changing technologies

Solution: Although there may be occasions when it is necessary to use a different technology during the execution of the project, any change must be carefully evaluated to determine its impact on the project objectives. There may well be a benefit in some areas but a loss in others. If technology is a significant element of a project, ensure that it is given adequate attention in a risk analysis where the potential for absolution, etc is addressed and mitigation defined. (Life cycle stage: Defining your project)

People

Personality clashes within and outside the project team

Solution: Undertake behaviour profiling of the team ensuring that the potential for conflict is reduced and that the team members understand each other. (Life cycle stage: Planning your project, Executing your project)

Individuals not up to the job
Solution: Careful selection of team members. Allowing for and providing
training where necessary. Introduce peer support within the team.
(Life cycle stage: Planning your project, Executing your project)

Poor teamwork
Solution: Gain an understanding of what motivates individuals in the team.
Deal with conflict within the team. Provide an acceptable working
environment. Undertake off-project team building / social events.
(Life cycle stage: Planning your project, Executing your project)

Twenty actions to help ensure project success

TABLE 1.8   Actions for project success

Action	Results of successful performance
Defining your project	
1. Demonstrate the project need and feasibility.	• A document confirming the need for the project deliverables and describing, in broad terms: the deliverables, means of creating the deliverables, costs of creating and implementing the deliverables, benefits to be obtained by implementing the deliverables.
2. Obtain project authorization.	• A 'go/no go' decision is made by the sponsor (company).
	• A project manager is assigned.
	• A 'project charter' is created which:
	– formally recognizes the project;
	– communicates the success factors;
	– details the scope of the project and its deliverables;
	– is used as a communication document throughout the project.
3. Appraise fully all aspects of the project	• Outline the various ways the project objectives can be met.
	• Conduct a comprehensive risk analysis:
	– include Technical, Commercial, Environmental and Safety;
	– document all risks within the Project Risk Register.

TABLE 1.8   *continued*

Action	Results of successful performance
Planning your project	
4. Describe project scope.	• Statement of project scope. • Scope management plan. • Work breakdown structure.
5. Define and sequence project activities.	• An activity list (list of all activities that will be performed on the project). • Updates to the work breakdown structure (WBS). • A project network diagram.
6. Estimate durations for activities and resources required.	• Estimate of durations for each activity and assumptions related to each estimate. • Statement of resource requirements. • Updates to activity list.
7. Develop a project schedule.	• Project schedule in the form of Gantt charts, network diagrams, milestone charts, or text tables. • Supporting details, such as resource usage over time, cash flow projections, order/delivery schedules, etc.
8. Estimate costs.	• Cost estimates for completing each activity. • Supporting detail, including assumptions and constraints. • Cost management plan describing how cost variances will be handled.
9. Build a budget and spending plan.	• A cost baseline or time-phased budget for measuring/monitoring costs. • A spending plan, telling how much will be spent on what resources at what time.
10. Create a formal quality plan.	• Quality management plan, including operational definitions. • Quality verification checklists.

TABLE 1.8 *continued*

Action	Results of successful performance
Planning your project	
11. Create a formal project communications plan.	• A communication management plan, including: – collection structure; – distribution structure; – distribution structure of information to be disseminated; – schedules listing when information will be produced; – a method for updating the communications plan.
12. Organize and acquire staff.	• Role and responsibility assignments. • Staffing plan. • Organizational chart with detail as appropriate. • Project staff. • Project team directory.
13. Identify risks and plan to respond.	• A document describing potential risks, including their sources, symptoms, and ways to address them.
14. Plan for and acquire outside resources. *(if required)*	• Procurement management plan describing how contractors will be obtained. • Statement of work (SOW) or statement of requirements (SOR) describing the item (product or service) to be procured. • Bid documents, such as RFP (request for proposal), IFB (invitation for bid), etc. • Evaluation criteria – means of scoring contractor's proposals. • Contract with one or more suppliers of goods or services.
15. Organize the project plan.	• A comprehensive project plan that pulls together all the outputs of the preceding project planning activities.
16. Close out the project planning phase.	• Project plan that has been approved, in writing, by the client and a 'green light' or okay to begin work on the project.

TABLE 1.8 *continued*

Action	Results of successful performance
Planning your project	
17. Revisit the project plan and re-plan if needed.	• Confidence that the detailed plans to execute a particular phase are still accurate and will effectively achieve results as planned.
Execution of your project	
18. Execute project activities.	• Work results (deliverables) are created.
	• Change requests (ie, based on expanded or contracted project) are identified.
	• Periodic progress reports are created.
	• Team performance is assessed, guided, and improved if needed.
	• Bids/proposals for deliverables are solicited, contractors (suppliers) are chosen, and contracts are established.
	• Contracts are administered to achieve desired work results.
19. Control project activities.	• Decision to accept inspected deliverables.
	• Corrective actions such as rework of deliverables, adjustments to work process, etc.
	• Updates to project plan and scope.
	• Improved quality.
	• Completed evaluation checklists (if applicable).
***Closing* your project**	
20. Close out project activities.	• Formal acceptance, documented in writing, that the sponsor has accepted the product of this phase or activity.
	• Formal acceptance of contractor work products and updates to the contractor's files.
	• Updated project records prepared for archiving.
	• List of lessons learned.
	• A plan for follow-up and/or hand-off of work products.

Project manager's weekly checklist

Check your project's scope

Refresh your memory about your project's goals and boundaries. In particular, make sure you have a clear picture of what the desired results should be at this point relative to deliverables, schedule costs, quality, and so on.

Check your deliverables

Analyse the status of each project deliverable. Are they evolving as planned? If appropriate:

- Locate lists of quality criteria that may be applied to inspect the quality and completeness of the deliverables at this stage of the project.
- Check contractors' proposals or contracts to make sure you know what they should be supplying at this point.
- Inspect all project deliverables.
- Decide whether to accept inspected deliverables or to require rework.

Check your schedule

Examine your milestones, key dates, and critical path. Are you where you need to be?

Analyse variances by comparing 'estimated' to 'actual'

- Are activities taking longer than planned? (Are you exceeding estimates of duration?)
- Are you using more resource hours than you planned?
- Are your actual costs exceeding your estimated costs?
- If minor variances are discovered (variances that can be resolved easily without changing the plan or scope), then resolve them.
- If major variances are discovered (variances that change the scope or constitute significant project issues), then handle them as described in the steps below.

Address scope changes

- Identify changes in scope (changes in deliverables, schedule, costs, etc).
- Handle scope changes, if necessary.

List, track, and try to resolve open issues

- Make a list of all the unresolved issues. Or;
- Revisit the list of open issues from the last inspection period and try to resolve them.

Revisit potential project risks

- Locate the risk management plan, if one has been created.
- Note particularly whether any of the ongoing events or upcoming events are identified in the risk management plan as particularly vulnerable to risk.

Report project status

- After completing the checks above, if you haven't already done so, talk to your team members and determine their perspective on project status.
- Create and circulate a project status report.

Drive for close-out of activities and sign-off of deliverables as appropriate

- Ask yourself, 'What activities can I close out? Which deliverables can I get formally approved and signed off?'
- Prepare and get signatures on sign-off forms as appropriate.

Create a list of lessons learned

Create a list of lessons learned that describes the ways subsequent project activities must be modified in order to prevent the difficulties encountered up to this point.

Complete appropriate evaluation checklists

Complete evaluation checklists, if applicable, and file them as part of the official project records.

Ten tips for guaranteed failure

1 *Don't bother prioritizing your organization's overall project load.* After all, if there's a free-for-all approach to your overall programme management (ie 'survival of the fittest'), then the projects that survive will be those that were destined to survive. In the meantime, senior management need not trouble themselves aligning projects with strategic goals or facing the logical imperative that people simply cannot have 12 number one priorities!

2 *Encourage sponsors and key stakeholders to take a passive role on the project team.* Let them assert their authority to reject deliverables at random, without participating in defining project outcomes in a high-resolution fashion.

3 *Set up ongoing committees focusing on management process* (such as TQM groups, etc) and make project team members participate in frequent meetings and write lots of reports ... preferably when critical project deadlines are coming due.

4 *Interrupt team members relentlessly* ... preferably during their time off. Find all sorts of trivial issues that 'need to be addressed', then keep their beepers and mobile phones ringing and bury them in e-mails to keep them off balance.

5 *Create a culture in which project managers* are expected to 'roll over' *and take it when substantive new deliverables are added* halfway through the project. (After all, only a tradesperson like a plumber or electrician would demand more money or more time for additional services; our people are 'professionals' and should be prepared to be 'flexible'.)

6 *Half way through the project, when most of the deliverables have begun to take shape, add a whole bunch of previously unnamed stakeholders* and ask them for their opinions about the project and its deliverables.

7 *Encourage the client to approve deliverables informally* (with nods, smiles and verbal praise); *never force clients to stand behind their approvals with a formal sign-off.* (Give them plenty of room to wriggle out of agreements!)

8 *Make sure project managers have lots of responsibilities and deadlines, but no authority* whatsoever to acquire or remove people from the project; to get enough money, materials, or facilities; or insist on timely participation of the key personnel.

9 *Describe project deliverables in the vaguest possible terms* so sponsors and reviewers have plenty of leeway to reinvent the project outputs repeatedly as the project unfolds.

10 *Get projects up and running as quickly as possible* – don't worry about documenting agreements in a formal project charter, clearly describing team roles/responsibilities, or doing a thorough work breakdown analysis. After all, we know what we're doing and we trust each other. So let's get to it without a pesky audit trail!

Financial evaluation in projects

Financial assessment

Financial assessment is an activity generally conducted early in the project life cycle. In most cases it would be carried out prior to a project being initiated with the results forming a major part of the business case. Financial appraisal not only looks at the financial viability of a project but also allows the comparison of several projects or project options on a like for like basis. Income and expenditure should always be produced for each project option taking into account the whole project. These figures are usually based on historical data from similar projects. Once these figures have been calculated each project or project option is assessed and the financial position appraised.

If an option cannot generate sufficient income to cover its expenditure it will probably be excluded at this stage unless any other overriding factors are considered more important ie loss leaders, image, politics, regulatory commitments, necessary commitments (software upgrade).

Evaluation of the financial aspects of a project is very important due to the nature of project expenditure where:

- Expenditure is generally high.
- It is generally long term.
- It involves forecast of future events.

It is therefore very important that we have a method to compare the financial aspects of different projects and project options. We therefore:

- must have a clear objective;
- must have a procedure for assessing financial implications;
- must have a means of evaluating the benefits;
- need to be able to measure different projects against the objective.

Financial appraisal methods can be divided into two main techniques.

- techniques which ignore the time value of money;
- techniques which account for the time value of money.

Appraisal techniques which do not account for time

Payback

This method measures when the project will 'pay back' the initial sum of money invested.

TABLE 1.9   Payback calculation

	Method A	Method B	Method C
Investment at start year 1	£10,000	£10,000	£10,000
Income at end year 1	£3,000	£5,000	£2,500
Income at end year 2	£3,000	£5,000	£4,000
Income at end year 3	£3,000	£4,000	£5,000
Income at end year 4	£3,000	£2,000	£6,000
Payback Period	**3.3 years**	**2 years**	**2.7 years**

In the above example method B would be preferred due to the fact that it returns the initial investment quicker than the other two methods irrespective of the fact that method C's return would be much greater.

The main advantages of this method are:

- It is easily understood and applied.
- It reduces the uncertainty of long range cash forecast as it concentrates on early cash returns.

The disadvantages are:

- No account of cash flows beyond the payback date is taken into account.
- Projects with high early returns are favoured even though the risks may be higher.
- Projects with longer life cycles are penalized where the cash flow may initially be low.

Return on investment (ROI)

This approach makes use of concepts similar to the 'return on investment' concepts used to assess profitability in conventional profit and loss accounts and balance sheets. The method is illustrated in the following table.

TABLE 1.10   Return on investment

	Method A	Method B	Method C
Investment at start year 1	£10,000	£10,000	£10,000
Income at end year 1	£3,000	£5,000	£2,500
Income at end year 2	£3,000	£5,000	£4,000
Income at end year 3	£3,000	£4,000	£5,000
Income at end year 4	£3,000	£2,000	£6,000
Payback Period	**3.3 years**	2 years	**2.7 years**
Average income p.a.	**£3,000**	**£4,000**	**£4,375**
R.o.I (Av inc. / invest.)	**30%**	**40%**	43.75%

By appraising the ROI of each method, method C would be most favourable despite its longer payback period.

The main advantages of this method are:

- It is also easily understood and applied.
- It follows the traditional approach that will be used in determining return on capital employed and can be used to ensure that required financial constraints are satisfied by a project.

The main disadvantage of this method is:

- No account is taken of the effect time has on the predicted cash flows, ie money received in four years' times is treated as if it were received in year 1.

Appraisal techniques which do use discounting

Principles of discounting

The principles of discounting are based on the principle of compound interest. ie interest is applied and accumulated to the principal sum at an agreed time.

Assuming £1000 is borrowed at 10 per cent interest, compounded annually, then at the end of 3 years the borrower will owe £1331, as illustrated in the following example:

TABLE 1.11   Discounting example

Start of year 1	Principal	**£1,000**	
End of year 1	Interest	£100	£1,100
End of year 2	Interest	£110	£1,210
End of year 3	Interest	£121	**£1,331**

This also tells us (assuming interest rates stay the same) £1,333 received in three years' time is the equivalent of receiving £1,000 today.

Dividing the principal by the total accumulated at the end of each year, produces a series of discount factors, eg:

End year 1: £1,000/1,100 = 0.909

End year 2: £1,000/1,210 = 0.826

End year 3: £1,000/1,331 = 0.751

If we now apply these factors to the predicted cash flows we can equate them to an equivalent present-day figure, ie present value. This figure can now be used to give a more accurate effect of the cash flows.

Net present value (NPV)

The net present value (NPV) is the total of all the discounted forecasts, out and in, over the expected life of the project and its product.

All predicted forecast flows are discounted for the life of the project. If the sum of the discounted revenue flows for the life of the project is greater than the initial investment then the project would be seen to be successful. If the total was less then it would be questionable if the project should proceed.

The rate used to discount the cash flows is obviously crucial and would usually be based on the minimum rate of return (MRR) defined by the organization and is usually based on the rate of interest that could be earned on the initial outlay if invested in a more predictable area.

The following example illustrates the approach:

NPV calculation

Minimum rate of return = 10 per cent

TABLE 1.12 Net Present Value (NPV) example

	Revenues	Discount factor	PV
Investment at start year 1	£20,000	1.00	£–20,000
Income at end year 1	£5,000	.909	£4,545
Income at end year 2	£8,000	.826	£6,608
Income at end year 3	£10,000	.751	£7,510
Income at end year 4	£12,000	.683	£8,196
Totals	**£35,000**		**£26,859**
Net present value			**£6,859**

In the above example the net present value (NPV) is based on an MRR of 10 per cent. In this instance this project would seem to be viable based on this financial appraisal method. In addition it can be seen that it meets its payback in just over three years. Projects which meet their MRR quicker may also be viewed more favourably than others that don't.

Internal rate of return (IRR)

The internal rate of return (IRR) is the discount rate which gives zero NPV over the life of the project. It is the method that therefore solves a rate of interest for the project by working out what discount rate returns the present value of the outgoings equal to the initial investment.

For example: What is the rate of interest that makes £1,331 in three years' time equivalent to £1,000?

TABLE 1.13 Internal Rate of Return (IRR) example

Investment start year 1	£12K	0%	10%	15%
Income at end year 1	£2K	**£2,000**	*.909* £1,818	*.870* £1,740
Income at end year 2	£7K	**£7,000**	*.826* £5,782	*.756* £5,292
Income at end year 3	£6K	**£6,000**	*.751* £4,506	*.658* £3,948
PV		**£15,000**	**£12,106**	**£10,980**
Ratio		**0.8**	**0.991**	**1.093**

Two of the ratios are then plotted on a graph against the percentage rate and a straight line drawn between them. Where the line crosses the ratio at 1 this is the IRR that the project will return.

In the case below it is approximately 11 per cent.

FIGURE 1.6 Example IRR calculation

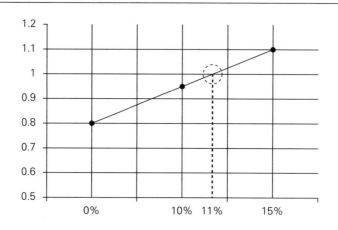

Things to consider

The tortoise and the hare

The initial phase of starting a project is often rushed, yet it is the most critical stage at which a project manager can add value to their project and ensure it has every chance of success. By stepping methodically through the starting phase you will lay the foundations for a successful project. There is often pressure to 'get on with the project' – caused by a lack of understanding in the organization – yet to rush this stage is to build on loose, unstable foundations without a clear understanding by all stakeholders of the project objectives. Time spent here will be rewarded later in the project. Time spent on a careful start-up of your project will lead you faster to a successful conclusion.

Being SMART

One way to check whether a project has met its objectives is to ask each stakeholder to wrote them down independently. It is common to then see significant differences in how some stakeholders view project success – usually because they themselves have differing objectives. The idea of SMART objectives is not a new one. Indeed it is well used in management and leadership theory. However, it applies especially well to project management. Objectives which are not SMART will cause project issues later.

Defining success

It sounds obvious but it isn't. Unless there is a clear measureable definition of project success how can a project manager know if they have delivered a successful project? The key here is to get all the stakeholders to agree – sometimes easier said than done.

Beware the terrorists

It is important to understand how a stakeholder can affect or influence the project. Sometimes even the most sublime stakeholders can, at a vital moment, have a major influence on the project. Often this can be avoided by careful stakeholder analysis but it is critical to ensure continued and appropriate levels of communication throughout the project to ensure that all the stakeholders remain 'on side'. This is especially true of politically sensitive projects in any organization – and especially so where there are external stakeholders in collaborative projects typical of government and public sectors.

The project management plan as a 'live' document

Like many of the documents we will discuss during this book, the project management plan must be a living document. It is best seen as a structured filing cabinet, accessible to many (in parts) and constantly evolving and documenting. A small project may have a project management plan of only a few pages, whereas a complex or high value project may have many pages. However, the content has to be at a relevant level of detail. For the wise project manager it is both an audit trail and ultimately a project closure report all in one.

Sometimes it is right to cancel a project

It is important to always remember the business case and financial or other criteria on which the project is based. A good project manager will not be reluctant to monitor that the business case is still valid. It is tempting and commonplace to continue a project even when the business case no longer stands, but this is not in the best interests of the organization and, in a mature project organization, the project manager and their team either.

Conclusion

This chapter is perhaps the most important of all the chapters as starting out correctly is crucial to project success. Laying suitable foundations can take time and there is always pressure to start 'delivering'. But following the steps in this chapter will lead to a successful project and ultimately, this is the fundamental of good project management. The following chapters will follow the project life cycle of phases from planning to completion.

CASE STUDY   Starting projects at Subsea 7

About Subsea 7

Subsea 7 is a seabed-to-surface engineering, construction and services contractor to the offshore energy industry worldwide specializing in seabed-to-surface design, fabrication, installation and commissioning. The company has a total of 12,500 employees spread globally.

They provide fully integrated services and have a proven track record in delivering complex projects in deep water and challenging environments. Many of these fall within engineering, procurement, installation and commissioning (EPIC) project delivery.

They achieve this by:

- using specialist knowledge and expertise in the design, fabrication, installation and commissioning of seabed-to-surface projects;

- deploying global resources in all major offshore hydrocarbon basins worldwide;

- operating one of the world's most versatile fleets comprising over 40 high-specification pipe-lay, construction, remote intervention and diving support vessels;

- always keeping safety at the heart of all operations and committing to an incident-free workplace, every day, everywhere.

Successful project management is one of the core competencies which sets Subsea 7 apart. It takes years of practical experience, know-how and dedication to safely deliver the toughest and most complex of offshore projects on schedule, on budget, to agreed standards, time after time.

Their project managers are responsible for organizing and managing multi-disciplinary, integrated project teams able to safely manage and deliver the demands of each undertaking in terms of safety, quality, cost and schedule. These teams have industry-leading logistical support, supply chain management and the assets needed to safely execute each project.

Through its project management expertise, Subsea 7 adds value to every phase of the project life cycle – from planning and design through fabrication, construction and installation to commissioning, operation and decommissioning.

Starting out with a framework for success

Subsea 7 use a proprietary online tool (PM7) designed to enhance their already proven capabilities by providing extended cross-functional guidance in the day to day management of projects, not just for the project manager, but for the entire project team.

PM7 breaks the project down into its constituent phases, from the initial identification of prospects in the win process to the closedown of projects in the execution phase, detailing each of the activities associated with that phase.

For each activity PM7 provides:

- guidance to the team in what to do, how they should do it, and how best to do it in practice;

- links to internal guidance and procedural documents within their business management system particular to that activity;

- ready access to a suite of global best practices, go-bys and templates for key activities.

In addition to this, a gate and health check system has been developed to allow project management teams to self-audit the project at any stage of its life cycle.

Across the full project life cycle from 'win' to 'close-out', five key phases of a project are identified as critical stages, and as seen from the diagram overleaf, project start up is identified as a stand-alone phase of a project.

Subsea 7 define project start up as the phase of the project between notice of project award and the execution phase, and consider it to be a critical point in the total project life cycle. There is a tendency to try and make this phase of the project as short as possible. This is particularly noticeable amongst the engineering community as engineers have a tendency to want to go straight out to the design and build phase. Historical evidence, however, shows that many of the problems occurring in projects can be traced back to failures or lack of attention during start-up.

Subsea 7 consider the work and effort put into ensuring all start up activities are properly performed will pay dividends by setting the foundations for the success of the project.

Generally Subsea 7 group the start up phase into two equally important components:

- review and set up;

- planning.

Review and set up

This component concerns:

- putting together the resources required to perform the project through to completion in terms of personnel, office facilities, IT facilities etc;

- gathering of input to the project eg contract, project scope, specifications etc;

- reviewing, verifying and accepting the work that has been performed up to this stage;

- familiarizing the team with the scope, contract, internal and external expectations, drivers and goals;

- familiarizing the team with the key stakeholders and ensuring alignment at this stage with the primary stakeholder, ie the client;

- establishing administration and internal/external communication routines.

FIGURE 1.7 Subsea 7 PMR life cycle vs phases

PM7

PROJECT MANAGEMENT IN SUBSEA 7

Life Cycle ------------->

WIN		PROJECT START-UP			EXECUTION				OPERATIONS		CLOSE OUT
100 BD PROSPECT	200 BA / ITT	300 PROJECT AWARD	400 REVIEW & SET UP	500 PLAN	600 MANAGE	700 CONTROL AND REPORT	800 ENGINEERING	900 SUBCONTRACTS AND PROCUREMENT	1000 ONSHORE MANUFACTURE AND FABRICATION	1100 OFFSHORE OPERATIONS	1200 CLOSE OUT AND HANDOVER

Activities

100 BD PROSPECT	200 BA / ITT	300 PROJECT AWARD	400 REVIEW & SET UP	500 PLAN	600 MANAGE	700 CONTROL AND REPORT	800 ENGINEERING	900 SUBCONTRACTS AND PROCUREMENT	1000 ONSHORE MANUFACTURE AND FABRICATION	1100 OFFSHORE OPERATIONS	1200 CLOSE OUT AND HANDOVER
105 The BD Process	205 Tender Summary and Approval Workbook (TSAW)	305 Contract Award/Non-Award	405 Project Organisation & Resources	505 Project Management and Execution Plan	605 Management/ Development of the Project Team	705 Planning	805 Engineering Management	905 Placement of Subcontracts	1005 Site HSEQ	1105 Personnel Logistics	1205 Technical Close Out (Client)
110 Pursuit Plan	210 Tender Preliminaries	310 BA to BE Handover	410 Handover Review	510 Start Up – Risk Management	610 Health and Safety Management	710 Cost Control/ Forecasting	810 Engineering Design Control	910 Procurement	1010 Third Party Manufacture and Fabrication	1110 Operational HSEQ	1210 Contractual Close Out (Client)
115 Client Contact Reports	215 Tender Planning	315 BA/BE Follow up	415 Project Strategy Meeting	515 Start Up – Subcontract/ Procurement	615 Quality Management	715 Accounting	815 Engineering Document Production	915 Subcontractor and Supplier Management	1015 PPG Fabrication Pipelines and Bundles	1115 Preparation for Vessel Mobilisation	1215 Internal Close Out
120 Estimating and Planning	220 Tender Subcontracts and Procurement		420 Start Up Plan	520 Start Up – Cost Control/ Accounting	620 Environmental Management	720 Document Control	820 External Interface Management	920 Logistics and Materials Control		1120 Mobilisation	1220 Subcontract Close Out
	225 Tender Preparation		425 Project Kick Off Meeting – Internal	525 Start Up – Pl...	625 Risk Management	725 Internal Management Reporting	825 Technical Package Management			1125 Offshore Operations	1225 Experience Transfer
	230 Ter...		430 Project Kick Off Meeting – Exter...		630 ...rd	730 Client Reporting	830			1130 Demobilisation	1230 Project Close ...own
						735					

Phase Levels ------------->

Planning

This component is concerned with effectively 'baselining' the project in terms of:

- generation of the key project control documents, processes and procedures to be used by the team throughout the execution phase: project management and execution plan, hse plan, quality plan, etc;

- definition of the documentation deliverables in the form of a master document register;

- establishing a schedule for performing all major onshore and offshore activities required to complete the work scope, which can be used in conjunction with the master document register to track and report progress;

- establishing the initial project cost and revenue forecast, and the means by which to control and adjust through the execution and operational phases as required;

- establishing a means of controlling all incoming and outgoing financial funds from the project;

- establishing the materials, goods and services to be procured and the strategy for procurement and supply of these;

- reviewing the inherent project risks and establishing a risk register which can be used to effectively control risk throughout the execution and operational phases;

- establishing a sound technical basis for the execution and operational phases.

It is all very well to have the process for project start-up laid out in clear and carefully defined steps; however, it is equally important to ensure that each project follows the 'road map' provided by PM7. To achieve this, Subsea 7 have introduced the concept of 'stage gates' into PM7.

There are two 'stage gates' associated with the start up phase of the project.

Gate 1 marks the transition phase between the works performed by the business acquisition team in winning the work, and the handover to the team who will execute the work.

Gate 2 marks the completion of all activities associated with the start-up phase such that the solid foundation for the continuing execution phase is successfully in place.

Each of the above gates can be opened within PM7 to reveal a series of audit type questions which allows the project management teams to self-audit the project at these critical phases. The gate audits can also be used by upper management to review the status of the project, and the system incorporates 'traffic lights' to provide a visual and 'at a glance' status of each of the audit activities.

One of the key elements of a successful project start-up within Subsea 7 is the development and approval of a project management and execution plan (PMEP).

The PMEP is considered as the core document for the management and execution of the project, and is the principal means by which the project is planned, monitored and managed. The document is owned and maintained by the project manager and is utilized by the project team members to ensure the successful day to day operational management and control of the project and the quality of the outputs.

The PMEP documents how the project will be managed in terms of why, what, how, how much, who, when and where.

FIGURE 1.8 Subsea 7 PMEP documents

Gate 2

Completion of Project Start up

This Gate acts as a checklist to ensure that all activities deemed to be an essential part of Project Start up have been succesfully completed

Item	Module	Compliance	Measure	Comment	Responsible
020 Project Management					
Is the Project adequately resourced in terms of personnel, hardware, software, office space and facilities?	405 Project Organisation & Resources	PM-GL-PM-007	Confirmation by Project Manager		
Has a Project organisation chart been produced?	405 Project Organisation & Resources	PM-GL-PM-007	Approved organisation chart in place		
Has a Manpower resource plan been developed to identify project man power requirements and input to the Regional planning system?	405 Project Organisation & Resources	NA	Confirmed by Regional Resource Co-ordinator		
Have all Project Team personnel completed mandatory Subsea 7 training	405 Project Organisation & Resources	NA	Training records		
Has the team been briefed on roles, responsibilities and communications protocol?	405 Project Organisation & Resources	NA	Briefing records		
Has the team been briefed on roles, responsibilities and communications protocol?	405 Project Organisation & Resources	NA	Briefing records		
Has the team been fully familairised with all aspects of the Project	405 Project Organisation & Resources	NA	Familiarisation records		
Has a familiarisation plan been considered, and if relevant has it been generated	405 Project Organisation & Resources	NA	Approved Familiarisation plan in place	At discretion of Project Manager or at client request	
Has the team been issued with Project specific job descriptions?	405 Project Organisation & Resources	NA	Signed Job Descriptions in place	At discretion of Project Manager, at Client request and/or regional legislation	
Has the BA to BE handover been performed according to Gate 1?	410 Handover Review	PM-GL-PM-007	Project Manager acceptance of handover		
Has a team review of all handover material been conducted?	410 Handover Review	NA	Records of review		
Has a team review of all handover material been conducted?	410 Handover Review	NA	Records of review		
Have relevant issues re the handover material been resolved and has feedback been provided to BA?	410 Handover Review	NA	Records of review		
Has a Project strategy meeting been performed with Regional ops?	415 Project Strategy Meeting	PM-GL-PM-007	MoM/actions from meeting		
Has a project Start Up Plan been developed covering the first 30–90 day period?	420 Start Up Plan	NA	Start up plan in place	At discretion of Project Manager or if required by Client	
Has an internal project Kick-Off meeting been held with the Project Team, including remote locations as applicable?	425 Project Kick Off Meeting – Internal	PM-GL-PM-007	MoM/action list from meeting		
Has a formal Kick-Off Meeting been held with the Client Project Team?	430 Project Kick Off Meeting – External	PM-GL-PM-007	MoM/action list from meeting		
Is the Project set up on SharePoint?	440 Administration/ Communication	NA	Sharepoint site set up		
Have specific Project document templates been set up	440 Administration/ Communication	NA	Document Templates for use		

Why: A statement of what is to be delivered by the project which includes a definition of the need, problem, or opportunity being addressed.

What: A description of the scope, the deliverables and the acceptance criteria. This includes the success criteria for the project, the objectives and the KPIs used to measure success. The 'what' needs to take into account the project's constraints assumptions and the dependencies.

How: Defines the strategy for management, the tools, resources, techniques, monitoring, control and reporting requirements. This will also include material and procurement requirements. Also defines how the work is to be technically performed.

How much: Definition of the project budget, and the budget and cost management processes.

Who: A description of the key project roles and responsibilities, the organization, and the plan for required resources.

When: Defines the timescales, including milestones, phasing and the overall plan.

Where: Defines the geographical locations in which all aspects of the work are to be performed.

The PMEP provides high level information on the project and then sets specific guidelines for successful management and execution, ensuring that all activities are compliant with Subsea 7 business management system and client's contractual and technical requirements.

The high-level table of contents for the generic Subsea 7 PMEP is presented below:

Section I: General information
Introduction
Executive summary

Section II: Project statement
Scope of work
Project schedule
Project organization
Work breakdown structure
Project objectives and measures of success

Section III: Project management
General project management
Project start-up
HSEQ management
Risk and opportunity management
Management of change
Project controls
Communications, information management and reporting
Contract and procurement management
Technical and operational management
Project close-out

Section IV: Project execution
Services/materials/equipment requirements
Engineering
Onshore fabrication/construction/manufacturing
Offshore operations
Risks and challenges
Contingency plans

Defining your project

02

Introduction

Running a project without a work breakdown structure is like going to a strange land without a road map. **J PHILLIPS**

Defining your project is all about 'scope management'. Scope management is the process by which the deliverables and work to produce them are identified and defined. Identification and definition of the scope must describe what the project will include and what it will not include, ie what is in and out of the scope. **APM'S BODY OF KNOWLEDGE**

The scope of the project is comprised of what has to be delivered (the project deliverables) and what work has to be done to deliver the project deliverables. Scope management should be continually addressed throughout the life of the project and includes regular monitoring and controlling.

The high-level scope of the project should have been defined and documented in the business case. The depth and detail of the scope will develop as the project progresses and will be a breakdown of the original scope held in the project management plan (PMP).

The scope can be broken down and refined by using a PBS (product breakdown structure) and a WBS (work breakdown structure).

The product breakdown structure (PBS)

The product breakdown structure (PBS) identifies and defines all the products (deliverables) that the project has to produce. The PBS will show the scope broken down in a hierarchical manner and at its lowest level each product (deliverable) will be identified.

FIGURE 2.1   Example product breakdown structure (PBS)

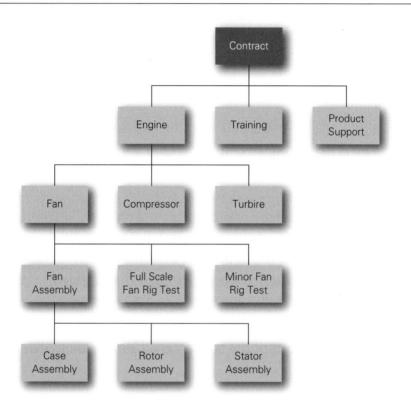

This shows an example PBS from the British Standard (BS 6079) for project management.

The work breakdown structure (WBS)

The work breakdown structure (WBS) defines the work that is required in order to produce the product or deliverables. It is represented as a hierarchical subdivision of a project into work areas with the lowest generally being a work package or sometimes even an activity. The lowest level of the WBS should be consistent and agreed at the outset of the creation of the WBS.

A simplified example of a WBS for the production of a new model of car is shown below. In this example the work is broken down to work package level where an activity list can then be produced.

FIGURE 2.2   Example work breakdown structure (WBS)

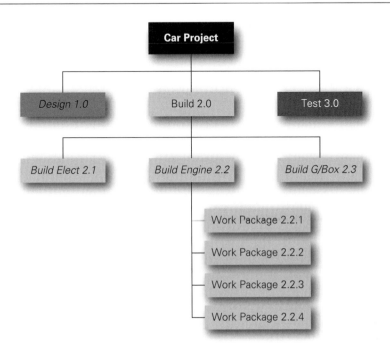

The rationale for creating a WBS is:

- It enables the definition of the total scope of work.
- It provides the ability to assign work to people responsible for carrying out the work.
- It establishes a control baseline.
- It measures accomplishments objectively when the work is done.
- It defines, collects and reports information at the appropriate level required.
- It defines the relationships between work, organization and cost.

The organizational breakdown structure (OBS)

Project organizations can be broken down in much the same way as the work or product can. The OBS is created to reflect the strategy for managing the various aspects of the project and shows the hierarchical breakdown of the management structure.

An example of a typical OBS is shown below where the company is divided firstly by region (east and west) then by division or department.

FIGURE 2.3   Example organizational breakdown structure (OBS)

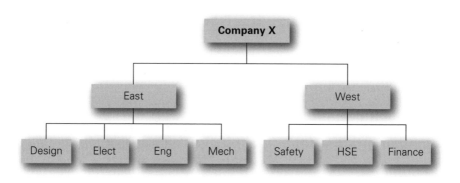

The cost breakdown structure (CBS)

Costs are allocated to the lowest level of the WBS. The tasks at this level can often be subdivided into discrete activities to be completed by different departments therefore one task may have several cost elements. Once costs have been assigned to tasks, it is possible to monitor the project in terms of actual, forecast and earned cost on a task.

In order to be able to summarize costs within projects and across projects a cost breakdown structure (CBS) needs to be developed.

The majority of organizations have a standard CBS that is applied across all projects and is nearly always determined by the finance department. Finance often refers to the structure as the code of accounts which includes other elements over and above pure costs. With some computerized tools, a separate CBS is set up which is normally a simplified version of the code of accounts so that it can be understood more easily by non-financial managers.

FIGURE 2.4   Example cost breakdown structure (CBS)

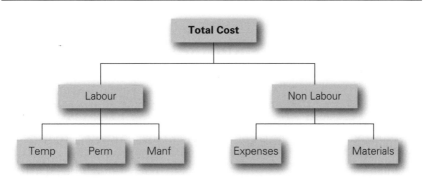

The responsibility assignment matrix (RAM)

The WBS and OBS can be combined to produce a responsibility assignment matrix (RAM) which links the work to be done with the assigned organization, department or person.

FIGURE 2.5   Example responsibility

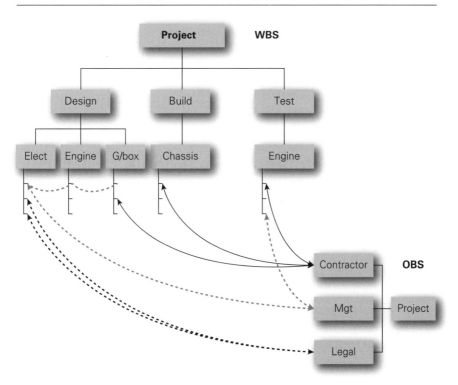

It can be seen in this example how the work to be carried out in the WBS can be associated to the responsible department within the OBS.

Assigning responsibilities to tasks

By forming a matrix with the work breakdown structure and the organizational breakdown structure, responsibilities can be assigned to lower level tasks. Each task is assigned a WBS and OBS code, the department responsible, the person responsible, and the scope of the work required (contained in a 'statement of work'). More than one department may be responsible for a task's statement of work (SoW) because it is often made up of several distinct activities.

SoW example

Task reference code: D01;

Summary description of the requirement: design unit 1;

Key deliverables: detailed design; documentation;

Timescales for the deliverables: start and finish dates;

Task dependencies/subsidiary tasks: succeeding tasks D03, M27;

Schedule of costs by cost element: £1,000 per deliverable;

Risk assessment: impact: low; probability: low;

Performance measurement and task completion criteria: client sign-off;

Description of work content: full description;

Reporting requirements: project manager;

Task ownership: drawing office.

Steps in developing a breakdown structure

- Start with project objectives.
- Identify the type of breakdown structure required: WBS, PBS, OBS CBS.
- Subdivide the work from the most general level to the most specific until manageable units are achieved, ie organize into a pyramid arrangement from the most general level to the most specific until manageable units are achieved.
- Define the objectives and interrelationships at each level within the structure.
- Allocate each discrete element of the structure a unique reference code.
- Estimate effort, time and cost at the lowest level of the WBS or PBS.

FIGURE 2.6 Developing hierarchical breakdown structures

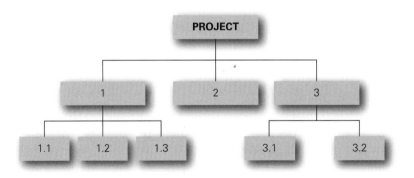

This process should be democratic with all project participants being represented so that nothing is left out and that all parties commit themselves, taking responsibility for their part in the project.

When developing a breakdown structure, the following areas should be considered:

- must represent how the work is going to be done;
- must be compatible with other existing processes (eg time recording, purchasing, finance, etc);
- consistency in size of the lowest level activities (or tasks);
- must reconcile the structure back to the requirements (or contract) to ensure that all elements are included;
- do not have a task crossing a phase or stage boundary;
- do not go into too much detail and develop too many levels.

When the WBS has been developed, and all tasks identified, it is useful to check that all tasks have the following attributes:

- results in a product;
- definable scope of work;
- measurable start (restraint);
- measurable finish;
- assumptions.

Common-sense guidelines

- Each project is different.
- Each project manager has a preferred approach.

- Customers may have a preferred approach.
- Tasks must not cross life cycle stage boundaries.

It is impossible to define a single set of workable rules on how to develop a breakdown structure. However, a number of common-sense guidelines do exist.

- Tasks should be of a size that they could be completed within two reporting periods.
- Project management or other support tasks should not be unnecessarily limited. They should cover a phase or stage of the project and should, ideally, have a duration no greater than twelve months.
- If an activity is to cover outside purchases that have a long lead time, it is counterproductive to split this work into separate tasks.
- If an activity is to cover intense activity over a short time period, it may be useful to subdivide the activity into elements (or tasks) smaller than two months.
- Do not develop the WBS to too much detail in the early stages of a project. A WBS that has been developed too early will require frequent changing. Once a WBS has been set up it becomes difficult to change.
- Minimize the number of levels. Too many levels will cause confusion and misunderstandings.
- Look at other successful projects. Copy their ideas and layout. Examine unsuccessful projects and learn from their failures. Use templates where possible.
- Leave gaps in any numbering system. Anticipate changes and variation orders. By leaving gaps, any new tasks can be built into the structure at a logical point.
- If projects are short term and can be completed in one or two reporting cycles it is pointless to develop a detailed WBS. In many of these cases, a single activity with associated tasks may suffice.
- Each task must have strictly defined entry and exit criteria with the scope of each work package being unambiguously defined.

Templates can be useful but do not slavishly copy them. If templates or structures from other projects are being used as the basis for developing the WBS, take care to ensure that elements are not omitted or that elements have not been included from the template that do not apply to the current project.

If possible, involve the customer when developing the WBS. Involve the project team. They are the people who have to accept responsibility for doing the work.

Requirements management

What is requirements management?

> Requirements management is the set of activities encompassing the collection, control, analysis, filtering, documentation and communication of the requirements of a project.
>
> (Source APM Pathways)

When discussing requirements management it should be considered in relation to work scope, change control, the business case and procurement and project success as the subject is very closely interlinked to these other content areas.

Requirements management is a subject which covers the understanding a project manager must have about the purpose of the project they are working on. In addition to this, the understanding must then be communicated very clearly and comprehensively to the team who will be delivering the work so that the project can be delivered within the previously discussed parameters of cost, time and quality. These requirements must also be traceable and testable and provide some sort of benchmark in terms of how the overall success of the project will be judged.

The fundamental issue we tend to find with a project is that it is initiated to solve some sort of problem or instil some form of change within an organization, the problem or change in turn tends to be ill defined. However, the solution we are responsible for developing needs to be very well defined in order for suppliers or sub contractors to bid/tender for this work or indeed for project teams to deliver against it. In order to create an environment where we can succeed in delivery we need to go through a process of evolving, refining and checking the features and requirements to inform the final design, build and test our product, thus achieving the traceability and provision of an audit trail on the work we have done.

The illustration overleaf best demonstrates requirements management.

FIGURE 2.7   Requirements management

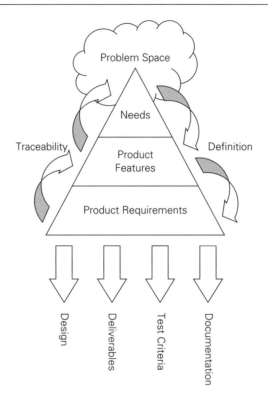

Why do we need requirements management?

The requirements of a project can change quite significantly throughout its life cycle. This is particularly true when considering requests for change, movement in objectives, stakeholder management, legislation etc which makes it extremely difficult to track our progress on the product/solution against our original plans and specifications. Therefore we need a suitable and effective management method to control, trace and test these requirements as they:

- have different levels of detail;
- can be very large in numbers and can become unmanageable;
- are not always obvious and can come from many different sources;
- are always subject to change;
- can be generated from cross functional groups;
- are unique;

- can have differing priorities;
- are time sensitive;
- can have common deliverables;
- can be related to other projects;
- can be difficult to articulate to others. (source: APM Pathways)

Project programme planning

Many projects are large and complex and in order that they can be efficiently managed they need to be sub divided into smaller areas of manageable work. A number of individual (sub) projects can then be managed as part of a programme of work.

Traditionally, this has been carried out by developing a work breakdown structure and managing each task as a separate package of work with:

- a definable start and finish;
- a budget;
- a person responsible;
- a scope of work.

With very large projects, even when they are sub divided into tasks they can still represent a complexity that is difficult to manage. In order to overcome this problem, very large projects should be first subdivided into individual projects and then each individual project divided into its own work breakdown structure. The creation of sub projects or programmes can be treated as just another level of the WBS.

When to use programmes

The reason for breaking a project down into sub projects (or for grouping projects into a programme) is often for organizational or contractual reasons.

Splitting projects into sub projects of a programme is recommended when:

- different sites using differing processes and tools are working on large elements of the programme;
- different companies are working on large elements of the programme;
- different contracts have been placed by the customer for different stages of the programme;
- different types of contracts have been placed for different elements of the programme;
- multitasking contracts have been placed where each task is treated as a separate contract by the customer.

Grouping projects into programmes is recommended when:

- there are many activity or task interfaces between the projects;
- a common pool of labour is supporting all the projects;
- the customer requires individual projects to be reported as a single entity;
- a part of the organization requires the projects to be consolidated and reported as a single entity.

How to set them up

Projects can be broken down into sub projects using a variety of approaches:

- by phase;
- by function;
- by process;
- by product.

The preferred approach would be to break programmes into sub projects using products or deliverables. Using this approach should minimize the inter-project relationships and will allow the project manager to focus on the project deliverables or objectives, rather than on a process or a part of a process.

Sub projects of a programme could be generated based on contract items, provided that the items in the contract are compatible with a product break-down structure approach.

If programmes are subdivided using functions or processes, many of the projects will only have input into other projects rather than resulting in end products themselves. Responsibilities are more difficult to assign; there would be more inter-project relationships and more inter-project coordination required. It would also be more difficult for the project team to focus on the project goals.

If programmes are subdivided into individual projects by phase, it means that the current phase of the programme essentially represents the overall work scope at any point in time. Future uncertainties will not be addressed, as the project covering the future phases will not be able to be defined until the current phase project finishes.

Each individual project in a programme should be treated as a separate entity with quality, finance, project management and support tasks being part of the project. There should *not* be a series of quality tasks encompassing all projects in a programme.

Thought must be given to subcontractors when developing the project breakdown structure. It is more efficient to place a subcontract for one project item rather than for many smaller items across many projects. The internal management of the subcontractor must be considered.

Managing programmes

The managing of multiple projects as part of a programme requires some additional effort over and above managing a group of individual projects.

Even though an individual project is part of a larger programme, it must still be treated as a stand-alone project with its own:

- project manager;
- requirements;
- acceptance criteria;
- budget;
- milestones;
- contingency;
- baseline;
- risk;
- support team (QA, finance, PSO, etc);
- subcontractors/suppliers.

Although it is a stand-alone project, an additional consolidation process must take place subsequent to any individual project reports being generated. Project priorities must be assigned, on occasion resources may be reassigned, and contract changes will take place.

In order to manage multiple projects within a programme, a separate programme manager must be nominated, together with a support team whose sole role is to manage the consolidation process and the interrelationships between the projects. This support group must comprise an overall design authority, quality authority and programme management authority. This support group would be set up as a separate team that would act as the prime contractor for the individual projects and would define the processes that each project would have to adopt. External customer contact, commercial arrangements, and financial trading information would all be managed by this prime contractor programme.

In essence, the programme manager and the central support team act as the customer for the project and manage all inter-project disputes and change orders. From time to time, changes will be required between projects without an external customer being involved. There must be this capability of internal changes and internal customers in order that a programme environment can operate.

Consolidations

When programmes of work are subdivided, thought must be given to any subsequent consolidations. If a large programme is subdivided into ten smaller projects, each with a quality assurance work package, then consideration must be given as to how the quality assurance elements across the projects can be consolidated into an overall quality assurance resource, cost or time plan. Attributes must be assigned across all projects so that this programme consolidation can take place.

As the individual projects will require to be consolidated for corporate reporting, all the projects must adhere to common data standards and a common consistent programme management process. They must all be using a common life cycle process and review cycle. To minimize costs, the projects should use common formats for management and reporting.

Things to consider when defining your project

Stakeholder agreement

It is as important to agree what is not in the scope of the project, as to what is. Defining the project scope sounds obvious in principle. However, it is easy for 'assumptions' to be made by various stakeholders on what is included in the scope. The easiest way to avoid this is to ask the project stakeholders to literally sign the work breakdown structure (or product breakdown structure if you prefer). Being asked to sign their agreement against the scope will force a careful analysis of the requirement which can save a lot of time and cost later.

Don't jump to the planning stage too soon

Without a clear knowledge of the scope, planning will be ineffective. It is tempting to make assumptions and jump too early into the planning stage, rather than painstakingly agree the detailed scope of work. This 'short cut' will lead to more problems later than it solves now.

Involve all those who know the work

The development of work or product breakdown structures gives the project team an opportunity to engage with anyone who knows the work better than they may do. Those who have previously been involved in similar projects will readily spot missing elements of scope using their experience and, even if they are not part of the formal team, they will usually be pleased to help at this stage. This stage is also an opportunity to engage the wider project team in working together – effectively team building but at the same time creating a common vision of the work involved.

Ignoring time

Creating a work breakdown structure allows the project team to define the work or products in a logical way, without being distracted by the 'timeline' which comes later in the planning stage. By ensuring each step of defining and planning your project is done methodically, it will lead to a better result, and increase the chances of project success.

Pre-planning benefits

Developing the responsibility assignment matrix (RAM) before the planning stage allows the project team to avoid the distraction of reality at too early a stage. It is too tempting to modify resource requirement because of assumptions about availability instead of simply and methodically agreeing who should have responsibility for what work. It is also important to keep the distinction between 'responsibility' (at this stage) and 'resource allocation' (who will do the work – agreed at the planning stage).

Programmes and projects

There is often much confusion between programmes and projects, and even the job titles of project manager, programme manager, project director and programme director. However, this chapter has sought to make the distinction clear. Programme management is briefly described in this chapter but is a large subject with many tools and techiques in its own right.

> Project management is like juggling three balls: time, cost and quality.
> Programme management is like a troupe of circus performers standing in
> a circle, each juggling three balls and swapping balls from time to time.
> (Source Geoff Reiss)

Project simulation

If we apply the processes discussed above in the creation of a WBS for our simulation project it may look something like in Figure 2.8.

For the sake of clarity we have only broken down some of the areas to task level, however, in an actual project we would break each level of the WBS down to its lowest point which then give us a list of activities for the project.

Continued overleaf

Project simulation *continued*

FIGURE 2.8 Simulation project: WBS

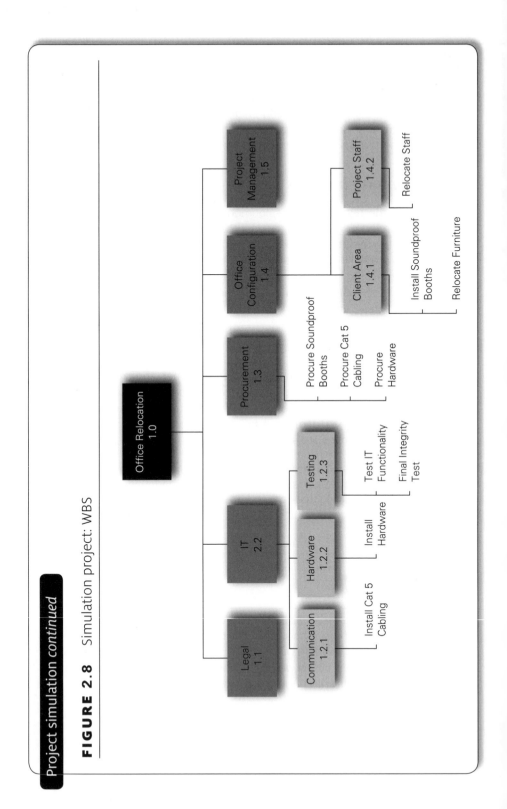

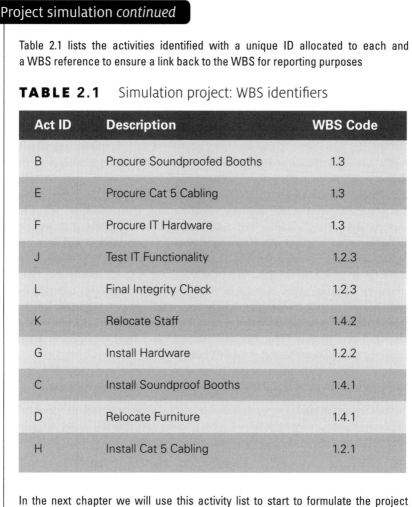

Project simulation *continued*

Table 2.1 lists the activities identified with a unique ID allocated to each and a WBS reference to ensure a link back to the WBS for reporting purposes

TABLE 2.1 Simulation project: WBS identifiers

Act ID	Description	WBS Code
B	Procure Soundproofed Booths	1.3
E	Procure Cat 5 Cabling	1.3
F	Procure IT Hardware	1.3
J	Test IT Functionality	1.2.3
L	Final Integrity Check	1.2.3
K	Relocate Staff	1.4.2
G	Install Hardware	1.2.2
C	Install Soundproof Booths	1.4.1
D	Relocate Furniture	1.4.1
H	Install Cat 5 Cabling	1.2.1

In the next chapter we will use this activity list to start to formulate the project schedule.

Conclusion

We have learned in this chapter how to define and agree the project scope using a number of similar tools depending on the type of project being considered. Ensuring that the work is scoped correctly is of paramount importance and sets the project team a known work scope when moving into the planning stage, described in the next chapter.

CASE STUDY   Halliburton and project definition

About Halliburton Pipeline and Process Services (PPS)

Founded in 1919, Halliburton is one of the world's largest providers of products and services to the energy industry. With nearly 70,000 employees in approximately 80 countries, the company serves the upstream oil and gas industry throughout the life cycle of the reservoir – from locating hydrocarbons and managing geological data, to drilling and formation evaluation, well construction and completion, and optimizing production through the life of the field.

As a Product Service Line of Halliburton, Boots & Coots is one of the largest pressure control providers in the world with the industry's most comprehensive and reliable technology, engineering expertise and personnel superiority. Combining its traditional strengths in pressure control with Halliburton's history of innovation in well intervention and global solutions offerings, Boots & Coots provides its clients with unprecedented solutions for all their requirements. As part of the Boots & Coots service line, Pipeline and Process Services offers multiple services in pre-commissioning, commissioning, maintenance and decommissioning services for the global pipeline and process industries.

Due to the unique and transitory nature of PPS work, each job we carry out can be classified as a 'project'. Therefore, the principles of project management are now implemented through every aspect of the PPS business.

Defining your project the Halliburton Pipeline and Process Services way

In a highly competitive market scope definition is key to ensuring a complete understanding of exactly what is required to be delivered, not only from a cost, time and quality perspective but also from a myriad of other potential deliverables, including:

TABLE 2.2   Scope definition examples

• Documentation	• Expertise
• Equipment	• Attendance at meetings
• Personnel	• Expectations (internal and external)
• Consumables	• Maintenance on products
• Products	• Servicing
• Engineering	• Etc.

Complex projects can have multiple interfaces and, as such, lines of demarcation within these projects can become blurry. In situations such as these, scope definition requires due diligence to make sure every aspect of the work is covered and assigned to a responsible party. During this key element of scope definition there is a need for clear and concise communication between all project stakeholders including, but not limited to, client, suppliers, other contractors/third parties and regulating authorities. Due to the nature of the projects in which Halliburton PPS are involved, in the early stages of the project life cycle the scope of work may not be clear. For this reason it is not uncommon to see very large scope changes between stage gates, eg between tender process and contract award. Even after contract award, it is not uncommon for project scope to grow (or shrink) and as such scope review should be carried out regularly.

Within Halliburton PPS a 'kick off' meeting is held with the client after award to ensure an agreed baseline is established to show where the boundaries of the scope reside. Once a clear picture exists of the project scope, a clear plan of delivery is required to ensure that identified deliverables are assigned to someone who is empowered to deliver that which is required. The level of involvement and detail required will be dependent upon the size and complexity of the project with smaller, less complex projects being much easier to handle than larger more complicated scopes.

FIGURE 2.9   Halliburton size vs complexity

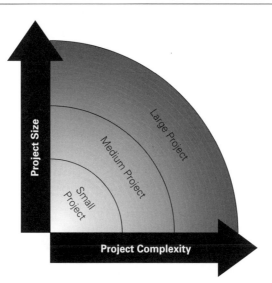

Scope definition of large projects within Halliburton PPS is managed through the use of a work breakdown structure or WBS. This is created soon after the overall scope has been identified and is formulated by the project team in a collaborative approach to capture all the tasks required to ensure scope delivery. A basic template exists within our digital project office to start the definition process with major headings such as engineering, documentation or procurement acting as an aide memoir for the top – or first level – packages in the creation of the WBS. Under each first level package further sub-level tasks are identified and as the WBS cascades to the lowest deliverable tasks, those responsible are assigned. Within Halliburton PPS our baseline WBS is agreed with our client and is considered a live document. Regular review is carried out with the project team not only to track progress but also to capture any scope changes and help in our variation order approval.

The WBS should capture all individual deliverable tasks but it does have its limitations. Whilst it is a very visual tool of what is to be delivered, it does not show how tasks are interlinked nor does it show a logical timeline for completion. High-level schedules can be used to help in the initial building of the WBS (to ensure all tasks are captured at least at a high level) but the WBS can conversely be used to help put the detail into more in-depth schedules.

Within Halliburton PPS, we see a wide range in project size. For smaller projects, a WBS could be considered overkill; however, it is still imperative to define all the required tasks for scope delivery and assign them to a responsible person for action. To this end a simple action tracker is utilized. The process of creating the action tracker is similar to that in building a WBS; however, for smaller projects the project team will be smaller and the process much quicker.

Planning your project

03

Introduction

Planning is an unnatural process; it is much more fun to do something. The nicest thing about not planning is that failure comes as a complete surprise, rather than being preceded by a period of worry and depression.

SIR JOHN HARVEY-JONES

Taking Sir John's comment into account, it is clear that to avoid failure (and especially failure as a surprise) planning is essential. It would seem reasonable to plan the work and therefore have an idea of the costs and timescale before we start to execute it. By spending time on planning, there will be rather more chance of it finishing on time and at the cost predicted and of course that it is delivered to a suitable quality.

At the first stage (just after the bright idea!) we need to have an overview of the reason for the project and its costs which will include labour, ours and any contract labour and the materials and non-labour resources required to complete the project. At this point in the process it will be 'broad brush' or high level estimated information which will be of enough accuracy to justify the feasibility of the project.

Once we have the agreement of the 'sponsor' that the project will deliver the benefits predicted within a suitable timescale, at an acceptable cost and that we have the skills to do the work, we need to further define the plan and determine a baseline against which we can measure success or failure.

In this chapter we will consider the purpose of managing time, define the concepts and terminology of the time-based schedule, and introduce tools for communicating the schedule, including activity listing and bar charts. We will look at how to calculate the duration of work elements, how to use networks to calculate the duration of work elements and the overall project, and show how to adjust the schedule by balancing resource requirements against resource availability.

It is important not to become tied up in the detail of parts of the work which will be carried out later in the project.

This is known as 'rolling wave planning' and in order to understand it, imagine you were planning a holiday overseas in two years' time, would you organize your taxi to the airport now or start shopping for holiday clothes? Probably not. However, you would book your flight and accommodation.

Following the concept of rolling wave planning, varying degrees of planning are carried out depending on when the work has to be executed. Work that is imminent is planned in detail while work that's in the future is planned at a high level. As the work in the future get nearer it is then planned in more detail.

This is a form of progressive elaboration and allows the project team to focus on planning the work that is pending as the project progresses.

There are four main planning documents and they are the network (sometimes referred to as a precedence network), the bar chart (sometimes known as the 'Gantt chart'), the resource histogram and the S-curve.

The four main documents used in planning

FIGURE 3.1 The four main planning documents

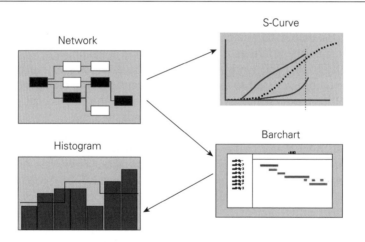

The best way to end up with these highly useful documents is to plan in steps. This chapter will take the reader, step by step, through the planning process and then demonstrate how these documents are developed and applied as project control tools.

Scope management

Breaking down the work and defining the activities

In the last chapter we discussed scope definition and the breaking down or 'decomposing' of the scope into manageable pieces. The main output from decomposing the scope baseline is the activity list, this is achieved by taking each work package of the work breakdown structure (WBS) and breaking it down into a list of activities that need to be conducted to ensure each work package is delivered and therefore the scope achieved.

The activity list is essentially an extension to the WBS as shown below.

FIGURE 3.2   Creating activity lists

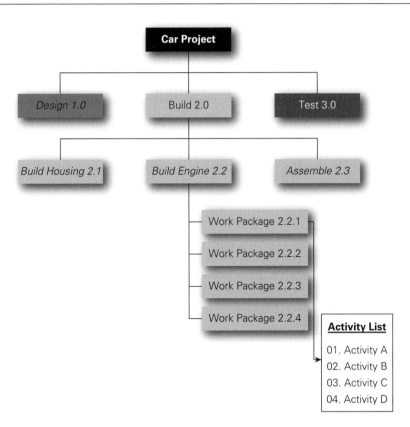

The typical attributes that need to be identified for each activity are:

TABLE 3.1 Typical activity attributes

Activity ID	A unique number that helps locate and identify the activity
Activity name	Cleary identifies the objective of the activity
WBS identifier	The relevant area in the WBS that the activity is linked to
Leads and lags	Any leads or lags that need to be added to the activity
Resource requirements	The people, equipment, material etc required to conduct the work
Relationships	Any relationships to other activities eg Finish to Start, Start to Start, Start to Finish, Finish to Finish etc
Dependency dates	Any dates that determine either start dates or completed dates
Constraints	Any constraints affecting the activity's progress
Assumptions	Any assumption made and additional information

Some of the areas above will be developed later in the chapter.

The above list is not exhaustive and should contain any relevant information for the activity to ensure it is defined clearly and concisely and covers all areas that will ensure the scope is suitably completed.

Remember that you need to break the work down to a level that you can trust the estimate!

Precedence networks

In precedence networks, activities are represented by boxes, which are in turn linked via logical links or dependencies. This is also known as an *activity on node* representation. The technique used to produce this network is called PNM (precedence network methodology) and is the process of identifying and documenting relationships among the project activities. The output of this action is a network diagram which will show the relationship between all the activities in the project.

The following example is a network shown in precedence notation.

FIGURE 3.3 Example precedence network

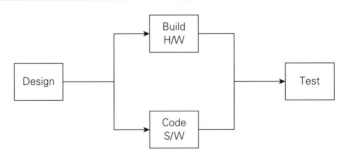

Logical links

There are three types of logical dependency which are represented below:

FIGURE 3.4 Example Finish – Start (FS) constraint

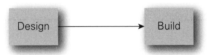

In this example (FS) you can't start building until the design activity is complete.

FIGURE 3.5 Example Start – Start (SS) constraint

In this example (SS), the pipe laying cannot start before the dig trench activity has started.

FIGURE 3.6 Example Finish – Finish (FF) constraint

In this example (FF) you cannot finish laying the tarmac until the drainage task is complete.

Leads and lags

In real life the sequence that activities need to be carried out in is not always as simple as highlighted in in the last examples. In order to add some reality to our representation we can apply leads and lags to the logical links between activities.

A *lead* indicates that the succeeding activity can start prior to preceding activity finishing.

The example below indicates the building can start five days before the design is complete. This is represented by a FS (finish–start) – five days being applied to the logic link between the two activities.

FIGURE 3.7   Example lead

A *lag* indicates that the succeeding activity cannot start until a predetermined time after the preceding activity finishing.

In the example below it may also be possible to start laying a pipe in a 500-hundred mile hole after only three days of digging, therefore the two activities would be linked SS with a three-day lag.

FIGURE 3.8   Example lag

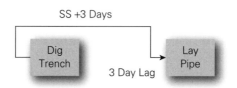

Example: Now that we have a list of activities, we can put them in an order which will allow us to determine the time it will take to complete the work package.

Consider the activity list we produced for the office relocation project in the last chapter. We have now added a value to each activity indicating the 'preceding activity', the task needed to be complete before the present activity can be started.

TABLE 3.2   Simulation project: activities

Act ID	Description	WBS Code	Preceding Activities
A	Project start		
F	Procure IT hardware	1.3	A
B	Procure soundproofed booths	1.3	A
H	Install Cat 5 cabling	1.2.1	E
D	Relocate furniture	1.4.1	C
K	Relocate staff	1.4.2	J
E	Procure Cat 5 cabling	1.3	A
G	Install hardware	1.2.2	D,F
J	Test IT functionality	1.2.3	G,H
L	Final integrity check	1.2.3	K
C	Install soundproof booths	1.4.1	B
M	Project end		L

Based on the activity list produced for the office relocation we can now create an activity sequence based on the added preceding activity information.

FIGURE 3.9   Simulation project: activity sequence

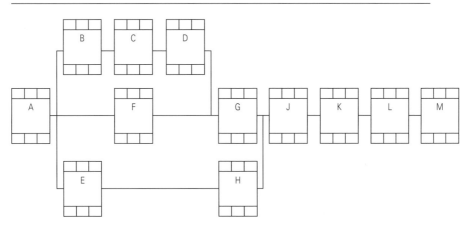

Analysing the network

Once we know how long each activity will take, we can roll up this information to understand the duration of the project.

The mathematical technique used to calculate the network schedule is called network analysis. The following are all types of network analysis: (CPM) critical path methodology, (CPA) critical path analysis and (PERT) programme evaluation and review technique.

Dependencies

We have spoken about logical links or dependencies. These dependencies can be divided into the three main categories described below.

Mandatory dependencies are often known as 'hard logic'. They involve physical restrictions which cannot be avoided; for example, you must dig the trench before you can lay the pipe.

Discretionary dependencies involve sequencing that is done because it is customary or the preferred method but could be done another way. It may be instructed by the client or another important stakeholder. However, it is not a physical constraint.

External dependencies exist where there is a relationship between project activities and events outside the boundaries of the project. These are normally outside the project team's control. However, the project manager needs to be aware of them and they may well also constitute a 'risk' (see 'Risk and your project').

Estimating

Before we can create a logical precedence network for the work package, we need to estimate the durations for each activity.

There are a number of methods which we can use to estimate the durations and costs for each activity and the project. For this reason 'Estimating your project' has been given its own unique reference chapter to help provide advice on how to get estimates right.

Once estimates are available, we can now develop a schedule for the work package by analysing activity sequences, durations and schedule constraints.

Let's take our office relocation network and add some durations to each of the activities.

FIGURE 3.10   Simulation project: durations

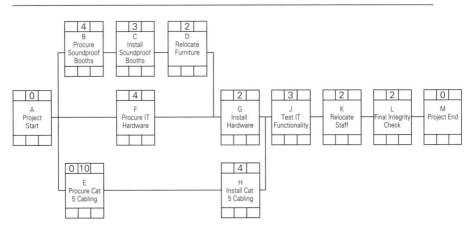

The durations in this example are in weeks but equally could be in hours, days or months.

In order to work out how long it will take to complete the sequenced work, we need to perform what is known as a forward pass on the network.

The forward pass

Early start and times are calculated by conducting a forward pass through the network. The early start of the first activity is zero and the early finish is calculated by adding the duration.

FIGURE 3.11   Forward pass early dates

For example, early finish (EF) = early start (ES) + duration.

This process is then carried through subsequent activities, adding or subtracting any leads or lags, until the whole network is analysed.

Where an activity has two or more preceding activities it is the latest time which is transferred:

FIGURE 3.12   Forward pass calculations

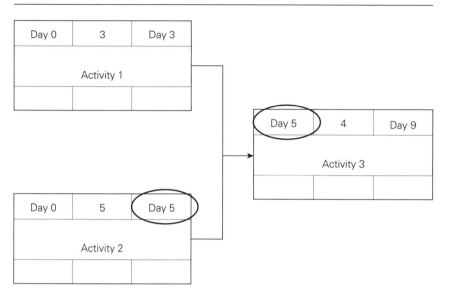

In the above example activity 3 cannot start until both activity 1 and 2 are complete. Therefore the earliest activity 3 can start is day 5.

This process is repeated throughout the network until the earliest end date of the network is established.

Let's perform a forward pass on our office relocation network.

FIGURE 3.13   Simulation project forward pass

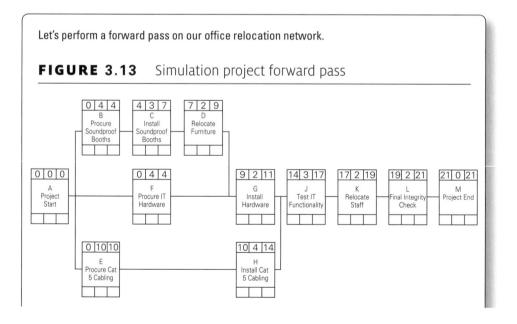

This now indicates that the quickest we can carry out the work we have identified is 21 weeks. However, what we don't know is which of the activities are critical and if we have movement available (float) on any of the activities.

The back pass

In order to establish the latest dates that an activity can commence without affecting the end date a back pass is performed. The early finish of the last activity in the network is transferred to the late finish. The duration is then subtracted from the late finish to obtain a late start.

FIGURE 3.14 Backward pass example

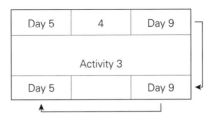

For example, late start (LS) = late finish (LF) – duration.

Where an activity has two or more succeeding activities, it is the earliest date that is transferred.

FIGURE 3.15 Backward pass calculations

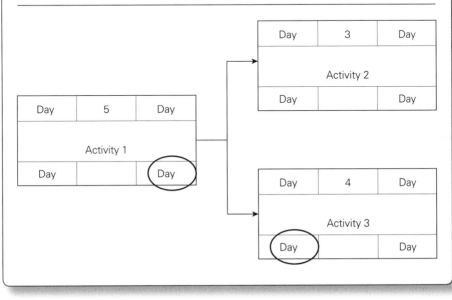

In the above example the latest activity 1 can finish without affecting the late starts of either activity 2 or 3 is day 5.

This process is repeated throughout the network until all late start and finish dates have been identified.

Based on this information we can conduct a back pass on the office relocation project.

FIGURE 3.16 Simulation project: backward pass

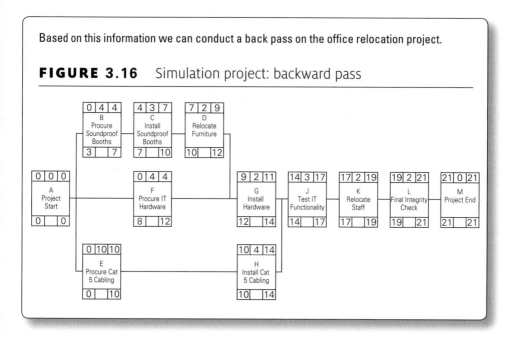

We now start to see a difference between the start and finish dates on some of the activities. This is an indication that those activities can be moved to their later dates without detriment to the project end date.

Float

Now that we have performed a forward pass which shows the earliest dates an activity can start and finish, and a back pass which shows the latest date an activity can start and finish, we can work out what flexibility we have in the network. This is known as 'float' and is very important to the project manager as it will allow for decisions to be taken with the allocation of resources to maximize their utilization.

There are two types of float: free float and total float.

Total float is defined as the amount of time which an activity can be delayed without affecting the end date of the project. Having completed a forward and backward pass, the total float can be calculated as:

Float = latest finish (LF) – earliest finish (EF)

Simulation example

In the network below we have calculated the float for each activity.

FIGURE 3.17   Simulation project: float

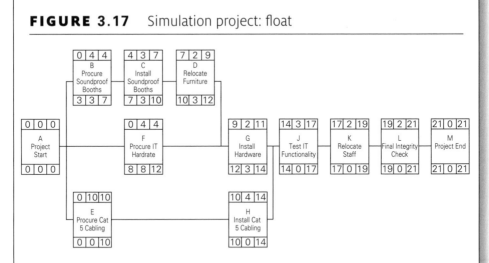

In our office relocation network activity F has a total float of 8 weeks [12(LF) – 4(EF)].

Free float is the amount of time a task can be delayed without affecting the succeeding tasks. This is can be determined by subtracting the EF of an activity from the ES of its subsequent activity.

In our office relocation network activity C has 0 free float [(ES of Act D)7 – (EF of Act C)7], although it has 3 weeks' total float [10(LF) – 7(LS)].

The table below shows the start, finish, duration, total float and free float for each of the office relocation activities.

TABLE 3.3   Simulation project: activity summary

Task	Duration (Weeks)	ES Early Start	EF Early Finish	LS Late Start	LF Late Finish	TF Total Float	FF Free Float
A	0	Week 0	Week 0	Week 0	Week 0	0	0
B	4	Week 0	Week 4	Week 3	Week 7	3	0
C	3	Week 4	Week 7	Week 7	Week 10	3	0
D	2	Week 7	Week 9	Week 10	Week 12	3	0
E	10	Week 0	Week 10	Week 0	Week 10	0	0
F	4	Week 0	Week 4	Week 8	Week 12	8	5

TABLE 3.3 *continued*

Task	Duration (Weeks)	ES Early Start	EF Early Finish	LS Late Start	LF Late Finish	TF Total Float	FF Free Float
G	2	Week 9	Week 11	Week 12	Week 14	3	3
H	4	Week 10	Week 14	Week 10	Week 14	0	0
J	3	Week 14	Week 17	Week 14	Week 17	0	0
K	2	Week 17	Week 19	Week 17	Week 19	0	0
L	2	Week 19	Week 21	Week 19	week 21	0	0
M	0	Week 21	Week 21	Week 21	Week 21	0	0

Critical path

Now that we have the early start and late start for each activity and have calculated the float available, we can now work out the critical path through the network.

The critical path is the series of activities within the network with zero *total float*. The following example shows two paths and their dependencies. The path through 1–3–4 is the critical path.

FIGURE 3.18   Critical path identification

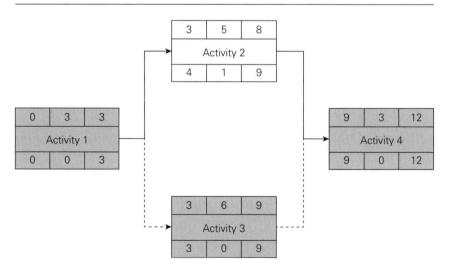

There must be at least one critical path through any network. The path must be continuous but it may branch into a number of parallel paths. It is possible for a network to be totally critical ie each activity will affect the end date of the network if it is completed beyond its late dates. Also, remember that a critical path can change during a project, as actual durations and dates vary.

Simulation example

The critical path for the office relocation project is shown below in grey.

FIGURE 3.19   Simulation project: critical path

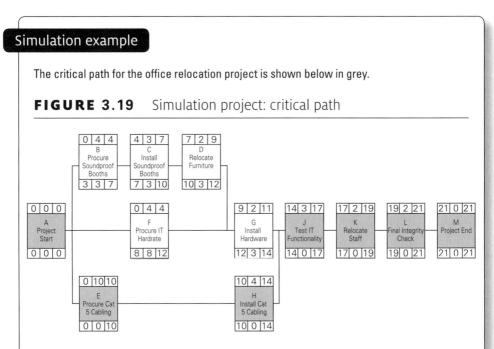

The critical path is very useful in helping to manage the project. When the critical path has been identified, it can be clearly seen where effort cannot be compromised. If any of the activities on the critical path change, the end date of the project will be affected. The critical path is often shown in red on bar charts and network diagrams so that they are easy to follow.

A helpful technique for controlling and managing the critical path is to invest some time in determining what is likely to go wrong in each of the main three project parameters, ie cost, time, quality. Although the critical path only reflects the time element, as discussed earlier a compromise in either cost or quality can have a time impact.

Although managing the critical path is very important, we should not forget the other planned activities. It may be that the project finished on time because the critical path was strictly managed and adhered to. However, another activity in the project was ignored as it had plenty of float, but cost 10 times more than it should have, consequently putting the whole project over budget.

Once the start and finish dates have been calculated they can be plotted on an activity bar chart. A bar chart (sometimes know as a Gannt chart) can show early dates, late dates, float, the critical path and even in some cases logical links.

The following is the bar chart representation of the office relocation network schedule above. The dark bars are critical activities, with the non-critical activities indication float with a lighter line extending from the bottom end of the activity.

FIGURE 3.20   Simulation project: Gantt chart

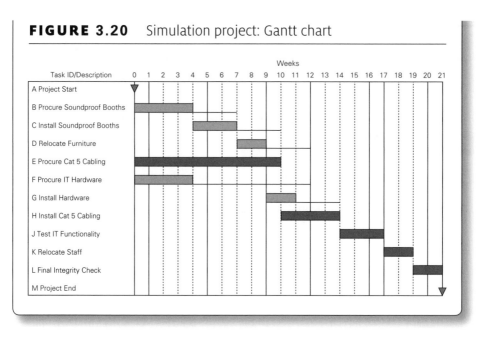

Now that we have a network of activities that stands scrutiny, we can look at the resources required for its delivery.

Project resources

Resources are the items that go into producing work and can be categorized as follows:

FIGURE 3.21   Project resource types

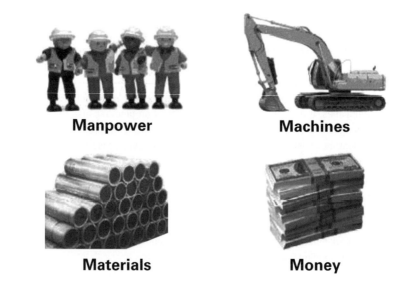

Manpower   Machines

Materials   Money

Resource allocation

We can allocate resources to each activity on our network.

If activity C which has duration of 3 weeks requires 2 labourers per day, we can value that activity at [daily cost of a labourer × 28 days]. (We will assume for this project that a week equates to 7 days per week and 10 hours per day.)

If we extend this calculation for all activities, we will have an estimated duration with estimated resources and therefore an estimated cost for the project.

Resource aggregation

In order to predict the demand for our resource requirement it is necessary to perform a resource aggregation. This entails looking at the demand for each resource on a day by day or week by week basis. Once an aggregation has been performed a resource histogram can be drawn highlighting any peaks or troughs in the demand.

The following bar chart shows two activities that are to be executed over a seven-day duration of the project. A daily aggregation has been carried out and shows the resource requirement for each day of the schedule.

FIGURE 3.22   Resource aggregation example

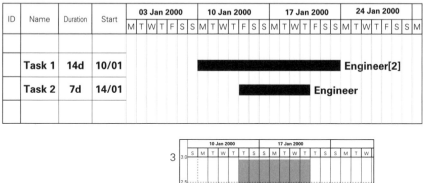

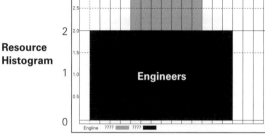

The resource histogram has highlighted three engineers are required from 14 to 18 of January and has also highlighted that the total available is only two.

It is obvious that it is not possible to execute the defined tasks within the timescales with the available resources. The following options are therefore open to us:

TABLE 3.4   Resource aggregation options

Action	Comments	Potential compromise
1. Redefine the scope of the task and reduce the manning required.	This would possibly allow us to reduce the manning requirement and potentially affect the quality aspect. However the optimum utilization should have been defined at the outset.	Quality Cost Safety
2. Increase the duration of task 1 to 28 Days therefore reducing the manning requirement to a maximum of 2.	This may not always be possible as task 1 may require 2 engineers at one time to complete the work.	Time Quality
3. Increase the resources available over the required period. Bring another engineer into the project team either by subcontracting or from an internal source.	This would solve our problem but cost us more money and may not be the best utilization of our resources. Equally we could utilize another resource other than an engineer on task 1. This may be cheaper but could have quality consequences.	Cost Quality Time
4. Move tasks earlier eg start task 2 before task 1.	This may be possible if the logic permits it. In the situation above there are no dependencies shown so this may be a feasible option.	Possibly none
5. Move the tasks later and try to spread the manpower requirement. eg move task 2 until after task 1.	This would have the effect of extending the end date of the project if the task was on the critical path.	Time Cost

Note: option 5 would be the only course of action a software planning package would automatically consider possible.

If option 5 were chosen the effect would be as follows.

FIGURE 3.23 Resource aggregation example solution

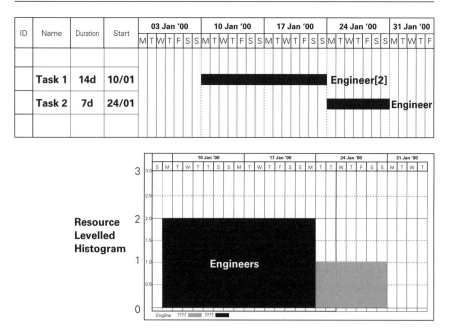

In order to enable task 2 to be completed using the available resources it needs to be pushed out to 24 January where there are sufficient resources to carry out the task.

Assigning resources

Resources must be assigned at the lowest level of detail of the schedule, ie the activity. When initially assigning resources, the approach to take is to assume that infinite resources are available at all times.

When assigning non-labour costs it is important to consider how costs are to be tracked and recorded. If the organization tracks and records committed costs, then the schedule should show committed costs (see Glossary of terms). If the organization records actual costs at delivery then the non-labour resources must be assigned in a similar manner.

Resource planning

The objective in planning resources is to optimize the use of these resources. The process of resource planning is a scheduling process and can be either manual or automated. If it is automated, the resource requirements for the different activities and the available resources can be added to the network and the computer itself will calculate where there are too many or too few resources and reschedule the activity.

Resource availability

Up until now, all resources have been assumed to be available as and when required. In order to carry out resource planning or scheduling, the availability of each resource has to be determined.

Availability of a resource can either be a total availability or availability over a time period. Total availability is normally reserved for consumable resources such as concrete whilst availability over a time period is used for other resources.

Availability is normally defined as a quantity or level over a time period, eg three people are available from 1 January until 4 April.

When defining availability, care should be taken to ensure that resource requirements and resource availabilities are compatible, eg do not assign a full-time resource requirement if the maximum availability profile being used is only 0.9 (to take account of holidays, etc).

From the work done so far, we can create a schedule baseline. This is a specific version of the project schedule and is developed from the schedule network analysis and reviewing the resource availability and allocation. This is a key component of the project management plan and is used to measure schedule performance.

Any deviations from the schedule baseline will impact on one or more of cost, time and quality and must be managed by a documented change control process, which is described in a separate chapter.

The amount of data will vary by application area; however, the project schedule data will normally contain the following:

- schedule milestones;
- activity attributes;
- identified assumptions and constraints.

It will be supported by a resource histogram, alternative schedules and scheduling of contingency reserves.

Against this background, we now need a process for monitoring the status of the project to update the project progress and manage changes to the schedule baseline and suitable reporting systems in order to communicate progress.

Managing the schedule

The project management plan contains the schedule management plan which describes how the project will be managed and controlled and the schedule baseline against which it will be measured and reported.

The most recent project schedule is required as is actual work performance information describing project progress.

There is a variety of tools and techniques that can be used to control the schedule.

First and foremost are regular performance reviews, which are meetings held to assess the current project status and progress. They are typically used with one or more of the reporting techniques listed below:

- *Variance analysis* is simply plan minus actual. Therefore if the task was planned to take three days and takes five, the schedule variance is minus two days.

- *Earned value analysis (EVA)* is the most commonly used method for performance measurement as it integrates scope, cost (or resource) and schedule measures to help the project management team to assess project performance. EVA is described in a separate chapter.

- *Resource levelling* is used to optimize the distribution or work among resources and schedule compression is used to find ways to bring activities that are behind into alignment with the plan. Both are described below.

Resource levelling

Developing the schedule is an iterative process with the optimization continuing as often as necessary, until an acceptable schedule is produced. A schedule is deemed acceptable when it satisfies the customer's delivery date requirements, contains a minimum amount of staff fluctuations and has an achievable build-up and run-down of resources.

Once time analysis has been completed and the schedule optimized, a resource-constrained or resource-levelled schedule should be created. When performing simple time analysis, only the durations and logic of the network are considered when calculating activity start and end dates. Conflicts will arise and alternatives have to be evaluated in order to meet contractual and management objectives. Schedule adjustments usually have to be made from the following options:

- constraints relaxed;
- manpower estimates revised;
- project scope revisited;
- network logic revised;
- critical path activities shortened;
- additional resources made available;
- activities worked on in parallel.

When scheduling, consider the different approaches that can be taken to a single activity to overcome resource problems. These approaches can be combined in order to overcome the shortfall.

Alternatively when the end date of the project cannot be allowed to slip, eg a major event like the Olympics where it is crucial that it starts on time, the method employed is *resource compression*. This method will utilize float within the project, increasing or decreasing the resources required for specific activities. In this way peaks and troughs in resource usage can be smoothed out.

However, if after employing these techniques you are still in danger of missing the end date of the project your final recourse will be to employ more resources to protect the project's end date or to renegotiate new end date by presenting your evidence to the relevant stakeholders.

Simulation example

The following bar chart indicates the resources required for each week of the project. In all cases in the chapter, resources used have been manpower; equally, machines and materials should be treated in the same way.

FIGURE 3.24   Simulation project: Gantt chart

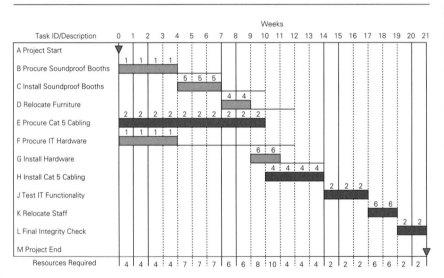

This resource information can be translated onto a resource histogram for a better understanding of requirements.

FIGURE 3.25 Simulation project: resource histogram

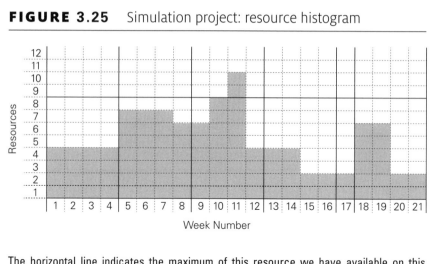

The horizontal line indicates the maximum of this resource we have available on this project. This means the work we have planned is not achievable as it is scheduled at present.

Consider the activities contributing to the overload and decide on the most appropriate action to resolve the issue.

The S-curve

The adequacy of any schedule should be reviewed and achieve the following criteria:

- clear presentation of the critical path, including activities which are critical and areas of risk;
- identification of any 'float' available in the schedule along with identifying key decision points;
- key interrelationships between activities and key dates and milestones within the schedule.

Having these criteria in place will enable you to determine the cash forecast and allow you to communicate to the project sponsor the work that has to be accomplished. This will in turn provide a sound base for monitoring progress. Importantly you will carry out resource levelling to ensure optimum utilization of staff and equipment.

Once the schedule has been finalized the resource information can be represented by means of an S-curve. This will show the cumulative resource requirement over time. In the example below the S-curve shows the cumulative labour resource required over time but equally could show cumulative costs over time. This information will then provide a basis for the monitoring and control of the project. This is discussed further in the Executing your Project chaper.

FIGURE 3.26 Simulation project: S-curve

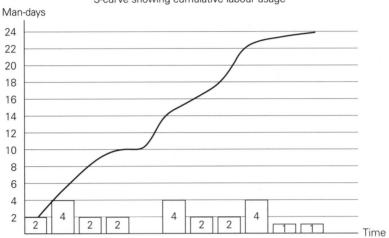

S-curve showing cumulative labour usage

Simulation example

The following example assumes each of our resources costs £10,000 per week. By applying this cost to each week and calculating the cumulative costs for each week we can produce a cost histogram and a cumulative cost curve for the project.

FIGURE 3.27 Simulation project: cost histogram

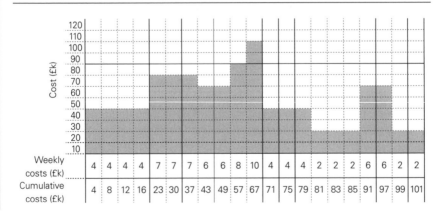

FIGURE 3.28   Simulation project: cumulative cost curve

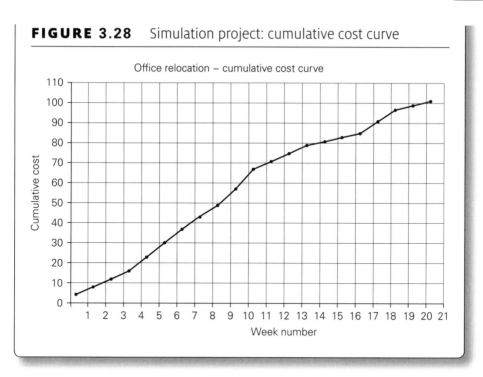

This can now be used to compare forecasted money out against the project cash flow. Once the expenditure of £101,000 and spread of expense over the project duration has been approved by the appropriate stakeholders these numbers would be locked and become the budget for the project.

Things to consider when planning

Over-optimism

Human nature affects planning in many ways. Despite the awareness that few projects are delivered on schedule people tend to plan optimistically. Techniques involved in building a time-based schedule rely on each activity taking the length of time it should take, then leading neatly to the next activity and so on. Whilst a single activity may well be delivered on time and encounter none of the risk that may have been identified (see 'Risk and your project'), the chances of each activity going to plan are slim at best. Critical path analysis (see later in this chapter) encourages the project team to commit to the best possible outcome in terms of a time-based schedule. This is planning to fail. It is important therefore to be critical when developing resource and duration estimates and to be realistic. It is usually better to overdeliver than miss your project end date. As a project schedule slips the common approach is to throw more resources at the project – usually at a high cost – to recover the schedule. This is not an argument for 'sand bagging' and overestimating but it is an argument for realism and allowing risk contingency.

Owning the plan

A common argument in project management circles is whether a project manager needs to understand the technical aspects of the work in order to manage the project or whether the discipline of good project management in itself is the important competence for a project manager. This argument also applies to project planning as a discipline. In a large project it is common for specialist project planners to be used who may, or may not, understand the technical detail. These arguments will continue but the solution is for project managers and the project team to 'own' the plan rather than delegate the process. In practice this means critically analysing every element of the schedule and ensuring that those in the organization with experience of similar projects or smaller 'work packages' ensure a realistic plan is developed.

The pitfalls of planning software

In this section we have looked at how to build and develop a schedule manually. These skills have become a lost art since the widespread availability of desktop planning software such as Microsoft Project®, and more sophisticated corporate tools such as Primavera® for large-scale projects. However, these tools cannot think and they cannot apply experience; they simply apply mathematical logic. The tools themselves are essential to plan and manage the data and complexity of large projects. However, they are not a replacement for human thought and experience. The temptation to let the software tools do the work is significant. However, project managers need to challenge the plan in all aspects – the durations, the logic and the resourcing.

Time, cost or quality?

Every project has different emphasis on time, cost or quality. For some projects it is critical that they are delivered on time. For others, the budget must not be exceeded but time may be compromised. For others still (such as safety or legislation-based projects) the quality of the deliverables is key. For a project manager or project team to critically analyse the plan they must understand the project drivers and ensure the plan is 'weighted accordingly'.

For example, if the timescale is the key priority then realistic time estimates are essential. If the budget is fixed then minimizing cost, sometimes at the expense of schedule, is essential. It is common when project teams challenge these project drivers for them to be told that cost, time, quality are all essential. However, some elements are always more important than others. To apply the same emphasis to all three in a project plan is to plan to fail and nobody will thank the project team for this at the end of the project.

All projects contain uncertainty and risk and change is inevitable. To fail to acknowledge this is to give the project team an unrealistic challenge and the project will fail. It is the ethical duty of the project manager to understand the project drivers before committing to the project plan.

Avoiding 'reverse planning'

It is not uncommon for a project manager to be given the delivery date, the budget and the quality parameters before the project plan has been developed. This is applying reverse logic to the project plan and will set the project team up for failure. However, although sometimes reverse planning is inevitable, it is still the duty of the project manager to be honest with their organization. This problem can be mitigated by publishing the risk management plan (see 'Risk management') and by producing different planning scenarios for review. These techniques ensure that the project sponsor or organization's management are made aware of the risks and different scenarios that can be applied and the decision then ultimately rests with them. Apart from ensuring the project manager keeps their job (and their credibility), it also ensures there is sound corporate governance. Whilst unrealistic management demands are not uncommon, no organization likes surprises.

Level of planning

The level of detail that your project needs to be planned at will depend greatly on the size of the project, the amount of information that is available to the project and the amount of visibility and reporting that is required. In a large project it is important to provide a level of detail at which the project can be managed. Presenting the project sponsor or organization with a complex plan involving many thousands of activities will remove clarity from the plan overall. For this reason this section recommends a series of planning 'levels' so managers at different levels can review information at the appropriate level of detail.

For example, a senior manager may wish to view the key project milestones whereas a project team leader managing a specific element of the project will wish to see the detail.

By effective coding of the WBS and including WBS codes against each task, summary level plans can easily be obtained.

Conclusion

We have learned in this chapter how to put together a project plan, including a schedule and a budget that will be realistic to follow. Creating this 'baseline' plan is critical to everything that follows in the project life cycle. The planning stage is often too rushed or ill-considered. A good plan sets the project team up for success. A poor plan sets them up for failure.

In the next chapter we will look at project execution. From the beginning of this next phase your project plan will be crucial to guide you through the entire all-important project execution phase.

CASE STUDY   Planning the AMEC way

About AMEC

AMEC is one of the world's leading engineering, project management and consultancy companies. Their goal is to deliver profitable, safe and sustainable projects and services for their customers in the oil and gas, minerals and metals, clean energy, environment and infrastructure markets, including sectors that play a vital role in the global and national economies and in people's everyday lives. They design, deliver and maintain strategic assets for their customers, offering services which extend from environmental and front end engineering design before the start of a project to decommissioning at the end of an asset's life. Their customers, in both the private and public sector, are among the worlds biggest and best in their fields; BP, Shell, EDF, National Grid and US Navy, to name just a few.

They are truly international, with major operations centres based in the UK and Americas and offices and projects in around 40 countries worldwide. They work in diverse and often challenging environments, from sub-zero temperatures in the north of Canada to the sweltering heat of the Persian Gulf.

They employ over 27,000 people – ranging from scientists and environmental consultants to engineers and project managers, dedicated professionals who take pride in their work. The AMEC Academy helps them to attract, develop and retain the best talent.

Planning the AMEC way

AMEC's preferred tool for planning is Oracle Primavera P6 and this software allows for an enterprise project structure (EPS), which enables project managers to manage multiple projects, from the highest levels of the organization to the individuals that perform specific project tasks. Multiple users can access the same projects concurrently and it allows for centralized resource management.

AMEC's approach to planning and scheduling can be represented in two major stages.

Project planning and schedule development resulting in the creation of a baseline:

- top-down approach;

- based on the data compiled from the initial project planning;

- facilitated by the work flows and work breakdown structures.

Schedule management resulting in a schedule update as a continuous and regular cycle from update period to update period:

- status collection (bottom-up approach);
- schedule updating, analysis, review and mitigation;
- period close and reporting.

These stages and the steps within are depicted in the chart below:

FIGURE 3.29 AMEC planning stages and steps

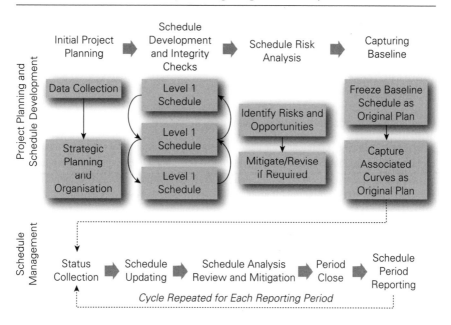

The planning process uses a 'top-down' approach for schedule development and a 'bottom-up' approach for schedule management. Each activity at a higher level is represented by a number of more detailed activities at the next lower level as shown in Figure 3.30 on the following page:

Project schedule definition

Level 1, 2 and 3 schedules are aligned with the work breakdown structure (WBS), plus milestones.

Level 1 and 2 schedules can initially be produced stand-alone before being replaced by rolled-up data from the level 3 project control schedule once this has been developed.

FIGURE 3.30   AMEC schedule levels

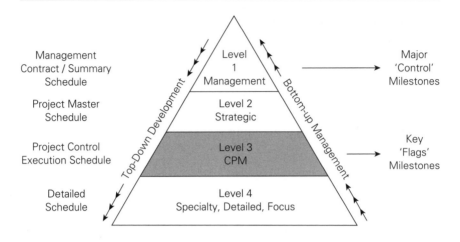

| Management Contract / Summary Schedule | Level 1 Management | Major 'Control' Milestones |

Level 1: Management
Level 2: Strategic
Level 3: CPM
Level 4: Specialty, Detailed, Focus

Management Contract / Summary Schedule
Project Master Schedule
Project Control Execution Schedule
Detailed Schedule

Top-Down Development
Bottom-up Management

Major 'Control' Milestones
Key 'Flags' Milestones

Level 1: the management/contract/summary schedule

This schedule level is principally for executive management (directors, project sponsors, etc) it typically has between 20 and 50 activities. It provides a very high-level schedule for the project life cycle including as applicable execution/implementation, commissioning and start-up, for each project/plant area, while highlighting key project milestones.

Level 2: the project master schedule

This schedule level is principally for senior management (project sponsors, project management, etc). It typically has between 50 and 500 activities and is broken down into major areas. It reflects major project/contract, areas, disciplines, and their main activities. It presents the sequence, interrelated logic and can be used on a stand-alone basis for schedule risk analysis. This is the detailed 'control' level for cost and schedule integration and earned value reporting.

Level 3: the project control/execution schedule

This schedule level is the key project coordination schedule developed to show the sequence and interrelated logic between activities, with activities logically linked to predecessors and successors. This will typically have between 200 and 3,000 activities (depending on project scope). It is pivotal to creating and validating all other project schedules, and rolls up into level 2 and level 1.

This schedule will define the project critical paths and activity free and total floats.

It is fully resource-loaded to validate manpower and peak requirements and to address forecast requirements; this will realize optimum resource and funding utilization and will be used to coordinate and control all activities on the project, and to perform critical path analyses and 'what-if' schedules.

In some instances, it may be expanded into more detailed activities that will be classified as level 4 activities.

Level 4: detailed schedules

This schedule level is optional and dependent on the size and complexity and needs of the project.

The number of activities is unlimited and will be dependent on the project's scope and might only be represented for portions of the level 3 schedule.

This schedule will show significantly more detail in the production and issue of engineering deliverables, procurement packages, contract packages, and detailed construction work programmes.

It might be expanded from the level 3 schedule as the project evolves, with level 4 activities being created at each regular update period as more detailed planning data becomes available; providing a rolling window of detail.

Executing your project

Introduction

> *If you always do what you've always done, you'll always get what you've always got.*

ANTHONY 'TONY' ROBBINS, US SELF-HELP AUTHOR
AND MOTIVATIONAL SPEAKER

There are endless statistics available which demonstrate how most projects are delivered late, or over budget, or don't deliver the benefits they had promised to.

The concept of the 'learning organization' does not seem to have progressed much in organizations involved in project delivery. Lessons learned need to be widely disseminated and organizational knowledge and experience harnessed to ensure that they deliver projects more successfully.

The first step towards improving project execution performance is to examine best practice – the subject of this chapter.

The primary purpose of setting a project schedule in the last chapter was to enable us to measure and control the project parameters of cost, time and quality. The four main steps required in the control process are as Figure 4.1.

Set the measure

Before execution, and to allow for effective control, a snapshot of the project should to be taken and held for the duration of the project. This is known as a baseline. A *baseline* provides a base to measure the progress of a project against and therefore highlights any variances from the original plan.

If progress is measured against the most recent version of the plan the control required is then lost. It is not uncommon to see projects which claim

FIGURE 4.1   Progress monitoring

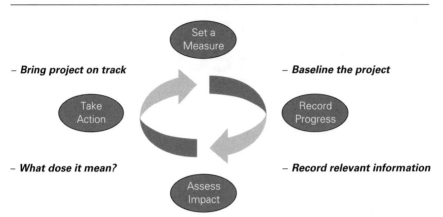

to be on schedule because they are updated after each review meeting and the original plan and targets are then lost and forgotten.

Although a baseline should be frozen and maintained in this state constantly, as far as possible, there are occasions when it may need to be changed. Changes to the baseline must be discussed thoroughly and only made in exceptional cases.

Some of the reasons for changing a baseline are:

- When the scope of work has changed or switched and costs have to be reallocated to different areas of the project, eg if a 'work package' has been subcontracted rather than carried out in-house.

- When new work is added, it is very difficult to add the estimated cost and dates of new tasks to an existing baseline.

- If the project becomes significantly overspent or delayed. There is no benefit in holding a baseline that no longer represents a realistic measure for control. In addition, trying to work to a grossly outdated baseline can be demotivating to those working on the project.

Cost reporting

An important aspect of monitoring and controlling the project is managing the project costs against the agreed budget. The budget is the amount of money that has been authorized to be spent on the completion of the project. Irrespective of the project measurement indications and the fact that the total project cost may exceed this amount the budget remains the same.

As discussed previously the project costs should be broken down by way of a WBS (work breakdown structure) which then forms the basis for the cost account. This is simply a breakdown of the project costs to a manageable and reportable level. As part of the planning process, costs should have been allocated at task level for all labour, material and equipment. In addition provision should also be made for any project risks identified. By tracking actual costs at this level, comparison against the budget can be examined and summarized at all levels and ultimately compared against the budget.

The cost account can then be used to:

- track actual costs against planned;
- give an early warning of any problems;
- highlight any uneven cost loadings and risk areas;
- show the total cost of the project to date;
- allocated individual budget areas;
- provide a basis for project forecasting.

The timing of the project expenditure is also important and is best shown as a cumulative amount over time.

Planned project cost over time

As was discussed in the last chapter, a cumulative S-curve should be produced as part of the planning stages. This can then be used to track progress throughout the project. The diagram below shows the planned expenditure over the life of the project.

FIGURE 4.2   Cumulative cost curve

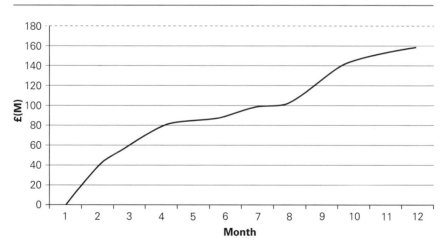

We can then show the actual cost against planned cost as the project progresses. This tells us we have spent less than planned up to the seventh month of the project.

FIGURE 4.3   Actual vs planned curves

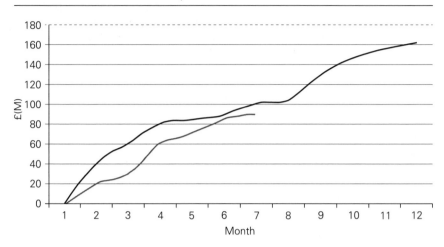

Cash flow

In addition to the monitoring of the actual spend against the planned it also important to monitor the cash flow situation of the project. Cash flow is the difference between the income and the expenditure. In the project shown below the cash flow is negative until the last month of the project. This is often the case as the customer will not pay out until the work has been done and invoiced.

FIGURE 4.4   Project cash flow curve

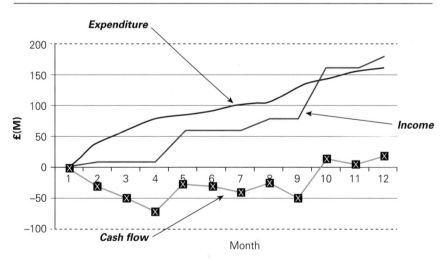

Cash flow should also be tracked and monitored to ensure it does not exceed what was planned for. It may be that the project is exceeding its planned achievement due to a more efficient workforce, additional hours being spent, early delivery of materials, etc. This will generally mean more money has to be paid out for the additional resources. However, if your customer is paying in monthly staged payments then this could cause cash flow problems and not allow enough funds to pay for the resources used.

Payment methods

The project payment terms are defined within the contract and they detail when, who and how payment will be made to the project. The contract will also define the terms of the payment and often the currency that the monies will be paid in.

Different payment terms can considerably affect the project cash flow and often the viability of the project, ie if the customer will only pay for the project at the final close-out milestone, someone needs to fund the project effort from beginning to end.

The following are some typical payment methods:

- *Payment on completion* – As discussed above, this is when payment is made on delivery of the end product or service; this is not a favourable payment method from the project viewpoint.
- *Advance payment* – This is the opposite from the above method and is where the customer will pay for all or some of the project in advance of it being undertaken.
- *Milestone payments* – Payment is made on the successful achievement of agreed project milestones. This can be on an agreed value or as a percentage of the phase or project, eg 20 per cent of contract will be awarded on completion of the approved design milestone.
- *Retention* – This is where the customer will hold back some payment for a period of time, often to ensure successful operation or functionality of the deliverables, eg 5 per cent of the contract value held for the agreed two-year warranty period. The full amount would then be released to the supplier after two years, assuming the warranty terms had been met.

Forecasting

As discussed, it is vitally important to record, monitor and compare our costs against the budget. This tells us how we are doing against what we planned to do. However, more importantly we need to know what has still to be done, the cost of it and how that compares against our final budget.

There are several forecasting methods, none of which will provide a totally accurate figure but they can give a reasonable indication of the project's expected performance. The following are common forecasting methods:

- *Actual plus remaining budget* – This is a simple forecasting method which adds together the actual costs occurred to the remaining budgeted figure. For example, assume in month 6 £15,000 has been spent out of a total budget of £30,000. However, our plan estimated that in month 6 we should have only spent £10,000. This would mean the forecast total would £15,000 + £20,000, ie £35,000.

- *Actual plus estimate to complete* – This takes the actual costs incurred and adds them to the planned cost of the remaining work. It may be that the productivity of the project labour had been underestimated and therefore the remaining work needs to be replanned. The new planned cost would then be added to the cost to date.

- *Trend* – This is where the trend of the costs or times to date are applied to the remaining work. Several calculations can be applied and are discussed later in this module.

Information for updating project progress

Project control is the process whereby the project manager determines the degree to which the project plan is being met. The focus generally tends to be on schedule, budget, scope/quality and resources.

The key aspect which control addresses is variance. Variance is, in its simplest form, the difference between planned and actual status. It is highly unusual for a project not to have some variance during its life cycle. Therefore the project manager not only needs to identify variance but also the magnitude of the variance – those activities where magnitude of variance is beyond an acceptable level must become the focus for corrective action.

A popular misconception is that it is a crime for a project manager to have a project with a variance. The reality of demanding zero variance on a project is that, apart from generally being unachievable in all but the simplest of projects, it will ultimately encourage corner-cutting. However, aiming for zero variance by addressing variances as they arise is a much more commendable approach.

Feedback on task performance should be obtained regularly. The greatest challenge is setting up a system which encourages honest, timely and accurate reporting by project staff. The first step to achieving this is to ensure that progress is reported against the plan. Using a simple pro forma with information from the project plan may well be ample (see Table 4.1).

The frequency at which progress is reported is relative to the length of duration of the tasks on the project. For example, in a project where tasks are typically a few weeks in duration, there is no point in reporting every other day as little progress will have been made; similarly, reporting every month is

TABLE 4.1 Capturing progress data

Task	Start	Finish	Duration	Hours	Cost
Build component X	Planned **1 May 11**	Planned **10 May 11**	Planned **10 days**	Planned **160 hrs**	Planned **€20,000**
	Revised	Revised **12 May 11**	Revised **12 days**	Revised **176 hrs**	Revised **€21,600**
	Actual **1 May 11**	Actual	Actual	Actual	Actual
	Reason for variances **Late delivery of assembly tools**				
Test section Z	Planned **5 May 11**	Planned **12 May 11**	Planned **8 days**	Planned **128 hrs**	Planned **€15,000**
	Revised	Revised	Revised	Revised	Revised
	Actual **5 May 11**	Actual **11 May 11**	Actual **7 days**	Actual **140 hrs**	Actual **€16,000**
	Reason for variances **Used up unused labour on component X task to get finished earlier. Cost more as other labour more expensive.**				

of no benefit as it will probably be too late to correct problems with progress measurements made so far apart. In such a situation, a weekly progress report would suffice.

In more sophisticated project management environments using information technology tools, it is possible to automatically generate much of the data required for progressing, eg:

- hours worked, from a timesheet system;
- task costs, from a purchase order/stock control system.

This becomes particularly effective if a set of standard work, organization and cost breakdown structure codes is used.

A rough indication of project progress can be obtained from an updated project Gantt chart. However, this tends to only show schedule-based progress – to take a consolidated view of project progress, earned value analysis provides a number of tools for measuring project performance in terms of a set of indicators.

Analysing the plan

Once all the progress elements have been collected the data can be analysed and reviewed and compared to the baseline.

If the project has slipped, critical areas can be examined and the plan adjusted.

Areas to consider are:

- relaxing constraints;
- revisiting manpower estimates;
- revising network logic;
- putting more activities in parallel;
- passing work to subcontractors.

It is not advisable to simply reduce the duration of future activities in order to achieve the overall schedule.

Variances

Any discrepancy from the plan or baseline is a variance. When the progressed plan is analysed, all variances should be detailed and a cumulative record of all variances maintained.

Bear in mind that the variances may have been caused by an inadequate estimate and this information must be recorded so that the next project does not fall into the same trap.

The two key variances are timescales and costs and in order to understand the correlation between time and cost, performance measurements or earned value should be used.

Performance measurement terminology

Most projects regularly progress their plans and generate status reports indicating what events have occurred and what milestones have been achieved. They also predict what events will occur in the future and when these events will occur. They also record what money has been spent and estimate what money is going to be spent in the future. In most cases, however, physical progress or achievement is measured and reported separately to financial spend and forecasting.

Few projects measure their efficiency of working or the value of work that has been achieved, ie few projects measure their performance.

A method of measuring project performance which enables efficiency of working or the value of work that has been achieved is *earned value*.

Earned value is a process that assigns a value to the achievement of project work. Ideally, achievement is in terms of milestones or deliverables. The value is usually monetary but can be expressed in any appropriate units such as man hours.

Earned value is the comparison of the amount of money (or man hours) actually spent with the amount of money (or man hours) which should have been spent to achieve the progress made.

The value to be earned when a specific milestone or deliverable is achieved is based on the planned cost of achieving the milestone or deliverable.

What are earned value measurements?

The purpose of earned value measurements is to compare the amount of money actually spent with that which has been earned by performing the work to date.

This is normally achieved by comparing spend to date with the amount of money that should have been spent to make the actual progress that has been made.

To achieve this three things are needed:

- a budget subdivided into measurable packages of work;
- a method of measuring achievement or progress;
- a method of collecting costs against the measurable packages of work.

Using performance measurements

Earned value techniques provide a discipline that ensures sound management and, what is more important, provide an early indicator of the state of the health of the project from, primarily, a cost and schedule perspective.

Any measurements of performance must be treated with caution. They are *indicators* of the efficiency or performance of a project and should be used as one of the criteria on which project managers base their decisions, after having interpreted the information and placed it in context.

Performance measures indicate where shortfalls are occurring and where extra resources, or management action, or other support is required in order to overcome the problem. It is an early indicator of problems and gives a pointer as to what may happen to the project if actions are not taken.

The earned value process can be applied to any type of project, irrespective of size.

What are the benefits?

The figure below shows the traditional budget vs actual graph.

FIGURE 4.5   Example budget vs actual

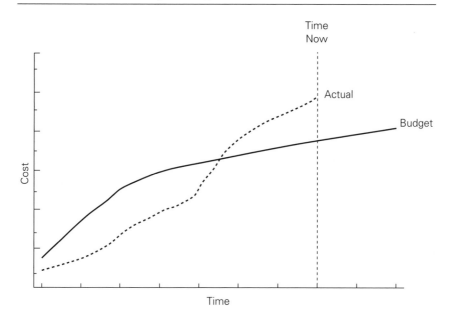

This graph is traditionally used to compare budget spend with actual spend. It shows how much has been spent to date and compares it to the budget that was planned to be used by the report date.

It does not show:

- if the project is ahead of schedule;
- if the project is truly over or under spent;
- if the project is getting value for money;
- if money has been spent on the right things;
- if the problems are over or have only just begun.

The graph below is similar to the previous graph except that a measure of performance (or status value) has been included. The line included is the *earned value* or *achievement* line.

This additional line represents the proportion of the budget that has actually been achieved.

FIGURE 4.6 Example budget, actual and earned
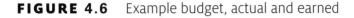

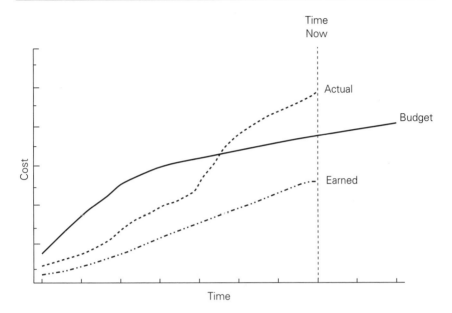

It indicates the following additional information:

- The project is behind schedule because the amount of work completed is less than that scheduled.

- The project is overspent because the cost of the work completed is greater than the budgeted cost of the work.

- The project is spending money incorrectly, as it is costing more to achieve less than budget.

- The problems do not appear to be contained, since the slope of the actual cost line is greater that the budgeted cost line which indicates that the overspend is going to increase, even though the earned value line does look like it will intersect the budget cost line some time in the future.

Terminology

Performance measurement baseline (PMB)
The PMB is the time-phased budget plan against which contract
    performance is measured. It is formed by the budgets assigned to
    scheduled cost accounts and undistributed budgets. It equals the total
    allocated budget less management reserve.

Actual cost (AC)
The cost incurred and recorded for the work performed in a given period.

Planned value (PV)
The planned cost for a defined scope of work that is scheduled to be
    done during a given period. Specifically PV is the sum of all budgets
    for all packages of work and in total forms the PMB.

Earned value (EV)
The sum of the budgets for completed work packages and completed
    portions of open work packages. Also referred to as earned value.

Cost variance (CV)
The difference between the EV and AC. A negative value indicates a cost
    overspend and a positive value indicates a cost underspend.

$$Cost\ variance = earned\ value - actual\ cost$$

Schedule variance (SV)
Schedule variance can be considered in terms of cost or time. The
    schedule variance (cost) is the difference between the EV and PV.
    A negative value indicates less work has been done than planned
    and a positive value indicates more work has been done than
    planned.

$$Schedule\ variance\ (cost) = earned\ value - planned\ cost$$

The schedule variance (time) is the difference between original
    duration (OD) planned and the actual time expended (ATE)
    on the work to date.

$$Schedule\ variance\ (time) = the\ original\ duration\ (OD)\ planned\ for\ the$$
$$work\ to\ date - actual\ time\ expended\ (ATE)\ on\ the\ work\ to\ date$$

Example of an earned value calculation

This example shows how to measure the progress made on building a wall
using earned value.

FIGURE 4.7 Brick wall example: specification

Here are the original estimates to build a wall of 20 rows of bricks:

Timescale = 2 weeks (10 days)

Estimate (budget) = £1,000

Size of wall = 20 rows

FIGURE 4.8 Brick wall example: progress

Progress after 5 days (50 per cent of the original time estimate): up to that point the costs were £600 (partly due to the fact that the bricks cost more).

The actual cost of the work performed is therefore £600 and the budget cost of work scheduled is £500 (original cost × elapsed time as a percentage of the original time estimate). If we were to graph this we would get a typical project cost curve:

FIGURE 4.9   Brick wall example: actual vs budget

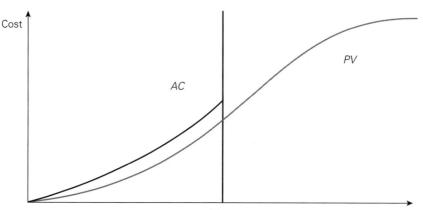

What does this graph tell us?

Nothing, in fact!

Why? Because although it looks on the graph as if the project is overspent, nowhere does it take into account the percentage of work completed. Therefore you might have completed more work than you needed to at this point, in which case, there might not have been overspending.

If the amount of work completed to date is added to the graph (budget cost of work performed) then we get a clearer picture.

In this case, 8 rows were finished at this point in time (40 per cent of what should have been completed), in other words £400. Here is the performance measurement curve that can now be drawn:

FIGURE 4.10   Brick wall example: variances

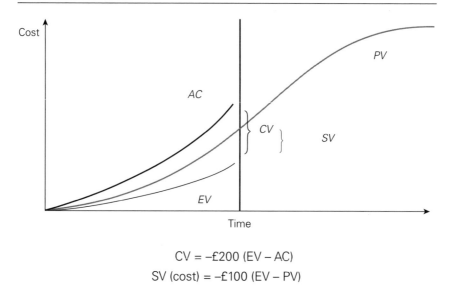

$$CV = -£200 \ (EV - AC)$$
$$SV \ (cost) = -£100 \ (EV - PV)$$

The fact that the cost variance and schedule (cost) variance are negative values tells us that we have both a cost overrun and a time overrun.

The performance measurement curve therefore takes into account both the cost and the work completed: it objectively measures the value of work achieved to date.

Future trends

Based on the earned value analysis, future trends can be tested for reasonableness.

If the project has been consistently underperforming in the past, the outstanding work can be multiplied by the earned value to give an indication of what will happen if nothing changes. The same can be applied to the schedule. You must bear in mind that efficiency will not improve in the future unless there is some action taken.

There are two other indicators which can also be derived directly from the graph:

FIGURE 4.11 Brick wall example: forecasting

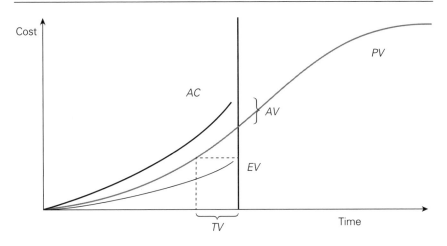

AV: Accounts variance
   This value gives an indication on the status of the project cash flow.

$$AV = PV - AC \text{ (cum to date)}$$

A positive value indicates a healthy cash flow, whereas a negative value indicates that funds will be required to pay for the work carried out.

TV: Time variance
   By determining the date at which the current EV value is equal to PV, it is possible to compute a variance as to how ahead or behind the project is.
   See also the definition for schedule variance (time).

Efficiency

From all of these discrete measures, two overall efficiency indicators can be derived which indicate the overall health of the project.

CPI: cost performance index
   This value gives an indication on how well the budget is in terms of the work performed.

$$CPI = EV / AC$$

A value greater than 1 indicates a healthy situation, whereas a value less than 1 indicates that the project is overspent for the work done.

SPI: schedule performance index
   This value gives an indication of how the project is progressing in terms of the costs incurred.

$$SPI = EV / PV$$

A value greater than 1 indicates a healthy situation, whereas a value less than 1 indicates that the project is behind schedule for the money spent.

Forecasting

Finally it is important to forecast what is now expected to happen to the project. Two key indicators are used to highlight this. These are EAC (estimate at completion) and VAC (variance at completion).

   In its simplest form EAC can be calculated by estimating the work that still has to be completed and adding to the actual figures to date. For example, if you have spent £10,000 (AC) and you estimate that there is £1,500 of work still to be completed then the EAC would be £11,500. This basic formula can be applied to both cost and time. For cost, this can be represented as EAC = AC + ETC where ETC = estimate to completion (money).

   However, statistical estimates can be produced based on the efficiency of the work to date. There are several calculations that can be used, all of which are based on the work achieved to date. In most cases the remaining work will not be carried out in the same way so the statistical forecasted figures given will not guarantee a 100 per cent correct answer and should only be used as a guide.

$$EAC = AC(cum) + ((AC/EV)(BAC - EV(cum)))$$

Or:

$$EAC = AC(cum) + (BAC - EV(cum))$$

Or: assuming work is to be carried out as it has to date:

$$EAC = \frac{Budgeted\ cost\ (BAC)}{CPI\ (cost\ performance\ index)}$$

Once the estimate at completion has been estimated it allows us to calculate the VAC (variance at completion) which is calculated as:

$$VAC = BAC - EAC$$

We can also look at forecasting the final end date which requires the pre-determination of a time based schedule performance index (SPI). This can be calculated as follows:

$$\frac{\text{schedule performance}}{\text{index (SPI) (time)}} = \frac{\text{original duration for the planned work to date}}{\text{actual time expended on the work to date}}$$

$$\text{final project duration} = \frac{\text{planned project duration}}{\text{time based schedule performance index}}$$

Simulation exercise

Let's look at our simulation project and assume we are now at the end of week 8 in the schedule.

We have asked for a report on actual percentage (%) complete on each of the activities along with the actual spend on each activity which has been captured via timesheets and invoices.

The progress figures for activity A have been completed. Calculate the figures for the remaining activities and summarize your perception of progress to date. You will need to reference the last bar chart to find the budget at completion and the planned percentage complete for some of the activities.

Transfer your EV and AC figures to the blank S-curve below. For drawing purposes assume linear spend in each from the start of the project. In addition highlight the SV and CV values.

Continued overleaf

TABLE 4.2 Simulation project: progress table

Activity ID	Activity Description	Budget at Completion	Planned % Complete	Planned Value (PV)	Actual Cost	Actual % Complete	Earned Value (EV)	Schedule Variance (SV)	Cost Variance (CV)	Schedule Performance Index (SPI)	Cost Performance Index (CPI)
A	Project Start	0	100%	0	0	100%	0	0	0		
B	Procure Soundproof Booths	4000	100%	4000	4000	100%	4000	0	0	1.00	1.00
C	Install Soundproof Booths	15000	100%		20000	75%					
D	Relocate Furniture	8000			7000	75%					
E	Procure Cat 5 Cabling	20000	80%		10000	50%					
F	Procure IT Hardware				1000	100%					
G	Install Hardware				10000	100%					
H	Install Cat 5 Cabling				0	0%					
J	Test IT Functionality				0	0%					
K	Relocate Staff				0	0%					
L	Final Integrity Check				0	0%					
M	Project End				0	0%					

FIGURE 4.12 Simulation project: cumulative cost curve

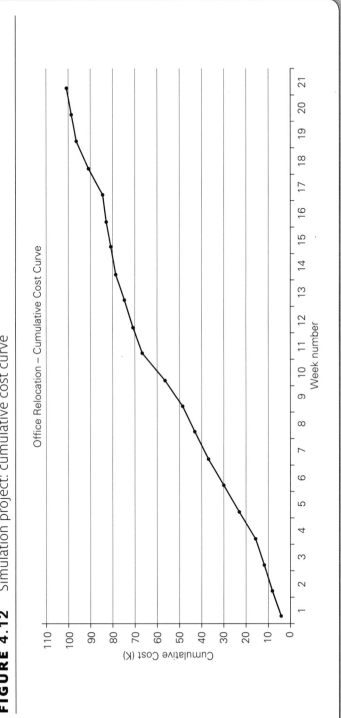

Office Relocation – Cumulative Cost Curve

Simulation example

TABLE 4.3 Simulation project: completed progress table

Activity ID	Activity Description	Budget at Completion	Planned % Complete	Planned Value (PV)	Actual Cost	Actual % Complete	Earned Value (EV)	Schedule Variance (SV)	Cost Variance (CV)	Schedule Performance Index (SPI)	Cost Performance Index (CPI)
A	Project Start	0	100%	0	0	100%	0	0	0		
B	Procure Soundproof Booths	4000	100%	4000	4000	100%	4000	0	0	1.00	1.00
C	Install Soundproof Booths	15000	100%	15000	20000	75%	11250	-3750	-8750	0.75	0.56
D	Relocate Furniture	8000	50%	4000	7000	75%	6000	2000	-1000	1.50	0.86
E	Procure Cat 5 Cabling	20000	80%	16000	10000	50%	10000	-6000	0	0.63	1.00
F	Procure IT Hardware	4000	100%	4000	1000	100%	4000	0	3000	1.00	4.00
G	Install Hardware	12000	0%	0	10000	100%	12000	12000	2000		1.20
H	Install Cat 5 Cabling	16000	0%	0	0	0%	0	0	0		
J	Test IT Functionality	6000	0%	0	0	0%	0	0	0		
K	Relocate Staff	12000	0%	0	0	0%	0	0	0		
L	Final Integrity Check	4000	0%	0	0	0%	0	0	0		
M	Project End	0	0%	0	0	0%	0	0	0		
		101000		43000	52000		47250	4250	4750	1.10	0.91

FIGURE 4.13 Simulation project: planned, earned and actual curves

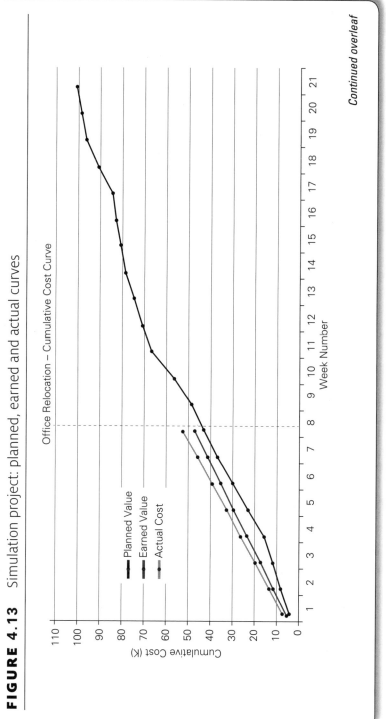

Office Relocation – Cumulative Cost Curve

Cumulative Cost (K)

Week Number

- Planned Value
- Earned Value
- Actual Cost

Continued overleaf

Simulation exercise *continued*

We can see from both the information in the table and the S-curve the progress situation. We have a positive SV (schedule variance) which indicates we have achieved more work to date than planned, however, we have a negative CV (cost variance), which implies we have spent more money than was planned on the work to date.

We need to deal with the important issue of identifying why we have overspent and what our forecasts at completion are. We should now forecast a final cost and time for the project using an appropriate method as discussed earlier.

Change control

As discussed in the planning chapter, unfortunately our plans will most likely change. This should not necessarily constitute a problem if handled correctly through a change control process. Change control is concerned with all aspects of managing the scope of the project and the project objectives during project execution.

Its purpose is to ensure that any proposed changes to the project objectives or project work packages are evaluated and approved, rejected or deferred before being incorporated into the project plan.

The project management plan and the work breakdown structure are two valuable sources of information which the project manager should use when a change becomes apparent. This will allow the impact of the proposed change to be investigated and evaluated in terms of the additional effort or benefit which it will bring, along with an indication of the impact on other aspects of the project.

Project change

Project change could arise as a result of:

- an omission, by the customer, in the original specification;
- an omission, by the project team, in the original work definition;
- an unforeseen external event;
- a request, by the customer, to make an addition/alteration to the specification;
- a request, by the project team, to make an addition/alteration to the work definition;
- design failure;
- personnel changes;
- advancement by competitors;
- new government regulations;
- new ideas being included.

Change should firstly be handled by the documentation of the change required. This should be done through a change request process and a change request form. An example of the change control process and a change request form are shown below. The change request form should be completed for a change request regardless of its source.

TABLE 4.4   Example change request form

Project				
Originator of Request				
Change Request #		Date of Request		
Description of Change				
Baseline/ Current Situation				
Reason for Change				
WBS Areas Affected		Effect		
WBS Areas Affected		Effect		
WBS Areas Affected		Effect		
Approve		Reject		
Comments				
Customer Authorization	Name		Signature	Date

Once the change has been logged it should then follow a change control process.

Change control process

The process of managing change control can be viewed as a five-stage process.

FIGURE 4.14   Change control process

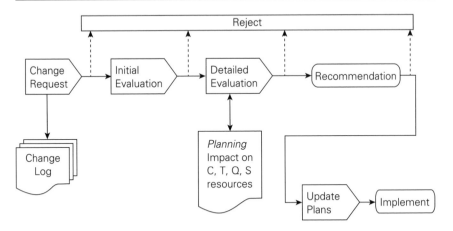

1 Log the change request and define precisely what is to be changed. Use the change request form.

2 Initial evaluation. Assess the impact which this change will have on the project. How will it affect the project objectives, the work packages, the schedule, the resources, the team, the environment, risks, etc?

3 Detailed evaluation. Determine the 'cost' of the change. Do not only consider the direct monetary cost of carrying out the change, but also the knock-on effect it may have on other aspects of the project. This should be done by incorporating the change into the existing baseline plan and determining the overall effect on time, cost, quality, safety and the resource availability. Also consider the 'benefit' of the change. Again, there may be more than pure financial benefit – the change may ultimately lead to reduced time savings elsewhere in the project or may lead to improved safety or quality.

4 Recommendation. Make a decision as to whether to accept or reject the change request. If the change is likely to result in a change to the project's terms of reference or objectives, then it is appropriate for this decision not to be taken by the project manager alone, but by a change control board which will include representatives of senior management and other business management functions.

5 Update plans. If the change is accepted then the plan should be updated, approved, re-baselined and published.

Note: If the change has come from the client it must be determined if the change is outside the contracted scope. If it is, then the additional cost should be signed off via a variation order before any of the work is undertaken.

Change register

It is important that once a change has been recorded through a change request that it is entered into the change register. The change register is often part of the project management plan and holds amendments to the original business case which are under consideration or which have already been approved. By keeping a change register as a supplement to the project management plan, you avoid the need for updating the main document for every change. It also provides an audit trail for the additional works that has been carried out.

Project close-out and handover

The goal of project management is to obtain client acceptance of the project result. This means that the client agrees that the quality specifications of the project parameters have been met. In order to make this go smoothly, the client and the project manager must have a well-documented criteria of performance in place from the beginning of the project. This information should be documented in the project management plan which should include all changes requested through the life of the project.

Objective, measurable criteria are always best, subjective criteria are risky and open to interpretation. There should be no room for doubt or ambiguity, although this is often difficult to achieve.

The project may not be complete when delivered to the client. Some final project areas that may need to be considered are:

- documentation requirements;
- complete drawings;
- final report;
- provision of people trained on operating product or facility;
- customer training;
- final report;
- project audit;
- update risk and work registers;
- settle all invoices;
- equipment and hire returns;
- warranties and guarantees settled;
- update financial systems;
- document lessons learned.

Although the project close-out and handover are typically the final phases of the project this does not mean that the relevant activities should only commence when the previous stage is complete. On the contrary, it can been seen by the list above that work such as as-built drawings should be developed as the project progresses through the earlier stages and be ready for handover as soon as the work is complete.

Finally, project team members need to be reassigned; surplus equipment, materials and supplies disposed of; and facilities released.

Post-project evaluation review

The final step of any project should be an evaluation review. This is a look back over the project to see what was learned that will contribute to future projects. This review is best done by the core project team and typically in a group discussion. If possible it can be beneficial to include the client, customer, users or any appropriate stakeholders. The post-project evaluation review will take place during project closure.

Why hold a post-project evaluation?

As the quote at the beginning of this chapter says, if we always do what we've always done, we'll always get what we've always got – meaning that if we always do things the same way we will get the same results. With all projects there are always areas that can be improved upon; however, it is typical for project personnel and managers, to get away from the project as soon as possible. This may be due to the fact that they are required immediately on the next project and they are glad to see the back of it and want to forget the results. Whatever the reason, the benefits of such a review are rarely seen, and dismissed as time wasting. It is therefore very important that the lessons learned from the project, whether good or bad, should be reviewed, documented and fed back to the next project.

What should be reviewed?

It is obviously very important that, first, an evaluation of what the project delivered against what was expected should be conducted. This again highlights the importance of agreeing the measurement for success at the outset of the project and with all the stakeholders.

We should therefore consider the three questions asked when we defined our project:

- Do we know where we are going?
- Do we know how we are going to get there?
- Do we have agreement of all of the stakeholders on the first two questions?

If we could categorically say yes to the above questions then we should now be asking:

- Did we get where we expected to get?
- Did we get there the way we expected to?
- Are all the stakeholders happy with the outcome and the way it was achieved?

If the answer is no to any of the above questions we should be asking why and what can be done to make sure they answer yes in the future. Equally, if the answer is yes we should be congratulating the project team and ensuring that we clarify what was done well so we can do it again and also what could be improved upon next time.

Some questions that could be considered are:

- Did everyone involved understand and agree on the project direction and objectives?
- Did we have the appropriate skills in the project?
- Did we have and use appropriate tools and techniques?
- Did all the team work well together?
- Were our stakeholders kept well informed of the project progress?
- Did we manage project changes effectively?
- Did we follow the agreed project life cycle?
- Did we encourage and deal with feedback effectively?
- Did we anticipate project problems effectively?
- Were our agreed procedures followed as planned?

Again if the answer to any of these questions is no, then we should ask why and put measures in place to ensure that in the future they are corrected. Likewise, if the answers are yes then ask why. Was it luck or was it good project management? Either way, the results should also be documented and fed back into future projects.

Things to consider when executing a project

Accuracy of progress measurement

It is often said that progress on an activity rushes to 95 per cent then slows down. There is also the issue of ambiguous progress measurement. The importance of accuracy in progress measurement cannot be overemphasized as, without accurate measurement, all of the benefits of best practice outlined in this chapter cannot be realized. Depending on the type of project involved, it may be possible to agree what needs to be achieved to 'claim' earned value percentages against different types of activities, or visual checks on progress may be necessary, but somehow the successful project manager needs to be sure that the progress measures being reported are accurate, to allow them to make the right decisions.

Cost versus schedule

The real value of earned value management (EVM) is that it compares cost *and* schedule progress measurements – providing the project team with accurate measures and forecasts. However, the timely reporting of actual costs (AC) is not realistic in some organizations. In these cases it is still possible to calculate a reasonably accurate costs-incurred figure based known payroll costs or committed costs through finance systems. To not measure costs and schedule simultaneously, as we have seen, is to make decisions based on potentially misleading data – which should worry any project team.

Forecasting and early warnings

The purpose of accurate forecasting figures such as estimate at completion (EAC) and budget at completion (BAC) provides an early warning to the project team, project manager and project stakeholders of all types. Hiding this bad news early in a project is a mistake that many project managers are tempted to make – convincing themselves that they will compensate for early problems later in the project. However, history tells us otherwise. A timely early warning of a negative 'trend' (schedule or cost, or both) can point towards poor estimating, planning or simply an expected or unexpected risk occurring. The best practice tools and techniques described in this book – if followed fully – allow for an honest appraisal and reappraisal of project success. All organizations need to know early if there are issues. No project manager is thanked for delaying bad news. Equally good news should be made available as it may allow an organization to channel much needed resources elsewhere if they are now available.

Variations and change management

This chapter has discussed the critical aspect of change management. Almost all projects will encounter change and it is the ability of the project team to recognize change, evaluate the effects of change, and make a reasoned decision (or refer it in a timely fashion) that can often make the different between a successful project and a disastrous one. Human nature often leads to variations or changes being accepted without challenge. The consequential effect of an ill-considered change is one of the most common causes of project cost or schedule overruns.

The learning organization

Capturing and recording 'actuals' has an importance to most organizations considerably beyond the project itself. If an organization is to learn lessons from the past and improve its project performance it is essential that the data recorded for progress reporting during a project is also analysed at project completion for 'lessons learned'. It is common in most organizations for project staff to be reallocated immediately (or before) a project is completed. However, a little time spent recording and disseminating lessons learned and actuals can pay immense dividends to the organization and is, in mature project organizations, an integral part of good project management.

Conclusion

We have learned in this chapter to measure progress against a baseline plan, forecast cost and schedule variances and manage change. These are some of the most critical tools and techniques available to the project manager and yet often the most overlooked. As some of the progress measurement techniques require timely and accurate data, and an understanding of earned value management (EVM), they are often avoided as 'too complex'. However, ignoring these best practice tools leads to projects being run 'blind' – in ignorance of their real progress and, therefore, the real cost and schedule outcome. In extreme cases this can lead to projects continuing when they should have been stopped – effectively gross misconduct within an organization.

CASE STUDY   Wood Group PSN project management framework

Wood Group PSN is a leading independent services provider for the oil & gas and power generation markets. Worldwide these services include engineering, procurement and construction management, facility operations and maintenance, and repair & overhaul of turbines and other high speed rotating equipment.

Underpinning the project management system is the project management delivery framework which provides direction and guidance on the key elements of the project management process, access to corporate procedures, guidelines on application of the procedures and corporate pro formas.

The project management delivery framework is based on best practice processes and systems distilled from recognized standards such as ISO 9001, Association of Project Management (APM) and Project Management Institute (PMI). It is used for guidance on what procedures, tools and processes are available and are expected to be utilized as a minimum during the delivery of projects and modifications. For each element of the road map for projects, the framework should be applied (Figure 4.15 and Figure 4.16).

FIGURE 4.15   WGPSN project management framework

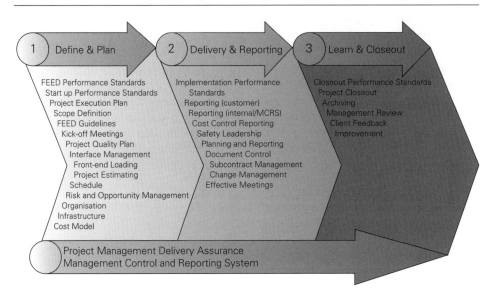

The project management road map provides an overview on how a typical project should be managed and illustrates the flow and the key issues from concept to close out. The road map for projects includes the following important information relevant to the conduct and management of projects:

- the project and contract management principles defining the essential minimum management controls and processes which must be formally addressed for all projects and contracts;

- performance standards applicable to feed and implementation project phases;

- definition of project phases some or all of which will be undertaken for each project;

- major project milestones some or all of which will be relevant dependent on which project phases are undertaken;

- milestone requirements for corporate reviews during each of the project phases.

Management control and reporting

An integral part of the PMS is the management control and reporting system (MCRS), which is designed to provide delivery assurance through a structured, hierarchical workflow, and a performance management and meetings schedule with clear objectives and expectations for those taking part in the process.

The MCRS is a graphic representation of how the business operates; presents what its business plan is for the next period (forecasting), how it will deliver the work required to achieve the business plan (planning), describes the controls and performance meetings (control) required to monitor the delivery, planned attainment, and reporting back into the

FIGURE 4.16 WGPSN road map

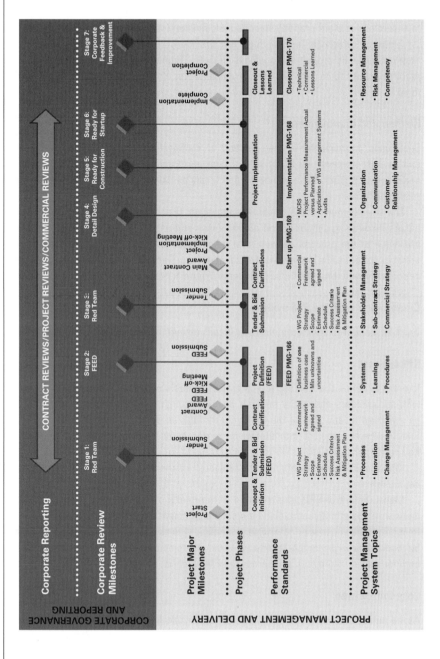

management systems (reporting) for adjustment to the forecast, up or down, or measures required to ensure the business plan is achieved (see Figure 4.17).

The MCRS model has been designed to focus on project delivery and provide details of the regular meetings expected to take place, at the varying levels in the organization, to ensure projects are properly managed and monitor (see Figure 4.17 for an example).

Terms of reference for meetings are provided, along with expected reports/data required for basic project management analysis. Outputs from any performance meeting requires actions to be captured with agreed dates for close-out and a nominated individual to do it.

Review and improvement

Continuous improvement is the lifeblood of successful future business. Improvement can be best achieved by firstly setting high performance standards, measuring actual performance against these standards and finally by having in place processes geared to raising performance.

The effectiveness of the project management system will continually be reviewed to ensure its ongoing suitability and effectiveness and ensure that continual improvements are made to the process as well as a mechanism for capturing lessons learned from previous projects. The improvement element of the project management system is modelled accordingly with three distinct components (Figure 4.18).

Compliance with the PM system

It will be monitored at different times by means of various peer and compliance reviews.

KPI success

In order to define the success of any project, suitable success criteria should be agreed with stakeholders during the concept phase although it is also possible that they may be amended at any time of the life cycle through an effective change control process. Success criteria require quantitative measures against which to judge meeting them. Key performance indicators (KPIs) are measures of success.

KPIs should be used throughout the project to ensure progression towards a successful conclusion.

Measurement of KPIs is a measure of the health of a project and to some extent a measure of the effectiveness of the project management system. It is therefore appropriate to consider the success or otherwise of meeting KPIs as a guide to both. KPIs will normally be reported through monthly reports by individual projects and a trend should be maintained both for individual projects and across the PM function.

Lessons learned

At the outset of a work, the assigned job responsible person (JRP) reviews the WGPSN lessons learned database in relation to the client, project type, proposed scope of work, systems/equipment involved, etc.

This action should assist in ensuring that lessons are learned from previous similar project work and overall performance is improved. As part of the close-out process for

FIGURE 4.17 WGPSN progress reporting: example of the processes related to project progress meeting

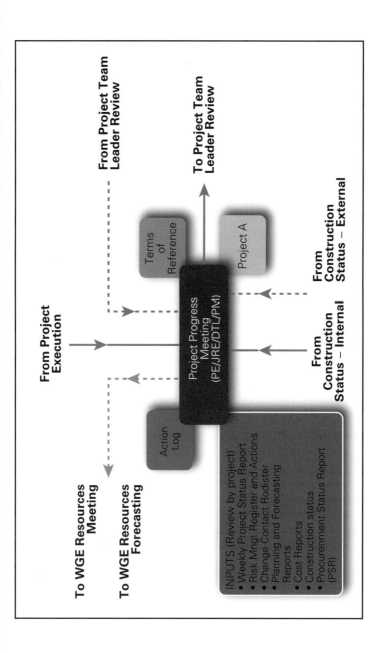

FIGURE 4.18   WGPSN PM system implementation

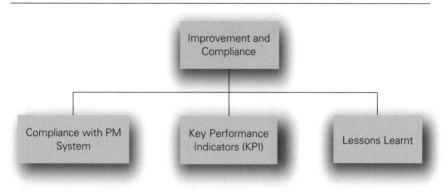

all work the lessons learned from the execution of the work is be documented. During the close-out stage of the work, the relevant JRP formally invites those involved, including the client representatives, to submit their written proposals for lessons to be learned.

For major projects the above requirement is supplemented by a project-specific lessons to be learned review, arranged by the relevant project manager, during the close-out phase of the work. The attendees at this review include the client representatives, operations/ maintenance representatives and the key members of the project team.

The project lessons learned list records the following data:

- originator;
- details of lesson learned;
- originator's recommended actions;
- reviewed date;
- actions taken;
- date of entry to database.

The relevant JRP records against each item on the project list of lessons learned recommended actions required to address the lessons learned. The project list of lessons learned is then submitted to the relevant assignment manager in order to document the actions taken to address the project lessons learned and highlight those items forwarded to the WGPSN management with recommendations for action.

Risk and your project

05

Introduction

As we know, there are known knowns. There are things we know we know. We also know there are known unknowns. That is to say, we know there are some things we do not know. But there are also unknown unknowns, the ones we don't know we don't know.

DONALD RUMSFELD, US DEFENSE SECRETARY

Mr Rumsfeld defines the issues of risk rather well, although in this chapter we will focus on the known knowns and discuss a process to expose and better define the known unknowns and then consider what the unknown unknowns might be and plan to reduce their impact on the project objectives as well!

So, what is risk management? The term refers to the systematic application of procedures for identifying and assessing risks to the successful delivery of strategic objectives, day-to-day business operations, programmes and projects.

The identification and management of risks relating to a project is an absolute cornerstone of the successful delivery of the project. Risks, when they occur, affect all the key areas of the cost, time and quality measures that are set when the business case is developed and the project baseline is set. Although the identification and management of risks is a continual activity which is performed throughout the life of the project, an analysis of potential risks will have taken place during the feasibility study stage and will have been built into the business case before the project was given the go ahead by the project sponsors. Typically, risk management is utilized at every stage of a project life cycle, which is why this supporting chapter should be referenced regularly.

As discussed earlier, uncertainty is an accepted part of project delivery. However, that uncertainty is often caused by a change in the scope of the deliverables and that level of uncertainty is normally something that can be managed by the change control process.

Risk management is different. If the process is correctly managed, risks can be foreseen, understood and managed accordingly. Risk can be defined in two distinct ways. First, a risk event is defined as:

> an uncertain event that, should it occur, will have an effect on achievement of one or more of the project's objectives.

This type of risk can be identified, assessed and managed through the risk management process.

For example:

- Will the new product launch date be achieved?
- Will our delivery of components be on time?
- Will the IT systems we use cope with the new project demands?
- Can our staff deliver the objectives we have set them on time?
- Will the design we have used satisfy the client's needs?

In addition, project risk is the cumulative effect of risk events and other sources of uncertainty. Although it is important to focus on the risk events the overall project risk needs to be the focus and managed accordingly.

> Project risk is the exposure of stakeholders to the consequences of variations in outcome.

This level of understanding and the subsequent open communication of exposure is key to good decision making and helps to deliver the consistency of information required for stakeholders and sponsors so that objective decisions can be made.

However, risks are not always negative events. Sometimes they can provide an opportunity. For example, if a major project is delayed this might – depending on the contract – result in additional revenues for the contractor. Whether risk is a threat or opportunity often depends on which side of the contract you are.

Risk is very much 'in the eye of the beholder'. For example, if the project budget cannot be altered, even the smallest risk can be a major risk. If the project delivery date cannot be altered then any risk to the project schedule being compromised becomes a major risk. How a risk is categorized will therefore be dependent on the needs and expectations of the project stakeholders.

Risk cultures

There is no textbook answer on how to handle risk other than to have a risk mitigation strategy prepared. The project manager or the organization must rely upon sound judgement and the use of the appropriate tools in dealing with risk. The ultimate decision on how to deal with risk is most often based upon the project manager's tolerance of risk.

The three commonly used classifications of tolerance for risk include risk averter or avoider, the neutral risk taker, and the risk seeker or lover.

FIGURE 5.1   Risk averter

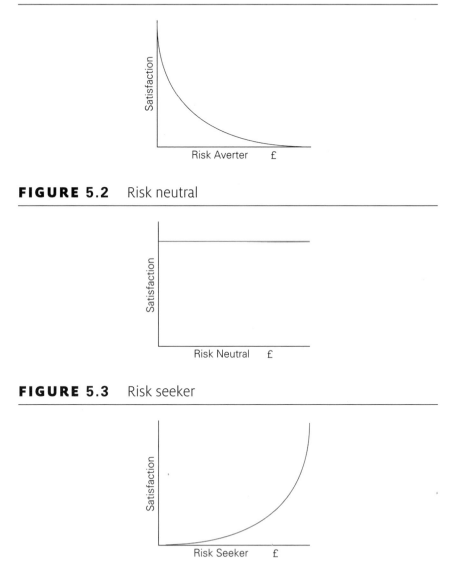

FIGURE 5.2   Risk neutral

FIGURE 5.3   Risk seeker

The above graphs show the amount of satisfaction, or pleasure, the project manager receives from a payoff; this is sometimes known as the project manager's tolerance for risk.

With the risk averter, satisfaction is reduced the more risk is at stake. With the risk seeker, the satisfaction increases when more is at stake, ie greater risk. A risk averter prefers a more certain outcome and will demand a premium to accept a risk. A risk seeker prefers the more uncertain outcome and may be willing to pay a penalty to take a risk.

Qualitative and quantitative approaches to risk

Whilst there are many methodologies and approaches that have been created to manage risk, let's look at two core approaches for identification and management: qualitative and quantitative.

A *qualitative* approach to risk involves analysing the types of risk that may occur in a project, their sources, knock-on effects, nature of impact, etc. Such an analysis is very much based on the expertise, experience and knowledge of the individual team members who take part in the risk analysis.

A *quantitative* approach to risk involves using statistical/historical data to predict the likely occurrence and impact of risks in a project. This method generally relies on there being available large volumes of historical and statistical data on similar projects or components of the project. It also relies on the processing of vast quantities of data and is best achieved using computers and custom-made software.

The first part of this chapter will primarily concentrate on the qualitative approach to risk analysis as due to the nature of the projects it is unlikely that large volumes of statistical and historical data exist for the types of projects concerned.

Later we will look at a quantitative approach to risk and will look at some of the methods and calculations used.

Informal risk management has been used for many years. For example:

- storing food (to reduce the risk of later shortages);
- the introduction of driving regulations (to reduce the risk of accidents).

In addition we all inadvertently conduct risk management on a day-to-day basis by buying insurance for our cars, using a pedestrian crossing when crossing a road, putting our money in a secure bank account. These are all simple risk management actions.

More formal risk analysis has only been developed quite recently, partly in response to the recognition of the magnitude of risks which are being faced on many projects and the need to either reduce the risks or at least prepare for their occurrence.

In fact many projects have now mandated the use of risk management for the parties to the project, including consultants, managing contractors, main contractors and subcontractors. Very often risk can be spread across the different organizational structures within a project.

Project risk

A project risk can be defined as follows:

- An undesirable development, about which there can only be a degree of certainty that it will happen, but if it does happen there will be a significant impact in respect of the project's timing, budget, quality, safety or performance objectives.
- Risk is an uncertain event or condition which, if it occurs, would have a negative impact on achievement of objectives (threat).
- Risk is an uncertain event or condition which, if it occurs, would have a negative or positive impact on achievement of objectives (threat or opportunity).

Account must also be taken of the effect of risk on issues such as safety, reliability, the organization's overall business and value for money.

Two aspects of this definition are important:

- Lack of certainty implies that there is a *probability*, but not a certainty, associated with the risk. If a risk is certain to happen it is not a risk but a problem, or an issue, to be dealt with using traditional project management and planning principles.
- The *impact* of the risk implies that there will be an effect on the project, in terms of time, cost, quality or safety. If there is no impact then the risk is irrelevant and can be ignored.

Risk management and opportunity

Although we generally think of risk as a threat, as can be seen from the definitions above it may also be looked on as an opportunity. This opportunity can be realized in a number of ways.

If a risk management process is implemented and managed properly it can provide a business opportunity that may not have existed previously, eg it may be prudent to bring a piece of subcontracted work in house in order to gain a greater control on enhancements and response to change. This in turn would offer a greater opportunity to the business in terms of flexibility to change and response to customers' needs.

In addition, a risk that has been defined as a threat to the project could also be turned around and an opportunity exploited, eg the risk may be that someone may be hurt during the construction phase of the project, therefore there may exist an opportunity to develop some new safety mechanism or procedure that could give the company competitive advantage or even be marketed outright.

One of the problems of risk management is identifying how well it is being carried out. If a risk does not happen it does not mean that the analysis was wrong. We can only assess the effectiveness of planning to the extent that we correctly identified the impact for those risks that did occur.

Risk assessment is like gambling in that the odds are assessed based on the available, often incomplete, data and you make your decisions accordingly. It is not necessarily a matter of blind faith where you just hope that risks won't become reality so do nothing.

Risk management

Several definitions for risk management exist; however, all follow the same key theme. Typically they are as follows.

- Risk management is the formal process by which risk factors are systematically identified, assessed, and provided for.
- Risk management is a formal, systematic method of managing that concentrates on identifying and controlling areas or events that have a potential of causing unwanted change.
- Risk management, in the project context, is the art and science of identifying, analysing and responding to risk factors throughout the life of a project and in the best interest of its objectives.

As you will see from the above definitions, risk management implies control of possible future events and is proactive rather than reactive. As an example, one activity in your project is to design a new piece of software for inclusion in your next product launch; the task has been estimated at six months. However after speaking to your design manager he informs you that it is more likely to be nine months. If you as the project manager are reactive you will do nothing until the problem occurs. However, at that time you must react rapidly to the crisis and may have lost valuable time when contingencies could have been developed earlier.

Proper risk management will not only reduce the likelihood of the event occurring but also the magnitude of its impact (Figure 5.4).

Consider the project above. It can be seen that the impact of reacting to risks later in the project life can have a significant impact on the project objectives. It should also be noted that it is in the early stages of the project that the greatest level of influence exists.

The benefits of risk management

It can be seen in the above example that there is potentially a cost benefit in effective risk management; however, several additional benefits can be delivered by implementation of a comprehensive risk management process.

Some of these benefits may be tangible ie in the form of a return or saving in cost or time. Others may be intangible, eg strengthen the team, improve morale, etc.

FIGURE 5.4 Influence vs risk cost

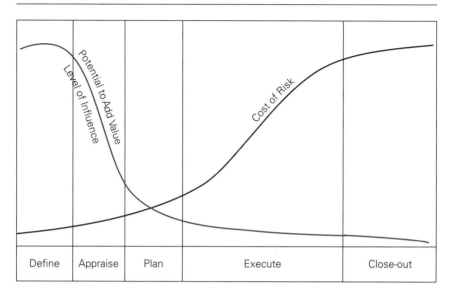

Define	Appraise	Plan	Execute	Close-out

Listed below are some of the benefits delivered by effective risk management:

- more realistic plans and budgets;
- allows the identification of alternatives;
- improves team spirit and team morale;
- increase the chance of the project delivering what it is supposed to deliver;
- gives the customer and team more confidence in the project data;
- assists future projects;
- assists with the justification of contingencies and additional spends;
- can provide justification for not proceeding with a project;
- helps focus the team on the project objectives and key project issues;
- helps eliminate the luck factor;
- helps to ensure sound contracts are awarded;
- gives more credibility with customers and clients;
- enables better communication within the project;
- can assist in future business;
- increases knowledge and experience within the project team.

The cost of risk management

There are several ways to address and manage risk; without exception these will all incur a cost in some way or other. The cost may be at the least the cost of time incurred in the risk management process or it may also be the cost of insurance, additional or alternative procurement or even the cost of totally redefining the project. In all cases a cost benefit should be conducted looking at the cost of managing a risk, the saving returned and the cost of ignoring the risk.

In some cases the cost of the proposed mitigation for managing a risk or a series of risks may exceed the overall project budget. It is then that there may need to be a decision made whether or not the project should proceed.

By conducting high-level risk management at the project conception risk management costs can be identified and be provided for by inclusion in the bid or the procurement strategy.

The risk management process

The aim of risk management is to reduce the undesirable consequences (impact) to a project of a risk occurring. In the example below, the aim is to reduce the undesirable consequence and reduce the probability. However, as we will see later, the reduction of risk impact can be very difficult and in many cases impossible. However, if the probability can be reduced to a low enough figure the magnitude of the impact becomes insignificant.

FIGURE 5.5   The purpose of risk management

The risk management process may be summarized as:

- Identify the events which may have a significant, undesirable impact on the project, ie the risks.
- Establish the impact of each event.
- Estimate the probability of each event occurring using appropriate techniques.

- Calculate the exposure to the project.
- Mitigate, if appropriate, against the risks.
- Review the effectiveness of the mitigation and review any changes in risk exposure.

So that: we can ensure that time, money and effort is allocated to those features which pose the greatest threat to successful completion of the project.

FIGURE 5.6   Risk management process

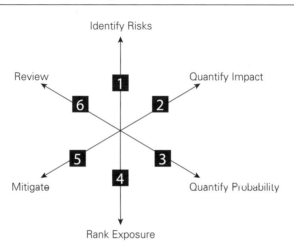

Three key steps

This process can be simplified into three key areas: *identify, quantify, manage* – IQM – where identification can include several methods as described later

FIGURE 5.7   Risk management steps

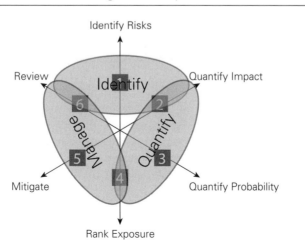

in this chapter. Quantification involves determining how the risk will affect the project. This may involve both quantitative and qualitative methods; however, the output of the quantify stage should be a measure of exposure to our project. In the manage stage we should use techniques to reduce the exposure to our project or maximize the opportunity.

The output at any stage of the process is to update the risk register, a register that contains the risk description, the exposure information, recommended responses and responsibilities. More details on the risk register can be found later in this chapter.

Stage 1: risk identification

The first step in risk management is to identify and assess all potential risk areas. The thoroughness with which this identification is accomplished will determine the effectiveness of the risk management.

There are several methods that can be used for identifying risks such as the following framework.

FIGURE 5.8   Risk identification framework

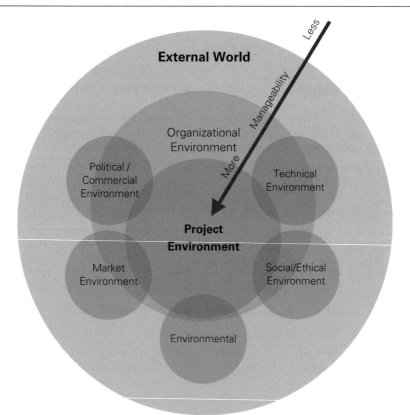

Risk management must be seen in its broadest sense – many of the risks are outside the project and outside the project manager's control, eg interest rate rises, currency fluctuations. In the diagram opposite the nearer the centre the circle we go, ie toward the project environment, the more manageable our risk should be.

Main sources of risk:

- *The project environment*: risks associated with project resources, project objectives, the client, project quality, schedules, the project organization and associated vendors and subcontractors. Most of the risk within this area should be manageable and within the project manager's control.

- *The organizational environment*: risks associated with strategic problems, finance and wider resources, management decisions, shareholders. Many risks in this area may be under the project manager's control although many may be outside their influence.

- *The external world*: risks associated with social, political and economic factors, legal and regulatory bodies, environmental pressure groups. Many of these risks will be outside the control of the project manager; however, the project manager may be able to affect the amount the project is influenced by them with the use of appropriate mitigation strategies.

- *Other influences*: It can be seen in the diagram opposite that several other factors can have an influence on our project and they are not limited to the few shown here. It is the project manager's job to explore all the areas of risk and ensure that where there is a reasonable exposure to the project effective mitigation strategies are documented and implemented.

Other areas of risk may include:

TABLE 5.1   Example risk areas

Assets	Equipment	People/Staffing	Resource and Contracts
Behaviour	Engineering	Partners	
Capability	Finance	Planning	Safety
Client	IT	Procurement	Schedule
Commercial/ Contracts	Infrastructure	Property	Security
	Innovation	Political/Country	Shutdown
Competition	Legal and Regulatory	Project Management	Social/Ethical
Construction			Subcontractors
Currency	Logistics	Quality	Technical
Delivery	Management	Recruitment	Terrorism
Design	Manufacturing	Reporting	Testing
Economic	Operations	Reputation	Vendors

Risk identification techniques

There is a variety of risk identification techniques available to the project manager and we will look at some of them here.

Brainstorming

Brainstorming is a commonly used technique in project risk management and is a great way of capturing a good quantity of risks in a relatively short space of time. It also is a good method for raising enthusiasm amongst the project team and can be used to engage stakeholders in the risk management process.

How it works is fairly simple. You need to gather a group of people with the necessary mix of skills and knowledge and allow them to come up with as many different risks to the project as possible. Based on the ideas of the other participants you should have a good element of free association, with the group members sparking off each other.

Of course, there is a downside to the method in that it can be weighted in favour of the extrovert members of the group and therefore needs to be controlled by a facilitator.

Nominal group technique (NGT)

One method that tries to prevent the attendant problems of brainstorming is NGT, particularly the problems caused by the participants who like the sound of their own voice. The way in which NGT commonly achieves this is through the use of Post-it notes. Rather than shouting out their ideas the members of the group will privately record their perceived risks to the project on the aforementioned Post-it notes. The project manager then asks each of them to nominate a unique risk event. While offsetting the impact of the extrovert members of the team it does lose that element of free association present in the brainstorming technique.

Interviews

As we know, it is often difficult to gather all of the project team in one place at the same time. Through the use of interviews the project manager can gather the risk information required without having to bring the team together. It is like a one-to-one brainstorm with the interviewer acting as a facilitator. The advantage to this method is that some people are more comfortable in a one-to-one situation. The main disadvantage is that you do not get the same cross-fertilization of ideas.

Delphi technique

This method uses expert judgement to determine the possible risk events on a project. The experts involved will generally be external to the project organization and the technique is used when embarking on a project where there is little or no experience held within the organization on projects of this type. To carry out the Delphi technique does not require the collocation of the experts and can be carried out remotely. The experts will be sent the scope of the project and will be asked to come up with risks relating to the scope. There will normally be several iterations as the analysis becomes more detailed but this can be time consuming and there is a need for care that you do not include too many iterations leading to drop-out from the experts.

Strengths, weaknesses, opportunities and threats (SWOT) analysis

SWOT analysis is a good method for identifying the areas of strength and weakness within the project and from this the threats and opportunities that may affect the project. In other words those things that expose the project to risk. The main advantage of using SWOT is that it is a technique that is used in other areas of organizations and is often used for dealing with issues. It is therefore a technique that can be integrated with other business functions,

FIGURE 5.9 SWOT analysis example

	Positive	Negative
Internal factors	**Strengths** > Technological Skills > Leading Brands > Distribution Channels > Customer Loyalty/Relationship > Production Quality > Scale > Management	**Weaknesses** > Absence of Important Skills > Weak Brands > Poor Access to Distribution > Low Customer Retention > Unreliable Product/Service > Sub-scale > Management
External factors	**Opportunities** > Changing Customer Tastes > Liberalization of Geographic Markets > Technological Advances > Changes in Government Politics > Lower Personal Taxes > Change in Population Age-structure > New Distribution Channels	**Threats** > Changing Customer Tastes > Closing of Geographic Markets > Technological Advances > Changes in Government Politics > Tax Increases > Change in Population Age-structure > New Distribution Channels

like business development and marketing, both of which will frequently be involved in the early phases of the project. This diagram shows the use of a SWOT analysis grid. If you look at the last point in both the opportunities and threats you will see that they are the same, 'new distribution channels'. This highlights the fact that even if there is an opportunity it will have a possibly negative impact as well.

Checklists

The checklist is used as a detailed aide-memoire, utilizing lessons learned from previous projects. By looking at previous projects we are able to identify risk events that have occurred, as many risks are common to the environment within which an organization operates. We also know that although projects can be defined as a unique endeavour it is common for projects carried out by an organization to have similarities. It is important that you do not use the checklist technique on its own, as slavish observance to it will mean that you will fail to identify the events that will be new to your current project. Therefore, checklists should be used in conjunction with a more proactive risk identification technique.

The risk register

One of the first priorities after risk identification is to record the identified risks in a risk register or risk log. This will allow us to collate, examine and draw general conclusions from the information gathered.

Risk fields

The information stored on each risk can be stored in fields. The fields used to hold your risk information can be boundless. However, it is important that the information held is useful, practical and is not too onerous in its maintenance. Bearing in mind the need for brevity, a few suggested fields are listed in Table 5.2.

Risk ownership

Identifying and documenting risk are essential to ensure project risks are monitored, controlled and responses monitored and measured. However, it is essential that the risks identified are allocated ownership. By allocating an owner to a risk, they then become accountable for that risk or risks and it is then their job to ensure that the relevant actions associated with that risk are carried out and documented. It is of no benefit to the project or the business if the risk management process is carried out but no ownership is allocated to ensure the relevant actions are implemented executed. There may be several people involved in the ownership of a risk ie there may be someone who will be involved in developing a risk response and then someone else will carry out the necessary actions related to that response.

TABLE 5.2 Example risk record

Reference	This should be a unique identifier assigned to each risk.
Description of Risk	This field should hold a comprehensive description of the risk and the issues involved.
Responsibility	Who is responsible for overseeing the risk and ensuing appropriate action is taken to minimize the exposure to the project.
Category	It is a good idea to highlight which category a risk is assigned to. This can be useful for examining the areas in the project that are most affected by risk. Category fields may link to the RBS (Risk Breakdown Structure) or may be generic. Ie Commercial, Financial, People, Management, Processes etc.
Impact	The impact can be held in a number of ways from, in it's simplest form, a straightforward High, Medium, Low categorization to a more sophisticated method which will break-out various components, eg cost, time and quality, individually. • **Cost** – The cost can be divided into actual values or percentage values representing change on budgets, eg a high risk could be 50% increase on the budget or a £5 million one-off cost • **Time** – This would generally be the delay in the schedule ie how late will the project be if this risk occurs • **Quality** – Quality is a more difficult category to define as quality is generally more of a soft issue. In general this will be the repository for all risks, which cannot be defined in terms of either cost or time. Ie "The tool keeps breaking down due to poor maintenance procedures". However, be careful because most can be translated into terms of cost or time that is in the main a better way of categorizing them.
Probability	The probability of the likelihood of the risk occurring. Similar to the Impact they can be ranked in a simple format or more complex using weightings etc.
Phase	The Phase is where in the Project Life Cycle the risk is going to occur. This is mainly useful on long projects where it can give you an indication how long you have to implement mitigation strategies. In addition it allows risks that apply to a particular phase that is complete to be closed out.
Risk Response	This information is key and should hold information regarding the mitigation actions that are to be implemented, who is responsible for them and when it should be carried out.

FIGURE 5.10   Example risk register

Ref No.	Description of Risk	Responsible	Category	Project Impact	Probability of Occurance	Exposure Pxl	Risk Response	Action Date
	Risk Register					Project: Office Relocation		
1.1.1	Delay of materials on site from client	Project Manager	Client	2	3	6	Work with client to bring delivery date forward and continually monitor delivery dates	17th January
1.1.2	IT hardware required obsolete	Procurement	Technical	3	1	3	Start procurement process as soon as project expenditure has been approved ensuring minimum spec is defined	14th February

Stage 2: risk impact analysis

This stage is concerned with assessing the impact of a risk. The aim is to identify those risks in our project risk register that will have a significant detrimental impact on the project. If the impact is insignificant then we do not need to manage it, and can remove it from the project risk register. Similarly, if it does not have a detrimental effect, then again we should not spend effort monitoring it.

Impact type

It is often easier to analyse the effects of a risk occurring if we concentrate on the primary impact types. These primary types are:

- time;
- cost;
- quality;
- safety;
- environment;
- reputation.

Each of these can have an impact on the project alone, or at a more strategic level. The purpose of this step is to define the impact type of each risk in order that we can assess the impact in the context of project and business constraints.

Impact estimate

Estimate the relative impact which each risk may have on the project. There are several simple yet effective approaches to quantifying the impact:

- A high/medium/low matrix, where the levels of impact are defined for each of the types described above.

For example, cost impact may be defined as >$1 million for high; between $100,000 and $1 million for medium, etc. However, these figures would not be relevant for a project that only lasted four weeks at a cost of $50,000.

In many cases it is more reasonable to apply a percentage figure to represent the level of impact, eg 70 per cent, 10 per cent. This method can be more useful than the high/medium/low matrix in that it allows for a greater level of detail in definition. This allows the same categorization to be used for different projects as it does not apply hard figures. However, some people find percentages very abstract and also tend to confuse them with probabilities of the risk occurring.

TABLE 5.3   Risk impact estimation

	Cost	Time	Quality	Safety
High	> $1M	> 4 Months	> 50 Defect	> 10 LTIs
Medium	$100K–$1M	1–4 Months	20–50 Defect	5–10 LTIs
Low	< $100K	< 1 Month	< 20 Defect	< 5 LTIs

FIGURE 5.11   Risk impact estimation

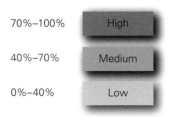

70%–100%	High
40%–70%	Medium
0%–40%	Low

In addition, it is often possible to relate all risks to an ultimate financial cost, should they occur. This method is useful in considering project cost contingencies but undermines the importance of safety and environmental risks.

As discussed earlier, some of the softer categories may be difficult to define, eg quality, safety, environment. When thinking in terms of these categories many people will use their knowledge and experience and go with 'gut feel'.

Stage 3: probability analysis

Every risk carries with it an uncertainty, ie a probability that it may occur. Probabilities are usually expressed as percentages. If a risk has a 100 per cent probability of occurring then it is not a risk, it is a certainty. It may still be an undesirable event, but nonetheless, we know it will happen so it should be accommodated in the project plans. Similarly, if a risk has a zero probability of occurring, then we can ignore it – it won't happen. Most of the time we can ignore risks that have a close to zero probability – except when the impact is extremely significant.

This stage is concerned with assessing the probability of a risk occurring. The stage will be revisited at each risk review point to reassess the probability of each risk in our project risk register.

Estimating probability

There are a number of ways to produce an estimate of probability of a risk occurring, such as a high/medium/low matrix, where three levels of probability are defined:

TABLE 5.4   Risk probability estimation

Category	Definition
High	Likely to occur
Medium	Possibility of occurrence
Low	Unlikely to occur

For example, high probability may be defined as 'likely to occur on most projects of this type'; 'has been known to occur on some similar projects' for medium, etc.

Use percentage figure to represent the level of probability, eg 70 per cent. This method can be more useful than the high/medium/low matrix in that it allows for a greater level of detail in definition. While the absolute values may not be scientifically based, this method does allow for better ranking of risk probabilities.

This method can be further adapted to take account of the distribution of views expressed as to the level of probability. The basic idea is to obtain a set of estimated probability values from people who have some knowledge and experience of the type of risk. Once the values have all been submitted the average is calculated. The most optimistic (Eo) is added to four times the average value (Ea) which is added to the most pessimistic value (Ep). The resulting figure is then divided by six to provide the estimate (PE).

$$PE = (Eo + 4\ Ea + Ep)/6$$

Stage 4: risk exposure

Having performed the previous steps it is now possible to automatically produce an exposure catalogue.

The threat of, or exposure to, any risk is a combination of the impact it would have, and the probability of it occurring.

The question is always: is a high impact, low probability risk more or less desirable than a low impact, high probability one?

Risk exposure calculations are intended to resolve this issue. Once we have calculated the relative exposure that the project has against the list of identified risks, we can choose the ones that present most threat, and concentrate our efforts on reducing and controlling them. The exposure catalogue gives us a ranked order of risks, with high exposure risks at the top and lower exposure at the bottom.

Once we have selected and ordered our risks we can decide on the extent to which we expend time and money managing them.

Exposure calculations

There is a simple method for determining exposure to a risk. By taking the product of the estimated impact the risk would have and the estimated probability of it occurring we have a relative measure of exposure to that risk.

$$\text{Exposure} = \int \text{impact, probability}$$

If impact was measured in cost, then the exposure calculation can provide a basis for estimating financial contingency in a project.

If impact and/or probability have been defined in non-numeric values, then an exposure matrix is the best way to represent the information. By plotting all risks in the matrix, each cell in the matrix will therefore define the relative level of exposure to each risk.

In its simplest form the exposure matrix may be used as seen here. However, it does not separate out quality, cost or time and in addition ranks high probability, medium impact risks in the same category as high impact, high probability. This may be suitable for some projects but generally a greater degree of quantification and differentiation is required.

FIGURE 5.12   Example Boston square

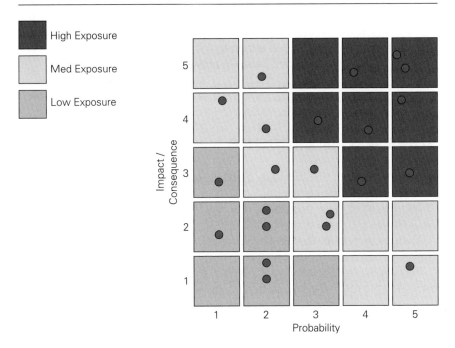

RBS (risk breakdown structure)

In the previous sections we have discussed risk identification and quantification. Although all very valid methods, the outcomes that are produced tend to be a linear and an isolated representation of each risk and do not really help with identifying the areas within a project that are most susceptible to risk. In the same way as a WBS (work breakdown structure) is recognized as a way of presenting project work in a hieratical, structured and manageable format, a RBS (risk breakdown structure) can be used in a similar way to represent project risks.

Risk data can be organized and structured, to provide a standard presentation of risks which will help to facilitate understanding, communication and management of these risks.

Following the pattern of a WBS, the RBS should be defined in a similar way to provide a source orientated grouping of risks that defines the total risk exposure of the project. Each descending level should represent an increased detail definition of the sources of risk. The RBS is therefore a hierarchical structure of the potential risk sources. As the WBS provides a basis for many aspects of the project management process, so the RBS can also be used to structure and guide the risk management process.

A generic RBS is shown below.

FIGURE 5.13   Generic risk breakdown structure (RBS)

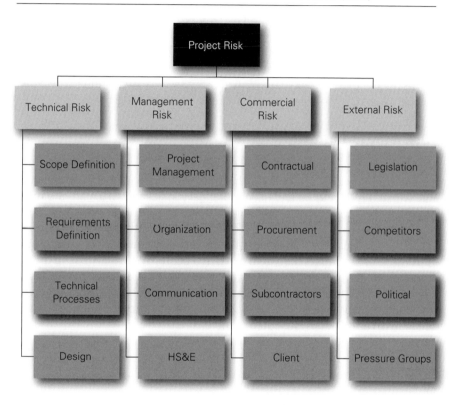

How to use the risk breakdown structure

Once the RBS has been defined for the project it can be used in a variety of ways. The main uses are highlighted in the following sections.

Risk identification

The upper levels of the RBS can be used as a prompt list in a similar way as key words were discussed in the previous module. As before each element of the RBS can be brainstormed encouraging participants to identify risks under each of the RBS levels. It also allows for specific risk interviews, where structured risk analysis can be achieved by interviewing individuals responsible for each of the main areas represented in the RBS and subsequently breaking each down.

Risk checklist

As with the WBS, the RBS is a useful tool for highlighting areas of risk that may have been omitted. By facilitating a brief brainstorm of the overall project the risks should then be placed within the relevant risk area. If a risk does not have a home, it is possible that a key area of project risk has been omitted from the RBS.

Similarly, it can be used in the opposite manner by checking to see if risks exist within each of the RBS categories. This will then reveal possible gaps or blind spots within the risk identification process. This should then provide an assurance that all the common risk sources have been explored.

Risk assessment

Identified risks can then be categorized by their source by allocating them to the various elements of the RBS. This then allows areas of concentration of risk within the RBS to be identified, potentially indicating which are the most significant sources of risk to the project.

This can be done by adding up the number of risks within each area, however, it can be misleading as it does not take into account the severity of each risk.

A more effective measure is to allocate a score to each risk based on the exposure to the project. This can be done in a number of ways as discussed before. This will then give a quantifiable value to each of the risk sources. In addition a percentage of the total can also be used to allow a comparison within each area. This is illustrated in the example below.

FIGURE 5.14   Example risk breakdown structure (RBS)

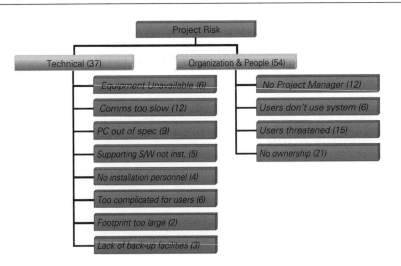

Risk reporting

The RBS can also be used to roll up risk information on an individual project to a higher level for reporting to senior management, as well as drilling down into the detail required to report on project team actions. Reports to senior management may include total numbers of risks or total risk score in each of the higher level RBS area. Project teams can also be notified of risks within their part of the project by selecting relevant RBS areas for each team member.

Lessons learned

One of the most important aspects of the RBS is it can provide a consistent insight to the project risks that have occurred after the project is completed. An RBS analysis can reveal risks which occur frequently, allowing generic risks to be recorded for future reference, together with effective responses. If routine analysis of post-project reviews indicates that a particular risk is occurring repeatedly, then preventative responses can be developed and implemented.

Stage 5: mitigation strategy

It is often not feasible to attempt to manage all risks remaining on the project risk register at any one time. Thus, it is important to select a manageable subset of the top grouping from the exposure catalogue to perform risk mitigation and actively monitor.

This stage firstly identifies all risks that are considered a threat to the next stage of the project. It defines the most appropriate mitigation plans to minimize the probability and/or their impact. In essence we will attempt to shift all of the risks identified on the exposure catalogue from the top right-hand corner (high risk, high impact) to the bottom left (low risk, low impact). However, it should be borne in mind that this will not always be possible.

Mitigation strategy

There are a number of ways to reduce the exposure of a risk. The purpose of this step is to define the most appropriate and cost-effective mitigation strategy for each risk remaining on the exposure catalogue.

The activities of this stage are ordered so the most desirable mitigation strategies are considered first, working down to the unavoidable options. In general, subject to cost considerations, mitigation should be conducted in the following sequence:

FIGURE 5.15   Risk mitigation process

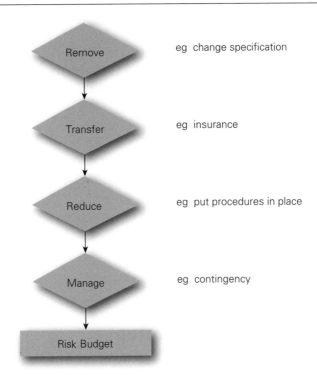

- *Risk removal*: Is it possible to remove the causes of risk by, for example, changing the project plan or changing specs, eg electric pump for diesel? It is important to remember that if you change the specification you will generate a new set of risks related to the new specification.
- *Risk transference*: Is it possible to transfer the risk away from the project, eg insurance, pass on risk via contractual terms to client or subcontractor? The problem with trying to transfer a risk by subcontracting is that if the risk is of a high severity the subcontractor may not be willing to take the job on.
- *Risk reduction*: Is it possible to reduce the exposure of a risk (reduce probability and/or impact)?
- *Manage*: If none of these options is available, then we must ensure the remaining risks are carefully managed, to ensure early detection should they occur so contingencies can be enacted. The reason for accepting a risk may be that the cost to mitigate may be higher than putting a risk mitigation strategy in place. It is a method that would not be used for risks with a high impact to the project.

Some mitigation strategies will introduce secondary risks. These will need to be fully evaluated. Thus there may be a number of iterations back through Stages 1 to 3 for some of the more complex risks.

Stage 6: risk monitoring and review

Risk monitoring is carried out by ensuring that adequate reporting mechanisms are put in place.

The task is to ensure that the risks are adequately monitored so timely action can take place. It should be noted that it is equally important to identify both if a risk occurs and if it does not. If a risk did not occur, it does not indicate that the analysis was wrong. Often the opposite is the case – it indicates that the mitigation strategy was effective.

Monitoring takes place at two levels:

- Proactive monitoring, where we continuously assess the effectiveness of our mitigation strategy for each risk, ie is the mitigation we have put in place being effective in containing the risk?

- Reactive monitoring, where a risk has occurred, and we now have to take positive – but hopefully anticipated – action to deal with it through contingencies.

This stage ensures effective and frequent reviews are carried out, and where necessary appropriate action is triggered.

Risk reviews

Risk reviews should be carried out at regular intervals. The purposes of risk reviews are:

- to identify which risks have occurred during the period under review, and whether or not the contingency was/is adequate;

- to identify which risks could have occurred during the period, but did not;

- to monitor the effectiveness of mitigation on risk that are on-going;

- to review risks that might occur during the next period and confirm that the mitigation strategy is still appropriate;

- to identify any new risks that might occur and instigate the necessary analysis (iterate through Stages 1 to 4);

- to keep the risk records up to date.

Risk evaluation review

Risk management, like any management discipline, relies heavily on experience – although some elements can be 'automated' or reduced to mathematical modelling, prediction based on past performance is still the most reliable source of data.

At the beginning, and as the project progresses, this risk analysis and management method aims to capture the decision-making processes and the conditions that existed in bringing about the elimination or realization of a risk.

This stage, carried out after the project has been completed, is designed to review the effectiveness of the risk analysis techniques and risk management process employed. If we successfully avoided a risk occurring then the procedures put in place on this project need to be made available to others. If our analysis was inaccurate or our mitigation strategy was ineffective, then we need to analyse why, and ensure the mistakes are not repeated in the future.

The purpose of this stage is to assess how well the risk management procedures operated. A number of questions need to be addressed:

- Did risks occur that were not identified? If so, what mechanism could be put in place to increase the chances of identification next time?
- Were risks identified, but inaccurately analysed? If so, what mechanisms can be put in place to improve both the impact analysis and probability estimates?
- Was the risk identified too late, ie did we fail to identify the fact that a risk had begun to occur in a timely manner? If so, how can we improve our detection procedures?
- Were our mitigation strategies effective? If not, why not?
- Was the level of risk analysis and monitoring appropriate? Did we spend too much/too little time on risk management? How can we improve the effectiveness of the analysis? How can we improve our techniques for exposure catalogue cut-offs?

Finally, the corporate risk register should be updated with the information from the project's risk register so that on future projects, the corporate risk register can be used as a reference for risks which were analysed on previous projects. As time progresses, the corporate risk register becomes a valuable resource for the company.

Quantitative risk management processes

Decision tree analysis

Decision trees are excellent tools for helping you to choose between several courses of action. They provide a highly effective structure within which you can lay out options and investigate the possible outcomes of choosing those options. They also help you to form a balanced picture of the risks and rewards associated with each possible course of action.

Drawing a decision tree

You start a decision tree with a decision that you need to make. Draw a small square to represent this towards the left of a large piece of paper.

From this box draw out lines towards the right for each possible solution, and write that solution along the line. Keep the lines apart as far as possible so that you can expand your thoughts.

At the end of each line, consider the results. If the result of taking that decision is uncertain, draw a small circle. If the result is another decision that you need to make, draw another square. Squares represent decisions, and circles represent uncertain outcomes. Write the decision or factor above the square or circle. If you have completed the solution at the end of the line, just leave it blank.

Starting from the new decision squares on your diagram, draw out lines representing the options that you could select. From the circles draw lines representing possible outcomes. Again make a brief note on the line saying what it means. Keep on doing this until you have drawn out as many of the possible outcomes and decisions as you can see leading on from the original decisions.

An example of a typical decision tree is shown below.

FIGURE 5.16 Example decision tree

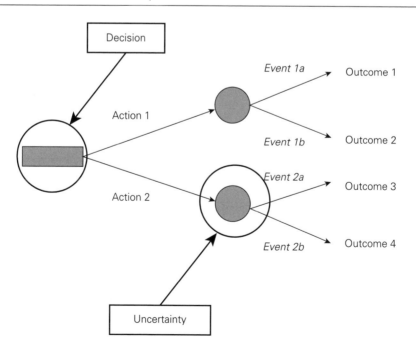

Simulation example

As part of our office relocation it has been decided it may also be an appropriate time to modify or replace our outdated project delivery system. There are number of options open to us:

- Do we buy a new product and get it customized fully to our needs or do the bare minimum?

- Do we keep the product we have and tweak it so it runs a little more efficiently or add new functionality?

We have represented these decisions in the decision tree below.

FIGURE 5.17   Simulation project decision tree decisions

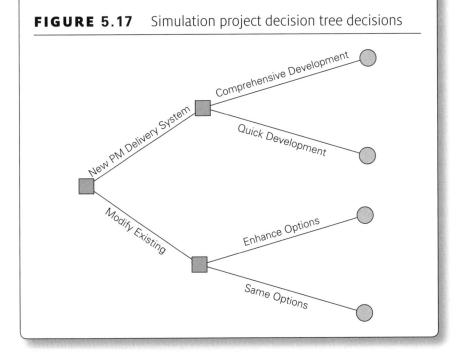

Evaluating your decision tree

Now you are ready to evaluate the decision tree. This is where you can work out which option has the greatest worth to you. Start by assigning a cash value or score to each possible outcome. Estimate how much you think it would be worth to you if that outcome came about.

Next look at each circle (representing an uncertainty point) and estimate the probability of each outcome. If you use percentages, the total must come

FIGURE 5.18   Simulation project: decision tree evaluation

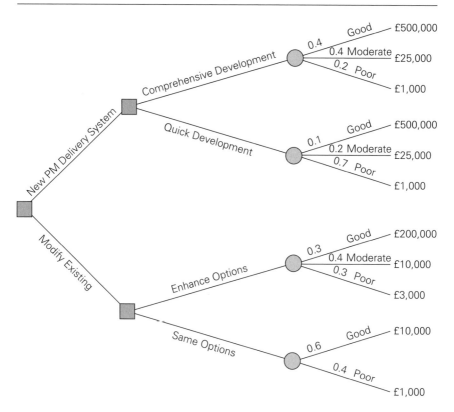

to 100 per cent at each circle. If you use fractions, these must add up to 1. If you have data on past events you may be able to make rigorous estimates of the probabilities. Otherwise write down your best guess.

Calculating tree values

Once you have worked out the value of the outcomes, and have assessed the probability of the outcomes of uncertainty, it is time to start calculating the values that will help you make your decision.

Start on the right-hand side of the decision tree, and work back towards the left. As you complete a set of calculations on a node (decision square or uncertainty circle), all you need to do is to record the result. You can ignore all the calculations that lead to that result from then on.

Calculating the value of uncertain outcome nodes

Where you are calculating the value of uncertain outcomes (circles on the diagram), do this by multiplying the value of the outcomes by their probability. The total for that node of the tree is the total of these values.

In this example in, the value for 'new system, comprehensive development' is:

TABLE 5.5   Simulation project decision tree values

0.4 (probability good outcome) x £500,000 (value) =	£200,000
0.4 (probability moderate outcome) x £25,000 (value) =	£10,000
0.2 (probability poor outcome) x £1,000 (value) =	£200
+	**£210,200**

The following figure shows the calculation of uncertain outcome nodes:

FIGURE 5.19   Simulation project decision tree node values

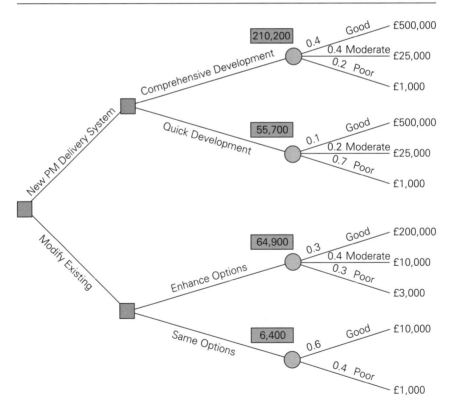

Note: The values calculated for each node are shown in the boxes.

Calculating the value of decision nodes

When you are evaluating a decision node, write down the cost of each option along each decision line. Then subtract the cost from the outcome value that you have already calculated. This will give you a value that represents the benefit of that decision.

When you have calculated these decision benefits, choose the option that has the largest benefit, and take that as the decision made. This is the value of that decision node.

The following example shows the decision node calculations.

FIGURE 5.20   Simulation project decision tree results

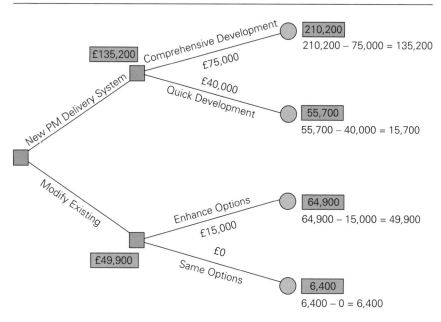

In this example, the benefit we previously calculated for 'new system, comprehensive development' was £210,200. We estimate the future cost of this approach as £75,000. This gives a net benefit of £135,200.

The net benefit of 'new system, quick development' was £15,700. On this branch we therefore choose the most valuable option, 'new system, comprehensive development', and allocate this value to the decision node.

The result

By applying this technique we can see that the best option is to develop a new product. It is worth much more to us to take our time and get the product right, than to rush the development. It is better just to improve our existing system (£49,900) than to botch up a new system (£15,700) even though it costs us less.

Key points

Decision trees provide an effective method of decision making because they:

- clearly lay out the problem so that all options can be challenged;
- allow us to analyse fully the possible consequences of a decision;
- provide a framework to quantify the values of outcomes and the probabilities of achieving them;
- help us to make the best decisions on the basis of existing information and best guesses.

Monte Carlo simulation

The main objective of creating a risk model for our project is to introduce some realism into our costs and our duration. This can be achieved by estimating a range of possible values for our costs and durations.

The simplest and most common range of distribution is the triangular distribution where values of minimum, most likely and maximum are selected. The probability of any value increases in value from the minimum to the most likely and reduces from the most likely to the maximum.

If you draw this distribution out you get a triangle shape, hence its name. Let's consider one of the activities in the office relocation project. Activity B was 'Procure soundproof booths'. When we look at this activity we will find there are several items making up this procurement activity. The items to be procured are shown in the table below along with their individual estimated costs.

TABLE 5.6 Example costs

Item	Cost
Soundproof Booths (60 @ £1,000)	£60,000
Floor Fixings (240 @ £50)	£12,000
Corner Units (180 @ £20)	£3,600
Lighting (60 @ £25)	£1,500
Electrical Sockets (120 @ £10)	£1,200
Total	**£78,300**

Let's assume this estimate was undertaken without any formal quotes but was estimated on a 'gut feel' basis. However, we needed to have a rough estimate quickly for the PM's first budget submission.

Many industries use a rule of thumb, such as:

- project estimate based on actual price +/–10 per cent;
- project estimate with no supporting data +1–20 per cent.

Using a Monte Carlo simulation, we can get a better idea of what the likely cost could be, and what we could expect to pay.

In the example we are only going to include the risk of estimating uncertainty, ie we will exclude specific risks, such as:

- You decide the booths need to be better quality than originally specified.
- Electrical sockets now need to be bought in gangs of 4 instead of 2.

Our next step is to consider each of the line items in our estimate and apply a range of possible costs. As we are only considering triangular distributions, this will be in the form of a minimum, most likely and maximum cost.

Minimum, maximum and most likely

When entering minimum and maximum values they should be extremes. Let's look at the purchase of the soundproof booths. Our procurement department staff have a good relationship with some suppliers and may be able to purchase them for a discounted price of £40,000. However, if their stock levels are low they may need to utilize another supplier who tends to sell at the high end for a premium, therefore the costs could be as high as £100,000. If we are confident with our initial estimate the most likely should remain as before at £60,000.

FIGURE 5.21 Example cost distribution

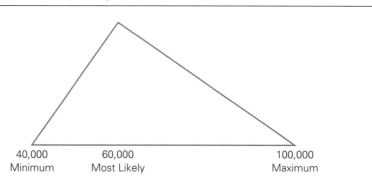

| 40,000 | 60,000 | 100,000 |
| Minimum | Most Likely | Maximum |

From the shape of the triangle you can tell that we are obviously expecting to pay more than our original cost.

If we apply this principle to the rest of the procurement items we can see the results below.

TABLE 5.7 Example cost distributions

Item	Cost	Minimum	Most Likely	Maximum
Soundproof Booths (60 @ £1,000)	£60,000	£40,000	£60,000	100,000
Floor Fixings (240 @ £50)	£12,000	£8,000	£12,000	£15,000
Corner Units (180 @ £20)	£3,600	£2,000	£3,600	£4,000
Lighting (60 @ £25)	£1,500	£1,000	£1,500	£2,000
Electrical Sockets (120 @ £10)	£1,200	£1,000	£1,200	£1,500
Total	£78,300	£52,000	£78,300	£122,500

So now we have a very simple risk model which only considers the risk of estimating uncertainty.

We can now apply a simulation tool to the costs we have entered. The simulation tool will randomly run through thousands of values within the range specified in the distribution model.

Due to the shape of the distribution, values close to the most likely are more likely to be selected than those near the minimum or maximum. After around 3,000–5,000 iterations, the values randomly produced will come near to the defined triangular distribution.

Table 5.8 is an example of just five iterations and the randomly selected values.

From this simple example it can be seen that there is quite a range of possible costs. By running thousands of iterations, the computer will build a picture of all, or at least most, of the possible outcomes and the percentage likelihood of each outcome being achieved.

We will now plot the results of just the soundproof booths. The differing costs are shown along the X-axis and the bars show the number of iterations on the Y-axis which indicates the amount of times a particular cost has been selected. As we would expect, the most selected is the most likely cost (£60,000) and the total results reflect the triangular distribution we selected.

TABLE 5.8 Example cost Monte Carlo iterations

Item	Run					
	1	**2**	**3**	**4**	**5**	**n**
Soundproof Booths (60 @ £1,000)	45	100	90	70	65	X
Floor Fixings (240 @ £50)	10	8	12	15	14	X
Corner Units (180 @ £20)	3	2	3.5	4	2.5	X
Lighting (60 @ £25)	1	1.5	1.8	1.2	2	X
Electrical Sockets (120 @ £10)	1.5	1.3	1	1.1	1.4	X
Total (K)	**60.5**	**112.8**	**108.5**	**91.3**	**84.9**	

Simulation result for the cost of the soundproof booths

FIGURE 5.22 Example Monte Carlo simulation results

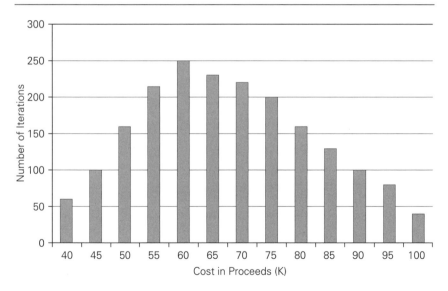

When we combine all the line items (the fixing units, corner units, lighting and sockets) we get a much smoother chart like the one shown overleaf.

It is sometimes more beneficial to show the cumulative distributions as a percentage. Once this is done we can show the results as per the graph below.

FIGURE 5.23   Example cost probabilities

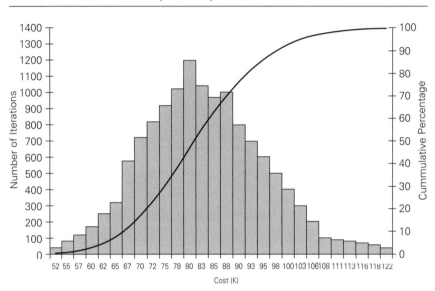

The S-curve now shows the probability of each cost being achieved.

FIGURE 5.24   Example probability of achieving planned costs

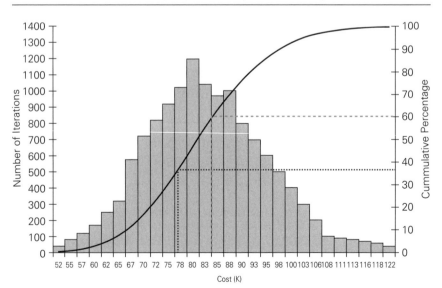

It can be deduced from the graph above that there is only a 38 per cent chance or less of us meeting our original estimate of £77,100. Realistically we should be using the P60 (60 per cent) or greater as our new estimate, which is £84,000.

We can apply the exact same techniques to the duration of our network to gain a more realistic schedule.

Distributions

So far we have only talked about three point estimates: a worst case, a most likely case and a best case. However, there are numerous other 'distributions' available to the professional statistician. In this book, we will only cover those that are likely to be most applicable to risk analysis exercises.

Uniform distributions

Uniform distributions are used when the cost or duration could be anywhere between two points, and you don't have a clue what the most likely value is. The simulation tool will, on each iteration, randomly select a value between the two extremes.

FIGURE 5.25   Uniform distribution

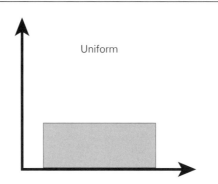

Uniform

Discrete distributions

Discrete distributions are used when you have a set of discrete values that could be selected, like in an either–or situation. This can occur when you have a risk that may or may not occur. If it doesn't occur, there will be no cost impact; however, if it does occur it will cost you a flat fee of £100,000. Percentage likelihoods can be attached to each value; for example, there might be an 80 per cent chance of the risk costing zero and a 20 per cent chance that the risk will cost £100,000. The percentages when summed should be equal to 100.

FIGURE 5.26   Discrete distribution

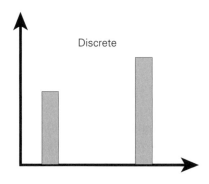

Custom distributions

Custom distributions can be used when there is no specific data on which to base your model and/or the data cannot easily be fitted to one of the standard statistical distributions.

Example: A pipeline has to be laid in a particularly hazardous stretch of water. The pipe-laying vessel can only work if the wave heights are less than 1.5 metres high. Weather statistics are available and give the probability of particular wave heights for each month. An example for June is shown below:

TABLE 5.9   Custom distribution data

Wave height in metres	<0.5	0.5 – 1	1 – 1.5	1.5 – 2	>2
Probability	20	25	40	10	5
Cumulative probability	20	45	85	95	100

This data can be added straight into the model as a custom distribution (Figure 5.27).

FIGURE 5.27 Custom distribution

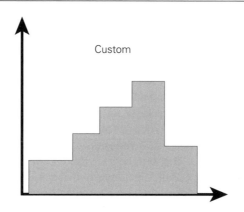

The values are entered as shown in Table 5.9. When sampling, the simulation will treat individual elements in the table as a mini-uniform distribution, eg 40 per cent of the sample should lie between 1 and 1.5 metres, and will be evenly spread between these extremes.

Normal distributions

Normal distributions are bell-shaped curves which tend to represent many natural events, such as the spread of results during an examination. Normal distributions are not used very frequently but are defined as a function of the mean value, and the standard deviation. One problem with using the normal distribution is that the data we wish to enter is skewed towards the pessimistic values. The normal distribution is, by definition, symmetrical. We also have to take account of the possibility that negative values may be sampled, which is usually not sensible if we are talking about costs or durations.

FIGURE 5.28 Normal distribution

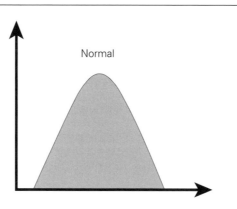

Things to consider with risk and your project

This is not a 'one-off' exercise

Most project managers consider risk at the start of a project. It is even common for a risk management workshop to be run, a risk management plan developed, and then the results carefully filed for review after the project. However, risk management is a continuous process for the professional project manager. It is important to ensure that risk is reassessed at every stage of the project life cycle, when any major change occurs, when a risk occurs, or otherwise at regular intervals throughout the project. Risks will disappear and new risks will emerge. Better risk mitigation strategies will become apparent. It is essential that risk management is 'live' throughout every stage of a project life cycle.

Involve anyone relevant and use a facilitator

My experience has been that the wider the group, particularly in risk identification, the better. Selecting workshop participants from a diverse range of backgrounds, roles and experience will provide a better list of risks to examine. The following steps of the process quickly focus minds on the important risks – and again, using those with previous experience or knowledge, will help find the best risk mitigation strategies. It is also wise to use a facilitator for these workshops or exercises as they can concentrate on the risk process, leaving participants to focus on the best strategies.

Monte Carlo or bust?

Monte Carlo method risk analysis (or probabilistic analysis) is an incredibly useful tool if there is good historical data (or 'norms') and an experience practitioner involved. In these cases the technique can be highly sophisticated and give meaningful cost and schedule predictions. However, a lack of sound historical data or experience in its application can lead to meaningless outputs, so please beware.

If you take only one thing from this book

It should be risk management. It is the single most common failure of projects – either failure to identify or to mitigate against a risk.

Conclusion

We have learned in this chapter how to put together a risk management plan which can be used and reviewed throughout the project. Following the simple steps of risk analysis is not complicated but is rarely done methodically or regularly enough in projects. Understanding the risks in a project leads to a better-informed project team and project stakeholders. There is less chance of a 'surprise' that derails the project and – above all – the project manager can lead their project honestly and openly in the full knowledge that the risks are known and mitigated against wherever possible.

This chapter on risk is referenced through the chapters covering the project life cycle as it is relevant at all times.

CASE STUDY   Managing risk the Mott MacDonald way

About Mott MacDonald

Mott MacDonald's £1 billion business spans 140 countries with over 14,000 staff working in all sectors from transport, energy, buildings, water and the environment to health and education, industry and communications. The company's breadth of skills, sectors, services and global reach makes it one of the world's top players in delivering management, engineering and development solutions for public and private sector customers from 30 centres throughout the UK and offices in some 50 countries across Europe, Asia and the Pacific, the Middle East, Africa and the Americas.

Mott MacDonald adopts a holistic approach to project development using its complete spectrum of skills across all stages of the development cycle – right from preparing the business case and advising on related issues to devising and implementing the solution and providing ongoing support.

Mott MacDonald's portfolio ranges from supporting major infrastructure projects in London such as Crossrail and Terminal 2 at Heathrow to programme managing the US$7.3 billion East Side Access project in Manhattan, New York and designing and managing delivery of India's largest-ever water transmission and treatment project.

Project and programme management the Mott MacDonald way

Mott MacDonald has a developed and published methodology for undertaking project or programme management commissions for customers. This recommended practice is termed Pathfinder and is captured within a set of good practice manuals, as well as a body of associated resources all hosted on an internal practice website.

The Pathfinder manuals which set out 'the Mott MacDonald Way' are aligned with international best practice. The methodology is structured around the PMI PMBoK, ie the five process groups of initiate, plan, execute, monitor and control and close.

FIGURE 5.29   Mott MacDonald's pathfinder manual

FIGURE 5.30   Mott MacDonald PMI-based project life cycle

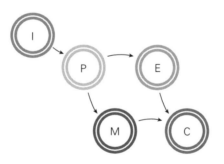

This was a deliberate choice, which reflects the global reach of the company and the wish to develop a methodology that was not seen to be a UK-centric approach. However, the methodology has also taken account of both the APM body of knowledge and the guidance given by OGC – for example, issues management (from APM) is included as is the concept of gateway reviews (from OGC).

Pathfinder provides guidance on all components of good project and programme management including risk management which is discussed further in the following section.

Managing risk the Mott MacDonald way

Whilst risk activities run throughout the Pathfinder life cycle – for example during the initiate phase risk assessment helps the selection of options – it is at the planning stage that the effort accelerates. In the Pathfinder guidance the planning stage of the project life cycle is of great importance, and practitioners are required to define clearly in a project (or programme) management plan how they will undertake the necessary project activities. This will often require the drafting of a specific risk management plan.

The guidance describes the purpose of the risk management plan, when it should be done, by whom, what the inputs should be and tools and techniques that might be used. It also provides guidance on the process of producing the plan through the use of a mind map, which is reproduced below:

FIGURE 5.31   Mott MacDonald risk management Mind Map

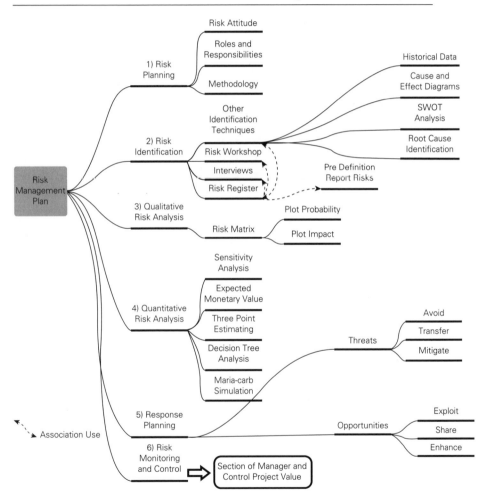

The mind map acts as a checklist to help the skilled project manager decide what is necessary and appropriate for risk management on his project – a shopping list from which the manager can select based on professional judgement.

To illustrate how this works in practice a case study is now considered.

Risk management on the Southern Region New Trains Programme (SRNTP)

As a result of the catastrophic UK rail accident at Clapham Junction in 1988 where 35 people lost their lives legislation was introduced which included the requirement to retire the aged 'slam door' trains, due to their poor crash worthiness. The deadline for implementation was December 2004.

FIGURE 5.32   Original 'slam door' train

A fleet of over 2000 new vehicles was purchased, but their introduction required an equivalent investment in rail infrastructure such as depots, power supplies, platforms etc. Mott MacDonald was appointed programme manager for this £2.9 billion programme in 2003, a role which included risk management across the numerous stakeholders.

In this case, following review of the client's risk policy, Mott MacDonald adopted a risk management process with the following key elements from the Pathfinder mind map:

- *Risk planning.* Early consultation was used to identify risk owners across the complex stakeholder environment and to gain consensus on the risk methodology to be used. Allocation of risk ownership is key to securing accountability.

- *Risk identification.* A combination of risk workshops and one-to-one interviews was used to help build the risk register. Previous risk registers were also reviewed to minimize gaps and overlaps.

FIGURE 5.33 Replacement train

- *Qualitative risk assessment.* Risks were assessed using a 5-by-5 matrix looking qualitatively at impact and probability. The impact assessment considered both time and cost. The risks were then mapped onto a probability impact matrix, which provided direction on where greater levels of focus and energy should be directed.

FIGURE 5.34 Mott MacDonald example risk register

Risk register for 58. 2. | RAS 5.1

● Risk 9. Late vehicle delivery from Bombardier.

Status	Active			
Owned By	Mike Dickinson			
Risk Leader				
Review Date	30 Mar 2005	Start Date	31 Dec 2003	
Customer Aware		Expiry Date		
Customer Risk Ref				
Send Reminder		Approved	√	

PRE MITIGATION

Score				
Probability	High		Performance	20
	Critical			80%
	Cost	Time	Performance	
Min	Very Low	High		
Likely		4 Weeks		
		8 Weeks		
Max		12 Weeks		

POST MITIGATION

Cost	Time	Performance

Risk Classification »Category 1: Delivery »Category 2: Delivery – Trains
»Risk Description: Vehicle manufacturers Bombardier fail to deliver vehicles to planned schedule – 376 delivery at risk as from Dec 04 & again at March 05
»Cause: Risk caused by manufacturer/sub-contractor delivery failure.

ACTIONS

Action 8. Ascertain current situation with manufacturers

»Owned By: Mike Dickinson
»Status: Action complete
»Action Deadline: 4 Feb 2004
»Approved: Yes
»Action Description: Meetings with the manufacturers – Bombardier and Siemens – are required – Siemens meeting required by 11th February – to be arranged by 4/2/02. This will identify current production schedule and how they relate to the overall programme schedule. This action becomes ongoing and will ascertain the actual level of this risk, for further RMA's to be considered

FIGURE 5.35 Mott MacDonald risk capture

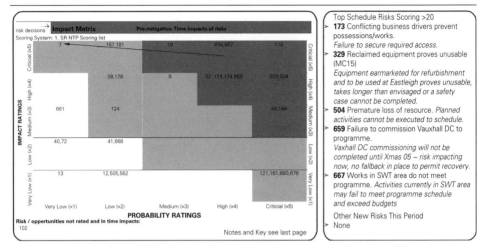

- *Quantitative risk assessment.* Risk software Predict! Risk Management System (PRMS) was used to capture, manage and analyse the risks. This included use of three-point estimates of cost impact and Monte Carlo analysis to generate a cumulative distribution curve. This would be run at regular intervals to inform the programme team on the levels of risk exposure across the various delivery elements and the movement on this exposure month to month.

FIGURE 5.36 Mott MacDonald risk exposure

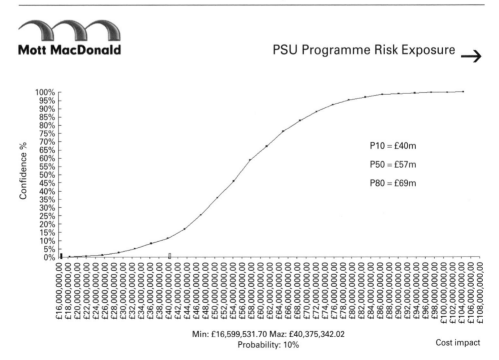

- *Response planning.* The use of the PRMS drove efficient allocation of responses, both for the opportunity items as well as the threats. The tool also captures action owners and timescales thus driving response planning.

FIGURE 5.37   Mott MacDonald response planning

● Opportunity 102. Opportunity for introducing re-generation braking.

			PRE MITIGATION			POST MITIGATION		
		Score	Medium	10				
Status	Active	Probability	Critical	90%				
Owned By	Tim Lowe, Ian Wearden		Cost	Time	Performance	Cost	Time	Performance
Risk Leader			Low					
Review Date	30 Mar 2005	Start Date	Min					
Customer Aware		Expiry Date	Likely					
Customer Risk Ref			Max					
Send Reminder		Approved	✓					

Risk Classification » Category 1: Systems Integration
» Risk Description: There is an opportunity to implement re-gen braking across the network
» Cause: Sponsor seeking to fund opportunity from programme savings – however, safety cases costs require considering.

ACTIONS

Action 85. Ascertain Safety Case costs
Owned By: Mike Dickinson
Status: Action complete
Action Deadline: 28 Feb 2004
Approved: Yes
Action Description: An estimate of what is required to provide a safety case for this opportunity is to be completed by

FIGURE 5.38   Mott MacDonald risk monitoring

Actions and linked risks Register

Action Details	Risk Details					
Action 40. Monitor PSU schedule adherence	● Risk 11. Delay by SWT to remove MK1 vehicles					
» Owned By: Dave Higginson	Status	Active	Approved ✓	Customer Aware		Customer Risk Ref
» Status: Active	Start Date	31 Dec 2004	Expiry Date	Review Date	15 Dec 2004	Send Reminder
» Action Deadline: 11 Feb 2004	Risk Leader			Pre Score	4	Post Score
» Approved: No	Owned By	Mike Dickinson				
» Action Description: PSU Programme slippage is source of risk 11, the potential of this threat occurring requires monitoring and weekly reporting.	Risk Classification » Category 1: Delivery » Category 2: Delivery – Trains » Risk Description Failure to remove the required/agreed numbers of passenger carrying Mk 1 vehicles by December 04. Risk now pending HMRI/ToC agreement on programme » Cause: Various – see related Actions					

- *Risk monitoring and control.* The risk management processes adopted on SRNTP allowed risks (threats and opportunities) to be swiftly captured as they arose, ie a live system. This was then supplemented by the formal monthly process of review, with the risk manager leading meetings with risk owners including progress checking against actions. Summaries of the top risks plus key movements were then rolled up to executive-level reports.

The PRMS tool with its database functionality provided a configuration-controlled medium to record all data as the project progressed, which is retained as historical data and evidence of successful – or otherwise – risk treatment actions.

Estimating your project

06

Introduction

Every time I make a picture the critics' estimate of American public taste goes down 10 per cent.

CECIL B DE MILLE (1881–1959), US FILM PRODUCER AND DIRECTOR

The *Oxford Dictionary* defines an estimate as 'a judgement of a thing's approximate value, amount, cost, etc'. While this gives an accurate generic definition, BusinessDictionary.com presents a definition more suited to industry needs:

> Approximation, prediction, or projection of a quantity based on experience and/or information available at the time, with the recognition that other pertinent facts are unclear or unknown (BusinessDictionary.com, Dec 2009)

The importance of estimating

Estimates are required, to varying degrees of accuracy, at all stages of the project life cycle. Before an organization can make an investment decision, an estimate needs to establish how much capital investment is required. An estimate needs to be made on likely business benefits. The likelihood is that an estimate would be needed before any shareholders or stakeholders authorized any funding for investment. Further along the project life cycle an estimate is required for tendering and bidding processes and throughout the life cycle the estimate is a control: a document that project stakeholders can reference progress against.

The estimate is a crucial part of the project process; organizations that underestimate in order to place a more competitive bid are likely to risk their profit margins if the contract is a lump-sum contract or risk repeat work if the client is meeting all of the costs. Conversely, the company that overestimates by building in too many contingencies or allowances is unlikely to be competitive.

So what makes a good estimate? A good estimate can only really be measured on completion of the project or phase that has been estimated. If the project out-turn is within the parameters of the estimate stated at the time, then the estimate was good.

The key to producing a good estimate is quality of information. As far as possible each item, resource, indirect cost, overhead, logistical element, staple, paper clip or paper cup needs to be known if it is to be included in the cost of the project. Of course, at varying stages of the life cycle a lot of this information is not available so quality of information has to be generated from sources such as scope of the project, internal expertise, previous known projects, quantities required, factors that affect productivity, location, experience of the project team – the list goes on. What is crucial in producing a good estimate above all else is that the basis and assumptions made for the estimate are accurately recorded, signed by the estimator and dated so that whoever is making decisions knows what the estimate is based on.

Estimating techniques

An estimate can be best defined as:

> a probabilistic assessment, based on skills, experience and judgement, of the time and resources required to successfully deliver a deliverable/product.

There are many ways to estimate. Most of these methods can be applied to both tasks and projects overall but a project which consists of poorly estimated tasks will be poorly estimated overall.

Introduction to estimating

When estimating we need to use a wide range of tools, techniques and knowledge to produce estimates. An estimate is in essence an approximation of project time and cost targets, refined throughout the life cycle of the project.

There are four main methods of estimating:

- bottom-up estimating (analytical);
- comparative estimating (analogous);
- parametric estimating (statistical modelling);
- top down.

Also used in conjunction with the above is:

- three-point estimating (most likely, mid range, optimistic).

There are challenges with all forms of estimating and these will be considered in this chapter. It is also important to estimate resource requirements for all four of the major resource types:

- labour;
- materials;
- equipment;
- financial (cash).

When examining the effect of durations on resources, it is important to remember which costs are fixed and which are variable. For example, equipment hire costs may be variable depending on the final duration of the activity, whereas materials will generally be fixed.

The importance and practical difficulties of estimating

Throughout the project life cycle the accuracy of an estimate will change. Estimates are, after all, only quantified approximations of project costs, durations and resources. Estimates however are vital to any project, without them you cannot put together a schedule, find out what your resource needs are or even draw up a budget. An important factor to keep in mind is that an estimate can never be 100 per cent accurate (unless you are extremely lucky), therefore it is best not to mention accuracy and estimate in the same breath.

When referring to estimating we will use the term 'range'; this is breadth of tolerance around the expected result.

The start of a project is the hardest time to estimate, due to the level of uncertainty over key factors like what is to be done, when, by whom, etc. At this stage an estimate's range is likely to be wide, compared to the latter stages of a project when the detail is more clearly known.

It is quite common to update estimates throughout the project life cycle. However, probably the most important estimate is the one that features in the project management plan (PMP). The reason for this is that it is the estimate upon which the project will be authorized.

The estimating funnel

The concept that estimates improve as the project life cycle progresses is commonly called the estimating funnel.

FIGURE 6.1 The estimating Funnel

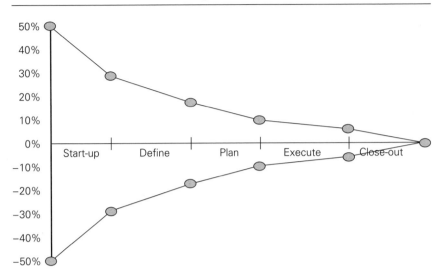

The above diagram illustrates how this process works; as we progress through the project our estimate becomes more accurate.

Classes of estimate

We can see from the diagram below the practical application of the estimating funnel on an engineering project where the accuracy of the estimate only

FIGURE 6.2 Classes of estimate

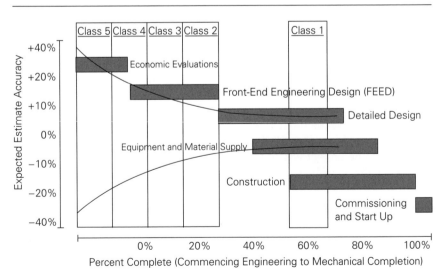

drops with +/− 10 per cent after the FEED (front end engineering design) has been completed.

In this chapter it is not the intention to provide a comprehensive approach to estimating but some guidelines and techniques that will allow you gain a better understanding of the pitfalls of estimating and arm you with some tools to allow for overall estimates for your project.

However, it is worth spending a couple of minutes reviewing what the AACE (Association for the Advancement of Cost Engineering) define as class of estimate to give us a better understanding of what to expect in terms of accuracy as we go through the project life cycle.

Cost estimating matrix

Table 6.1 on the next page shows a generic estimate classification system from the AACE. The type in bold represents the specific process industry matrix also produced by the AACE. We can then relate the class of estimate to the life cycle shown above.

Estimating techniques

As mentioned above, there are four main estimating techniques, which are listed below. Each of these techniques is useful in determining durations, resources and costs.

Bottom-up estimating (analytical)

Bottom-up estimating requires the identification of each discrete activity required to complete the project. For each activity the resources (labour, materials, equipment or financial) and the elapsed time required to complete the activity are estimated. During this process it is important to allow for normal staffing overheads (leave, training, sickness). Once you have identified any known constraints (limited skills, staffing, fixed dates before which certain activities cannot begin, equipment availability, etc), the network analysis process allows you to build up activity totals into a detailed estimate for the project. The bottom-up approach is usually used when the fine detail of the programme and/or its component projects (work packages in the case of projects) are well defined. Because this approach is based on more information and is completed in more detail, the estimate can be more precise than a top down.

Let's take a look at a snapshot of activities from our office relocation project. In our network we have durations estimated for all of these activities. However, they were estimated by breaking down the activity into its smallest tasks then rolled up to give us the overall duration. Figure 6.3 shows a snapshot of some of relocation activities.

TABLE 6.1 Cost estimate classification

Estimate class	Level of Project Definition — Expressed as % of complete definition	End Usage — Typical purpose of estimate	Methodology — Typical estimating method	Expected Accuracy Range — Typical +/– range	Preparation Effort — Typical degree of effort as % of total cost
5	0–2% (Initiation phase of project)	Concept screening	Stochastic or judgement **Capacity factored, parametric models**	Low –20 to –50% High +30 to +100%	0.005%
4	1–15% (Initiation phase of Project)	Study or feasibility	Primary stochastic **Equipment factored, parametric models**	Low –15 to –30% High +20 to +50%	0.01–0.02%
3	10–40% (Planning phase of project)	Budget, authorization or control	Mixed but primary deterministic **Semi-detailed unit costs with assembly level line items**	Low –10 to –20% High +30 to +100%	0.015–0.05
2	30–70% (Execution phase of project)	Control or bid/tender	Primary deterministic **Detailed unit costs with forced detailed take off**	Low –5 to –15% High +30 to +100%	0.02–0.1%
1	50–100% (Execution phase of project)	Check estimate or bid/tender	Deterministic **Detailed unit costs with detailed take off**	Low –3 to –10% High +3 to +15%	0.025–0.5%

FIGURE 6.3 Simulation project: activity estimate

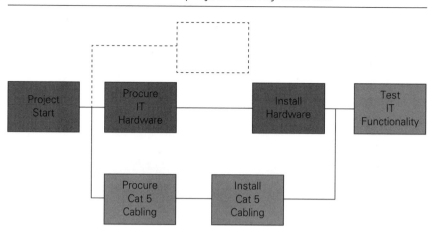

Activity H (Install Cat 5 cabling) is estimated at 4 weeks; this was estimated by firstly breaking the tasks down to their lowest level as shown in the example below.

FIGURE 6.4 Simulation project: estimate breakdown

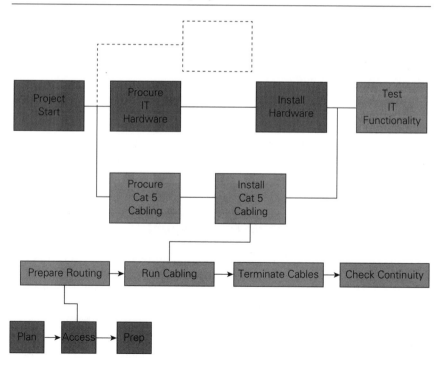

At the lowest level we can more accurately estimate the effort and duration of the work to be done. Once this has been done the results can be rolled up to the higher level.

FIGURE 6.5   Simulation project: estimate breakdown durations

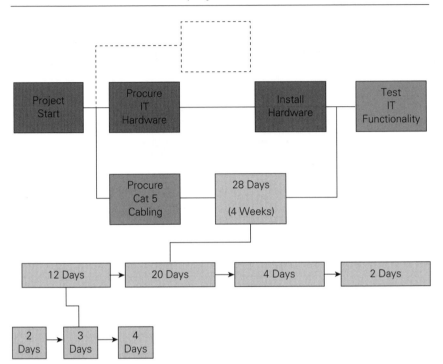

Although time consuming and onerous, breaking down each activity to its lowest level (where we should have most confidence in our estimate) will allow us to create a higher level of accuracy in our estimate.

However, bear in mind if lower level estimates are out by 50 per cent this will translate up the chain.

Comparative estimating (analogous)

Comparative estimating involves comparing current or completed tasks or projects for which you have some measures of the time and resources required. This method is based on actual past experience rather than opinion, but is only useful if the analogy is valid. The previous task or project will be different in some respects – do these differences mean that the task or project is not really comparable without having to make assumptions and thus reintroducing a large measure of opinion? The comparative method provides a firm basis for estimating if information is available, this information would then need to be scaled up or down to meet the needs of the project which is being estimated.

The following diagram highlights the fact that you are using comparisons with previous projects to base estimates upon.

FIGURE 6.6 Comparative estimating

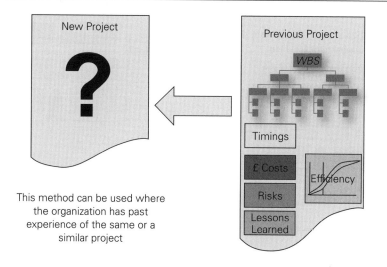

Parametric estimating (statistical modelling)

Parametric estimating uses defined parameters by which a project can be measured, such as the time or cost involved to build a specific project deliverable. This process can be repeated for a number of different deliverables, multiplied by the number of each of the parameters required to fulfil the project requirements. The parametric approach requires a reasonable amount of robust data in order to make this an easily accessible estimating technique.

An example for estimating the cost of a housing development is seen below (Figure 6.7). Type A house could be costed using the formula A = 4X+2Y+3Z, and Type B would be B = 2X+Y+Z.

Top-down estimating

In the early stages of a project, management needs some sense of the overall cost of the project, as well as the expected benefit.

As we have discussed the most accurate way to estimate is usually to build a work breakdown structure and to estimate all of the lowest level, individual work components. As discussed, this bottom-up approach is, unfortunately, the most time consuming. It is also not appropriate for initial estimating that this level of effort is expended at the early stages as a rough estimate may be all that is required to give the project a go ahead or not.

FIGURE 6.7   Top-down estimating

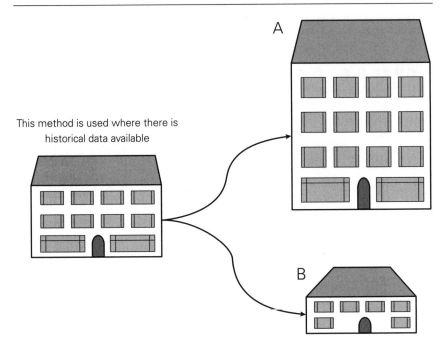

This method is used where there is historical data available

We can therefore utilize a top-down approach to gain as much estimating confidence as possible, while also considering as short a timeframe as practical in its preparation. The following are top-down techniques that should be considered.

Top-down techniques include the following:

- *Previous history*: This is using some of the comparative techniques discussed earlier. In all the techniques this is by far the best way to estimate work. Obviously this is dependent on delivering similar projects in the past and also relies on keeping track of actual effort, hours and costs from previous projects. If these parameters exist it is then possible to describe your project in the same terms to see if similar work was done in the past. If so, you will have a good idea of the effort required to do your work. Even if actual information from previous projects was not captured it may still be possible to find out how many people worked on the project, for how long, for how much and then adjust your final estimate as needed.

- Equally, *parametric estimating* can plan a major part in the top-down approach where we can use previous similar projects and multiply up or down costs and duration to reflect our new project.

- *Partial work breakdown structure (WBS)*: This approach involves building a traditional WBS as discussed in the bottom-up approach, but you only take it down one or two levels. We can then estimate the different components of work using your best guess or one of the other estimating techniques discussed.

- *Expert opinion*: In most cases an internal or external expert will be required to help estimating the work to be completed. For instance, if this is the first time you have used a new technology or technique, you may need help from outside the project team from someone who can provide the required information.

  Often benchmarking with other companies in the industry is useful where leverage from their experience can be utilized. Utilizing an internal expert can also be useful as although this may be the first estimate for a certain type of project, someone else in your organization may have done it many times.

- *Estimate in phases*: This is often called *rolling wave planning* or *progressive elaboration*. One of the most difficult aspects of estimating projects is not knowing exactly what work will be needed in the future. To reduce the level of uncertainty, you can break the work into a series of smaller areas of work, only estimating accurately the most current work with a vague or best guess estimate for the remaining work.

Often we can provide a high-level estimate for an analysis phase where we will collate business requirements. Once these requirements have been obtained we would be in a better position to estimate the rest of the project or at least the next major phase. At this point, management can perform a cost–benefit calculation to determine if it makes sense to proceed with the rest of the project.

A subsidiary technique we can use once we have established a good overall estimate for the project is to subdivide it down through the layers of the work breakdown structure; for example, design will be 50 per cent of the total, engineering 25 per cent, etc; then subdivide design and engineering into their percentages into their components parts.

Three-point estimating

The previously mentioned forms of estimating do not necessarily account for things like human error, inconsistent data or straightforward errors in the estimating. However, three-point estimating accepts a number of variations within the project values to produce a most likely outcome, eg 90 per cent probability, a mid range value, eg 50 per cent probability, and a least likely, eg 10 per cent probability. Some organizations will ask their project teams or subcontractors to provide a P10, P50, P90 estimate (where P stands for probability), although these numbers can vary depending on the organization's requirements and the level of risk they are prepared to accept. These numbers are simply a probability of the outcome of a budget or schedule as an example.

More details on the use of statistical modelling to achieve more accurate estimates can be found in Chapter 5, 'Risk and your project'.

The following equation is related to three-point estimating which is linked to PERT (project evaluation and review technique).

FIGURE 6.8   Three-point estimating (PERT)

$$\frac{\text{Optimistic} + (4 \times \text{Most Likely}) + \text{Pessimistic}}{6}$$

Simulation example

If we again look at activity G (Install hardware) from the office relocation project the estimate used is 2 weeks. Let's apply the three-point estimating technique to this activity.

We will assume the most likely is as used, ie 14 days (2 weeks). However, if all access is available in time and all the hardware runs up as required at switch-on, then we may be able to complete the installation in as little (optimistic) as 11 days. However, if we have access issues and power up problems the worst case estimate (pessimistic) could be 22 days. We can now apply three-point estimating to these figures.

FIGURE 6.9

$$\frac{\text{Optimistic (11 days)} + (4 \times \text{Most Likely (14 days)}) + \text{Pessimistic (23 days)}}{6}$$

In this case the new estimate for activity G equates to 15 days, a day longer than originally estimated. By applying this technique to the remaining activities in our network we should be able to provide a more realistic overall estimate.

More details on the use of statistical modelling to achieve more accurate estimates can be found in Chapter 5, 'Risk and your project'.

Uncertainty and risk

It should be noted that an estimate should not be treated as an exact value either by an external stakeholder (client) or indeed by the organization's management team. There are a range of outcomes that could occur around the estimate point; it is an important part of the estimating process to ensure the recipient of the estimate appreciates the range of potential outcomes. The range of outcomes can be achieved by using a probabilistic risk analysis (please see Chapter 5, 'Risk and your project'); this requires the estimator to produce a range of outcomes for a range of items such as quantities, unit rates, productivity ratios. These are called distributions and can be above and below the initial value of the estimate. This risk analysis is normally done through the software adopted by the estimator and produces a range of potential outcomes for the total estimate and a probability of achieving the stated outcome. As with other areas of the estimate it is important that any probability calculations and statements are included in the estimate documentation.

To deal with uncertainty and risk a contingency is normally established for 'specific provisions for unforeseeable elements of cost within defined project scope' (AACE).

Contingency funding is necessary due to risks and uncertainties, anything from lack of scope or design definition may lead to a cost overrun, rework caused by engineering or construction errors, productivity reduction due to labour disputes or limited supply of particular skills. The potential risks are many and varied and the amount of contingency will depend on the level of risk and probability of achieving the particular area of the project to the estimate. Again areas where contingency has been allocated to the estimate must be clearly communicated within the estimate.

Summary of the basic rules for estimating

- Remember to estimate labour, materials, equipment and financial resources.
- Assume that labour resources will only be productive for 80 per cent of their time.
- Labour resources working on multiple projects take longer to complete tasks because of time lost switching between them.
- People are generally optimistic and often underestimate how long tasks will take.
- Make use of other people's experiences and your own.
- Obtain an expert view.
- Include management time in any estimate.
- Always build in contingency for problem solving, meetings and other unexpected events.
- Cost each task in the work breakdown structure to arrive at a total, rather than trying to cost the project as a whole.
- Agree a tolerance with your customer for additional work that is not yet defined.
- Communicate any assumptions, exclusions or constraints you have to your customer.

- Provide regular budget statements to your customer, copying your team, so that they are always aware of the current position.

Common mistakes

- Not understanding what is involved to complete an item of work.
- Starting with an amount of money and making the project cost fit it.
- Assigning resources at more than 80 per cent utilization.
- Failing to build in contingency.
- Failing to adjust the estimate in accordance with changes in scope.
- Dividing tasks between more than one resource.
- Providing estimates under pressure in project meetings.

Things to consider when estimating

There are a number of considerations that need to be addressed when estimating; these are discussed below.

Diminishing returns. When estimating labour, if a job takes 1 person 100 days to complete it is rarely true that 100 people can do it in one day. Project teams work by sharing information; as a team grows so does the number of internal interfaces over which information must pass. A team of one has no internal interfaces, a team of 2 has one, a team of 9 has 36. If a task requires many people to work together, then some allowance for this effect must be made.

Failing to take account of the real world. Some people work faster than others, they always have other things to do, they get sick and they go on holiday. Don't estimate on the basis of the best, most dedicated and fittest person you have. People rarely deliver more than 4 days a week, when working full time on a task or project. Things will go wrong – allow time for problems to be investigated and solved.

Culture. The working hours, approach to work, work rate and work expectations of different international cultures vary considerably. Using norms from previous projects in a new culture can be dangerous; advisors with knowledge of local working customs should be used to assist in preparing realistic estimates.

Human optimism. It is a universal truth that people think they can achieve more in a given period of time than they actually can. People always estimate on the low side; be aware of this and be objective.

Differing skill levels. Due to different skill levels, duration cannot necessarily be halved by doubling resources. Therefore the productivity

and efficiency of each labour resource should be estimated
independently.

Using contingency. Remember to add project management time, as
well as contingency hours to reflect the risk associated with the
estimate. The size of the contingency will reflect the degree of risk. If
for example you feel relatively comfortable with your estimate you can
get away with 10–25 per cent. If, however, you feel that the brief is
unclear you may be justified in adding a 50 per cent contingency.
This should be added a separate figure rather than just padding
your estimate.

Allowing for communication. Remember that the more resources
applied to a task, the more they will have to communicate. This is to
ensure that work is not duplicated and that interdepartmental tasks are
carried out efficiently. This additional time needs to be taken into
account when estimating durations.

A useful rule-of-thumb calculation for estimating the number of communication channels in a project environment can be calculated as follows:

$$n(n-1)/2$$

where n represents the number of people requiring to communicate on a
task, eg if we have four people on a team the number of communication
channels would be six. If we add two more people to the team the communication channels increase to 15. This is very important to remember in estimating as the extra time required in clarification and repeat instruction can have a
significant effect on the work estimate.

Conclusion

We have learned in this chapter how to apply a wide range of estimating
techniques to your project and provided some guidance on which techniques
are most applicable and when.

This chapter can be referenced at various times in the project life cycle,
as indicated by the estimating funnel, depending on the level of detail available
and required.

Please remember that estimating begins early in the project, at feasibility
and conceptual stages well before the detailed scope has been defined,
and the use of historical data from past projects is invaluable until the design
information becomes available for estimating at the basic design and detail
design stages.

CASE STUDY   Estimating the AMEC way

About AMEC

AMEC is one of the world's leading engineering, project management and consultancy companies. Their goal is to deliver profitable, safe and sustainable projects and services for their customers in the oil and gas, minerals and metals, clean energy, environment and infrastructure markets, including sectors that play a vital role in the global and national economies and in people's everyday lives. They design, deliver and maintain strategic assets for their customers, offering services which extend from environmental and front end engineering design before the start of a project to decommissioning at the end of an asset's life. Their customers, in both the private and public sector, are among the world's biggest and best in their fields: BP, Shell, EDF, National Grid and US Navy, to name just a few.

They are truly international, with major operations centres based in the UK and Americas and offices and projects in around 40 countries worldwide. They work in diverse and often challenging environments, from sub-zero temperatures in the north of Canada to the sweltering heat of the Persian Gulf.

They employ over 27,000 people – ranging from scientists and environmental consultants to engineers and project managers, dedicated professionals who take pride in their work. The AMEC Academy helps them to attract, develop and retain the best talent.

They are proud of their core values: 'delivering excellence to our customers by believing in people, never compromising on safety and acting with integrity'.

Their shares are traded on the London Stock Exchange, where the company is included in the FTSE 100 index and listed in the oil equipment and services sector (LSE: AMEC).

Estimating: the AMEC approach

> There is no merit in attempting to achieve a level of accuracy that is inconsistent to the amount of information available, particularly as this could lead to the estimate being given a 'perceived' credibility it does not deserve.

The percentage accuracy of the estimate improves as the definition of the project is developed through feasibility, conceptual, basic engineering and detail design stages.

So for many projects the estimate is revisited and updated several times as the project definition moves through these stages.

Typically at the feasibility stage, when the project is not much more than an idea, the estimated accuracy is between −25 per cent and +50 per cent.

By the time detail design is complete, the overall project can be re-estimated to an accuracy of −5 per cent to +10 per cent, although the construction element itself might be a little less accurate (remember, at this stage detail design purchase order placement for equipment and materials will be 100 per cent or very close).

The four stages in detail

Feasibility

The estimate at this stage is often used for project sanction.

At feasibility stage, the project is not much more than an idea and there are very few details available. We may not even know in what country the construction will take place.

At this point the kind of information required to create the estimate will be as follows:

- generalized scope definition;
- required capacity of plant;
- approximate weights;
- preliminary project schedule.

Concept

The estimate at conceptual stage is often associated with studying various options for the final plant layout.

By this time, the country of construction is likely to have been identified and equipment lists and budget quotes will be available along with some of the early process definition.

During the concept stage the kind of information you will be working with is as follows:

- plant location;
- preliminary process diagram;
- main statutory requirements;
- equipment list;
- outline engineering specifications;
- preliminary 'block' plot plan;
- offsite and utilities by system and capacity;
- budget quotes for equipment;
- preliminary equipment data sheets;
- preliminary process and instrument diagram.

Basic design

During basic design, often known as FEED (front end engineering design), the number of options for the final plant layout will either have been eliminated or reduced so detailed plot plans will be available along with the other design information shown in the bulleted list overleaf.

The project master schedule and information on site conditions will also be available.

At this stage it is possible to establish target cost arrangements between the owner or client and the constructors.

- firm quotes for major equipment;

- detailed scope definition;

- finalized heat and mass balance calculations;

- P and IDs for process and offsite;

- detailed plot plans;

- detailed engineering specifications;

- preliminary material take offs;

- operators' requirements;

- local authority requirements;

- project master schedules;

- information on site conditions.

Detail design

As stated earlier, by the time detail design is complete, the overall project can be re-estimated to an accuracy of –5 per cent to +10 per cent, although the construction element itself might be a little less accurate (remember, at this stage detail design purchase order placement for equipment and materials will be 100 per cent or very close).

This is often known as the definitive estimate and the information used for this estimate will be:

- local availability of labour and materials;

- detailed equipment list;

- completed and approved plant layout;

- electrical single line diagrams;

- detailed equipment specifications/data sheets;

- detailed material take offs;

- firm quotations from potential vendors;

- quotations from potential contractors;

- commissioning and operating information;

- installation and fabrication specifications;

- construction subcontract enquiries;

- production design phase continues.

Estimating factors

At the feasibility stage, factors representing the ratio of total installed cost to cost of major process equipment are widely used in the refining and petrochemical industries.

These factors have been in use since the mid 1900s by various people including H J Lang in 1947 and K Guthrie in the late 1960s.

Different factors for different types of process equipment (pumps, exchangers, vessels, etc) are used.

Construction man hours, typically to +/–30 per cent, can then be estimated by dividing the expected construction percentage of total installed cost established from the factoring of process equipment by an average labour man hour rate.

Why is this important in the early stages of project definition?

It gives an idea of the total labour and number of jobs which will be provided during construction as regional benefits in the potential locations or countries in which the construction might take place, which will help improve the chance of the project going ahead.

In addition to factors, order of magnitude is often used for estimating during the feasibility stage. From historical information, a typical project might have costs divided as:

- engineering and home office: 19 per cent;

- procurement: 38 per cent;

- construction: 40 per cent;

- commissioning: 3 per cent.

At high level only, the percentages for the detail below these headings can be estimated, again using historical data as the basis.

At the concept stage, estimated principal quantities will be available for metres of pipe, tonnes of steel, etc, and using high-level composite rather than elemental 'norms' an estimate of construction man hours can be produced which is better than at the feasibility stage.

Onshore projects, offshore projects and shutdowns

Figure 6.10 summarizes much of what has been mentioned so far about estimating at the four stages, feasibility, concept, basic design and detail design, and provides a reminder of how the accuracy of the estimate improves as we move through the stages and the project scope definition becomes clearer.

Offshore

The main difference in offshore projects is that at the feasibility and concept stages estimated weights are used.

This makes sense as an offshore platform or oil rig is a fixed modular structure.

FIGURE 6.10 AMEC onshore estimating factors

1 Feasibility	2 Concept
(typically –25% to +50%)	(typically –15% to +25%)
– In house estimates for equipment and tagged items	– Preliminary details from suppliers for major equipment and tagged items
– **Factored from equipment and tagged items for bulk materials**	– **Principal quantities (approximate) for bulk materials**
– Order of magnitude from historical data on similar projects	– Base norms adjusted for location factors and productivity assumptions
– Estimate for project sanction	– Estimates for optioneering
3 Basic Design	**4 Detail Design**
(typically –10% to +15%)	(typically –5% to +10%)
– Firm details from suppliers for 80%–90% of equipment and tagged items	– Firm details from suppliers for 90%–100% of equipment and tagged items
– Preliminary MTO – in house, forced detail	– Intermediate and final MTOs
– Base component norms adjusted in house for location factors and productivity assumptions, or as provided by subcontractors	– Base component norms adjusted in house for location factors and productivity assumptions, or as provided by subcontractors
– Target cost estimate	– Definitive estimate

FIGURE 6.11 AMEC offshore estimating factors

1 Feasibiltiy	2 Concept
(typically –25% to +50%)	(typically –15% to +25%)
– In house estimates for equipment and tagged items	– Preliminary details from suppliers for major equipment and tagged items
– **Estimated weight**	– **Estimated weights for bulk materials**
– Order of magnitude from historical data on similar projects	– Base norms adjusted for location factors and productivity assumptions
– Estimate for project sanction	– Estimates for optioneering
3 Basic Design	**4 Detail Design**
(typically –10% to +15%)	(typically –5% to +10%)
– Firm details from suppliers for 80%–90% of equipment and tagged items	– Firm details from suppliers for 90%–100% of equipment and tagged items
– Preliminary MTO – in house, forced detail	– Intermediate and final MTOs
– Base component norms adjusted in house for location factors and productivity assumptions, or as provided by subcontractors	– Base component norms adjusted in house for location factors and productivity assumptions, or as provided by subcontractors
– Target cost estimate	– Definitive estimate

Shutdowns

Shutdown estimating has its own methods at the tender stage.

For poorly defined scope, the estimate will be in man-hour ranges plus a management fee which increases with the ranges.

If the tender information is better and includes a preliminary turnaround list from the client, a rough estimate can be made, based on the approximate number of jobcards, the number of associated activities, and the average man hours per activity.

As an example, the graph below shows the number of vessel inspections, control valves and other work types, each of which will require a job card.

This totals 500 job cards on the graph, which gives a total of 7,000 activities based on standard job card activities or work operations for each of the different work types.

The example shows an average of 20 man hours per job card so the 7,000 activities = 140,000 man hours.

In a real project, the man-hour estimate per job card will vary according to the work type for better accuracy.

FIGURE 6.12   AMEC estimating examples

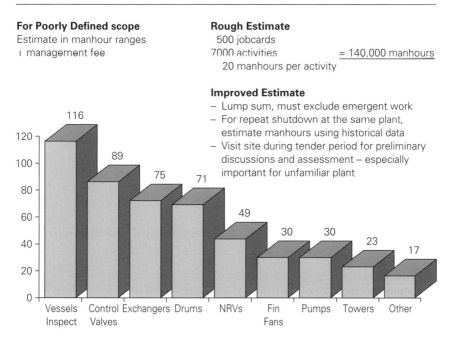

For Poorly Defined scope
Estimate in manhour ranges
ı management fee

Rough Estimate
500 jobcards
7000 activities   = 140,000 manhours
20 manhours per activity

Improved Estimate
– Lump sum, must exclude emergent work
– For repeat shutdown at the same plant, estimate manhours using historical data
– Visit site during tender period for preliminary discussions and assessment – especially important for unfamiliar plant

Bar chart values: Vessels Inspect 116, Control Valves 89, Exchangers 75, Drums 71, NRVs 49, Fin Fans 30, Pumps 30, Towers 23, Other 17

Norms

Adjustments to the base norms used in estimating will be made to take account of the country or location of construction, and also the use of estimating quantity allowances, all of which affect the construction man-hour estimate.

Base norms, dependant on the source, will be specific to that country or region.

For construction work in countries other than the country for which the base norms apply, a location factor adjustment to the base norms will be required.

For example, a productivity factor of 1.0 for US Gulf Coast (Houston, Texas) is the base. So using US Gulf Coast norms, there is no location factor adjustment necessary to the construction man hours for a project to be constructed in the US Gulf Coast location.

Other international locations, though, will have a productivity factor above or below the 1.0 base for US Gulf Coast.

For example, China has a location factor of 3.90, which means that if US Gulf Coast norms are used to produce an estimate for construction man hours, the man hours will need to be multiplied by 3.90 for construction in China.

Whether or not it has been necessary to apply location factors to the base norms, these will need to be adjusted to reflect project specific issues such as:

- climate;

- site layout and access;

- site location – how remote?

- clock in and walking time to workface;

- work days and hours;

- labour density;

- industrial relations;

- availability of skilled trades (competing projects, use of local and travelling labour);

- use of equipment, working methods (eg machine or hand excavate);

- permit to work on brownfield sites;

- conditions of contract.

Various quantity allowances will be included in the estimate for engineering growth, material take off and cutting and waste.

Construction increase allowance for anticipated engineering growth (including associated materials) will not increase the quantities against which the adjusted norms are applied in arriving at the total construction man-hour estimate.

Project leadership

07

Introduction

A leader's job is to look into the future, and to see the organization not as it is ... but as it can become.

WOODROW WILSON, 28TH US PRESIDENT

There are two typical questions asked when the subject of project leadership is discussed, the first being 'What is the difference between leadership and management?' and the second being 'Is there a difference between normal leadership and leadership in a project?'

This chapter will answer both these questions and examine the skills and behaviours required to successfully lead within a project environment.

In the project teams chapter we discussed the areas of team development and team management which tie in very closely with leadership in terms of skills and behaviours and each should not be treated in isolation but as integrated activities that need to be performed.

We are often asked how leadership is related to the main drive of a business, which is generally profit. Several studies have been conducted which show the relation between good leadership and profit. One such study was conducted by the CIBC (Canadian International Bank of Commerce).

In order to improve the quality of service that the CIBC provided to their customers, it was recognized that employees of the bank, who deliver the service, must feel motivated and loyal towards the company in order to do their best work.

This required major commitment and action by top management, who commissioned a series of customer and employee satisfaction surveys throughout all their branches (around 1,300) and then collated the results. They subsequently took action to address the results and measured the progress by conducting further annual surveys.

The following model charts (Figure 7.1) the progress in one year.

In summary, they deduced that an increase in profit of 2 per cent, which equated to $172 million, could be directly attributed to the change in leadership behaviour by their management.

FIGURE 7.1   CIBC leadership impact on profits

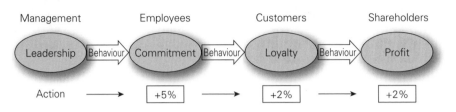

Dale Carnegie, author of *How to Win Friends and Influence People*, summarizes the importance of leadership in the following quote.

FIGURE 7.2   Dale Carnegie and leadership

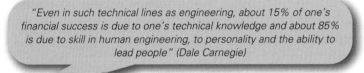

"Even in such technical lines as engineering, about 15% of one's financial success is due to one's technical knowledge and about 85% is due to skill in human engineering, to personality and the ability to lead people" (Dale Carnegie)

As a project leader you will be judged on the results of what your team achieves. This means much of your time should be spent supporting and encouraging your team to get the results you need.

This emphasizes the importance of effective leadership within business as a whole and equally in the project environment. In the following pages of this chapter I aim to highlight some of the important aspects of project leadership and arm you with some effective and useful tools to aid you in your leadership journey.

Leadership vs management

What is the difference between leadership and management?

The origins and meanings of the words 'manage' and 'lead' help to answer this question. Table 7.1 on the following page describes the origin of each word and three typical definitions.

Leadership is about deciding direction, knowing the next steps and then taking others with you to it, whereas *managing* is a later concept, and is more associated with handling a system or machine of some kind.

There are valuable elements of management not necessarily found in leadership, eg administration and managing resources. Leadership, on the other

TABLE 7.1 Leadership vs management

Manage:	
Origin	1560s, probably from Italian. *maneggiare* 'to handle', especially 'to control a horse', from Latin *manus* 'hand'. Influenced by French *manège* 'horsemanship' (earliest English sense was of handling horses)
Definitions	**1** to exert control over;
	2 to take charge or care of;
	3 to dominate or influence (a person) by tact, flattery, or artifice;
	4 to handle, direct, govern, or control in action or use.
Lead	
Origin	c.1300, 'to guide', O.E. lædan 'cause to go with one, guide' Anglo-Saxon 'the road or path ahead'
Definitions	**1** to go before or with to show the way; conduct or escort;
	2 to go first; be in advance;
	3 to influence or induce; cause;
	4 to guide in direction, course, action, opinion, etc.

hand, contains elements not necessarily found in management, eg inspiring others through the leader's own enthusiasm and commitment.

In conclusion, leadership is different from management. All leaders are not necessarily great managers, but the best leaders will possess good management skills. However, one skill set does not automatically imply the other will be present.

Obviously within a project environment the project manager needs to possess good management skills in order to plan and execute the project. However, often this is thought to be enough but, as we will explore, good leadership skills are as important if not more influential in the success of a project.

Leading in a project environment

Is there a difference between normal leadership and leadership in a project?

The basic definition of a project is 'a temporary endeavour undertaken to create a unique product, service or result'.

The project environment is very different from that of typical day-to-day operations or a regular team that performs similar activities on a day-to-day basis. The fact that a project is temporary has a huge impact on the staff employed within that project in respect of their motivation, their commitment to the work in hand and their loyalty to the project.

In addition the 'unique' aspects of the project will also lead to a different environment than that of a regular team which carries out similar, repetitive or comparable tasks on a regular basis. The impact of the 'unique' aspects on team members may be seen in a lack of confidence, fear, anxiety, aversion to responsibility and accountability and insecurity. This means the project manager may need to communicate with the team more than usual, adopt more of a coaching or mentoring role and overall spend more time with the team.

Examining the project life cycle below shows some of the transitions in styles and behaviours a project manager may need to adopt as the project progresses.

FIGURE 7.3   Leadership and the project life cycle

	Start-up	Definition	Execution	Close-out
Typical Major Tasks	• Gather data • Identify needs • Strategies • Goals • Stakeholders • Risks • Alternatives • Selling • Approvals	• Feasibility • Rationale • Tactics • WBS • Project Team • Schedule • Budget • Re-assess Risks • Project Brief	• Start-up • Motivate Team • Work Packages • Procurement • Execute Work • Control System • Progress Report • Forecasting • Resolve Issues	• Finalise Project • Review • Acceptance • Training • Transfers • Final Reports • Settle Accounts • Handover • Transfers
Leadership and Management Skills	• Visionary • Creative • Innovative • Communicator • Listener	• Facilitator • Integrator • Planner • Diplomatic • Coach	• Motivator • Decision Maker • Participation • Empowering • Team Builder	• Trainer • Morale Builder • Diplomatic • Energetic • Trustworthy

Action-centred leadership

Although there is clearly a difference between leadership and management and the fact that additional leadership skills are required in a project as opposed to a regular team, a good project manager will still have to balance both those areas effectively within the project.

John Adair's action-centred leadership model can be used effectively to reflect the balance of skills required in the leadership aspects of a project. He suggests leadership activities can be split into three key elements: achieving the task, developing the team and developing the individual. These elements are mutually dependent, as well as being separately essential to the overall leadership role. The diagram below shows the three elements depicted as overlapping circles.

FIGURE 7.4   Adair's action-centred leadership model

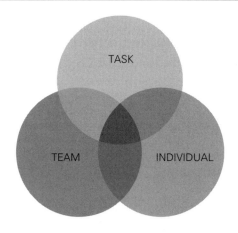

When considering projects, all of these elements are independently essential in ensuring success, but more importantly the dependence of each element on the other is essential in the successful execution of the project and its elements.

Good project managers should have full command of the three main areas of the action-centred leadership model, and should be able to use each of the elements according to the situation. Being able to do all of these things, and keep the right balance, gets results, builds morale, improves quality, develops teams and productivity, and is the mark of a successful project manager and leader.

Below is a summary of the key deliverables within each of the three leadership elements.

Your responsibilities as a project manager for achieving the *task* are:

- identify aims and vision for the group, purpose, and direction – define the activity (the task);
- identify resources, people, processes, systems and tools (including financials, communications, IT);
- create the plan to achieve the task – deliverables, measures, timescales, strategy and tactics;
- establish responsibilities, objectives, accountabilities and measures, by agreement and delegation;
- set standards, quality, time and reporting parameters;

- control and maintain activities against parameters;
- monitor and maintain overall performance against plan;
- report on progress towards the group's aim;
- review, reassess, adjust plan, methods and targets as necessary.

Your responsibilities as a project manager for the *team* are:

- establish, agree and communicate standards of performance and behaviour;
- establish style, culture, approach of the group – soft skill elements;
- monitor and maintain discipline, ethics, integrity and focus on objectives;
- anticipate and resolve group conflict, struggles or disagreements;
- assess and change as necessary the balance and composition of the group;
- develop team working, cooperation, morale and team spirit;
- develop the collective maturity and capability of the group – and group freedom and authority;
- encourage the team towards objectives and aims – and provide a collective sense of purpose;
- identify, develop and agree team and project leadership roles within group;
- enable, facilitate and ensure effective internal and external group communications;
- identify and meet group training needs;
- give feedback to the group on overall progress; and seek feedback and input from the group.

Your responsibilities as a project manager for each *individual* are:

- understand the team members as individuals – personality, skills, strengths, needs and aims;
- assist and support individuals – plans, problems, challenges, highs and lows;
- identify and agree appropriate individual responsibilities and objectives;
- give recognition and praise to individuals – acknowledge effort and good work;
- where appropriate reward individuals with extra responsibility, advancement and status;
- identify, develop and utilize each individual's capabilities and strengths;
- train and develop individual team members;
- develop individual freedom and authority.

The interaction of the three leadership elements

Using the example of a simple piece of project work which will require the project team to complete, it is then possible to illustrate how each leadership element is dependent on the next.

We need each *individual* within the team to be motivated, committed and willing to communicate with other individuals within the team to ensure the *team* works cohesively, is integrated in their approach and focused on the work to be done to ensure the *task* is completed in an efficient and timely manner. Equally, continuing in a clockwise direction, the definition, clarity and aims of the *task* need to be articulated to help with *individual* commitment and confidence.

FIGURE 7.5   Leadership element dependencies

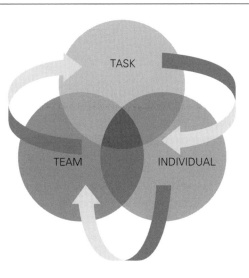

The dependency of each of the elements and the importance of each on each other in delivering a successful project is now clear.

Typical project balance

Possibly due to the perception that projects are often 'technical' and therefore task driven, many project managers focus on the task aspect of the project and less on the team and individual. The diagram overleaf shows the typical balance of focus of project managers. This may also be due to the fact that many project managers have spent many of their formative years honing, perfecting and mastering their trade which will often be technically based and therefore task orientated. When they are then appointed to the role of project manager, the perception of 'doing a good job' is seen to be delivering the task.

This is mainly true, but the realization that effective delivery of the task can be achieved by the team and individuals within that team is often overlooked and the project manager spends more time than is healthy on the task-oriented aspects of the project. In essence they are 'micro managing' the tasks rather than spending their valuable time on the people and softer issues of the project.

FIGURE 7.6   Typical task focus

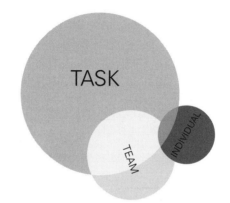

One other reason for spending less time on the people aspects of the project is because they are skills and behaviours that are often new to the project manager. The project manager has spent a minimum of five years at university learning the technical aspects of their trade, has then spent 10 years practising the technical aspects of their trade and been rewarded throughout those years for achievements in performing the aspects of their trade and now suddenly they are thrown into an environment where they are now expected to ignore the technical aspects of their trade and start to manage people – a whole new range of behaviours, skills and expertise that have very rarely been practised or performed before.

For project managers in this position, one consolation is that the skills required to manage people, although inherent in some people, can be learned. As with any skill, with direction, time and practice, the behaviours and skills required to effectively manage people can be learned and performed effectively over time.

The next few pages describe some of the key leadership behaviours and skills necessary to effectively manage people within a project.

Communication

If any single leadership skill is more important than another it is communication. In all elements of work life the most common complaint about an organization is 'lack of communication'.

The PMI (Project Management Institute) suggest a project manager should spend 90 per cent of their time communicating.

Effective communication

Communication 'messages' are perceived as dependent on the method of delivery.

Any communication is made of one or more of the following three elements:

- The first is the words used – ie written words through e-mail, text, memos, etc.
- The second is what we hear – ie how the spoken word is perceived based on tone: happy, sad, angry, etc.
- The third is the what we see – ie how the message giver's body language is perceived: defensive, aggressive, complacent, etc.

Several surveys have been conducted on this subject to determine the relationship between the three areas and how much of effective communication is attributed to each of these areas. The percentage split can be seen below.

FIGURE 7.7   Effective communication percentages

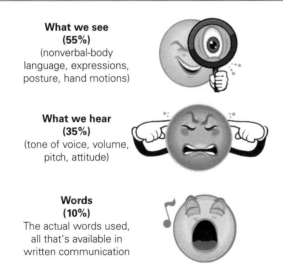

**What we see
(55%)**
(nonverbal-body
language, expressions,
posture, hand motions)

**What we hear
(35%)**
(tone of voice, volume,
pitch, attitude)

**Words
(10%)**
The actual words used,
all that's available in
written communication

Using as an example a situation where a manager is giving someone an appraisal and is saying 'I am so pleased with your performance to date and very impressed in the way you have motivated your team and managed the difficult client on your project.' However, they say this in a quiet monotone voice, with their arms crossed, body turned away while looking down at the desk and avoiding eye contact.

Although the words are loaded with compliments and praise, they are being negated by the body language and tone, which are overriding the true value of the message. Therefore 90 per cent of the message received is non-verbal and is indicating poor performance rather than the contrary.

If we consider each type of communication medium we can see how each can help or hinder the imparting of the correct message.

TABLE 7.2   Communication mediums

Written word: e-mail, letter, memo, text, IM	This means of communication is purely the words; it is difficult to convey emotion via this medium and is often misunderstood because of the lack of detail in the message or the perception of its content.
Voice communication: telephone, radio, voice to voice computer	This is an instant improvement on the purely written word because now emotion is included in the communication. In a telephone conversation we can start to determine if someone is happy, sad, angry, irritated, annoyed, distressed etc. It is also a more efficient form of communication as answers to questions can be received instantly.
Face to face: individual meetings, video conferencing, presentations	This is obviously the most effective of all communication mediums as it allows the three key communication elements to be used ie body language, tone and words. By communicating face to face with someone we can use these elements to ensure the correct message is being presented. **Note:** this will only be achieved if all the three elements are aligned.

Feedback

Irrespective of how we communicate with another party the impact of the message they wish to convey may be received differently from what we intended, again possibly due to a differing perception. In order to minimize misunderstanding we should always try and clarify by using feedback.

FIGURE 7.8   Misunderstanding feedback

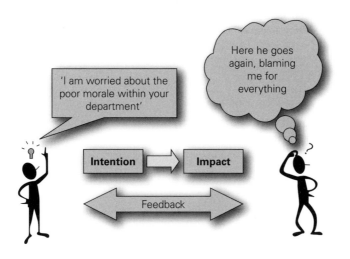

Types of feedback

There are two main types of feedback and they are the lifeblood of any project and project team; without feedback team members will not know what they are doing well and therefore what they should keep doing. They also won't know what they have done incorrectly and therefore what they must fix or improve. The two types of feedback are:

- *Motivational.* Tells a person what they have done well. Purpose: to encourage the person and reinforce their good behaviour or performance.
- *Developmental.* Tells the person what could be improved upon. Purpose: to help the person see how they could do a better job next time and/or understand the impact of their actions and behaviours on others.

How to give feedback

- Seek agreement from the receiver if appropriate.
- Keep motivational and formative separate.
- Make sure the timing is right.
- Focus on behaviour and not the person.
- Give specific examples.
- Deliver in a positive supportive manner.
- Demonstrate trust.
- Deliver frequently – don't store it up.

How to receive feedback

Receiving feedback is often more difficult than giving it even when it is motivational. The following are some pointers on how feedback should be received.

Motivational

- Accept the feedback graciously.
- Don't throw it back at the giver by saying 'You must want something!' or by denying it.
- Thank the person for making the effort to give you the feedback.

Developmental

- Listen and be receptive.
- Clarify understanding if unclear.
- Do not be defensive.
- Do not deny the other person's perception or experience.
- Think about it – remember we rarely see ourselves as others do!
- If you believe the feedback is unreasonable, seek the opinions of others in a positive and objective manner. This may help you to decide whether to accept and act upon it or not.
- Thank the person for the feedback. Treat it as a gift!

Five stages of receiving developmental feedback

Receiving developmental feedback is often difficult and by human nature we don't want to hear it or accept it. However, remember it should be treated as a gift and if delivered correctly (timely and with specific examples) it should be useful in developing an individual within their role.

Typically the stages an individual will go through when receiving developmental feedback are shown below.

1 Denial ('It wasn't my fault.')
2 Anger/emotion ('How dare they say that about me!')
3 Rationalization ('The only reason I did it was because ...')
4 Acceptance ('I think I can see now why they might think that way.')
5 Take action ('I had better do something about it.')

The early stages of this model should be expected. However, with the correct delivery, specific examples and time to reflect, the individual should get through to the latter stages quite quickly.

FIGURE 7.9   Early stages of development feedback

Practice makes perfect, the more regularly you start giving and receiving feedback the more natural it will become and the less defensive people will be in receiving it.

Examples of giving feedback

Giving either type of feedback can be challenging; below are some examples of how to deliver effective and useful feedback.

Motivational
'One thing I particularly like about you is...'
'I really appreciated it when you....'
'Something I've noticed you do particularly well is...'
'One of your real strengths is...'

Formative
'What I'd like you to consider the next time is...'
'When you did xxx it made me feel yyy...'
'One thing I feel you could improve upon in your job is...'
'I'm concerned that when you do xxx it will...'

Although motivational feedback can and should be delivered independently, developmental feedback should be delivered by first giving motivational feedback.
Example:

I really appreciated the detail that you included in the last performance report to the client. He reported back he was so glad to see those additional performance measures. (motivational)

One area to consider next time is additional time required in preparing this information as the client was a little concerned that the report was delivered two days late. (developmental)

Action

Make a point of giving at least one piece of motivational feedback daily to each of your immediate team; remember to be specific ('well done, good job' is not specific).

In addition practise giving development feedback as soon as it is appropriate. Again this should be delivered with specific, quantified examples.

Visionary

One of the key differences identified between management and leadership is that a leader needs to be visionary. This is the ability to look into the future and see the full picture of the project outcome.

A quote that sums up how a project team may feel at the beginning of a project:

> Give to us clear vision that we know where to stand and what to stand
> for because unless we stand for something, we shall fall for anything.
>
> (Peter Marshall)

It is therefore the job of the project manager to provide the clear vision the project team desires.

Visionary leadership is often associated with senior management or company entrepreneurs; however, it is an essential requirement of the project leader or project manager. In the early stages of a project the project manager must be able to provide a vision of the final project deliverables and deliver that vision to the team.

A visionary leader is effective in manifesting their vision because they create specific, achievable goals, initiate action and enlist the participation of others.

An effective project leader is often described as having a vision of where to go and the ability to articulate it. Visionaries thrive on change and being able to draw new boundaries. It was once said that a leader is someone who 'lifts us up, gives us a reason for being and gives the vision and spirit to change'. Visionary leaders enable people to feel they have a real stake in the project. They empower people to experience the vision on their own. They offer people opportunities to create their own vision, to explore what the vision will mean to their jobs and lives, and to envision their future as part of the vision for the organization.

Articulation of the vision

Projects often 'fail' because we simply fail to clearly articulate the vision and the project's 'success criteria'. We also don't successfully communicate it to each stakeholder and team member. Relating back to the last section and the importance of feedback, successfully communicating the vision and success criteria is a two-way process. Good project leaders need to verify that the message not only is received, but is translated to 'what it means to me' to each role, task and stakeholder.

Clearly communicating the project's vision and success criteria is a great start and can begin by having each member of the team paraphrase and articulate that same message – but specifically associating it with their role and responsibilities in the project. Having each member understand the other team members' roles (in regards to the success criteria and vision) will also increase the appreciation for each other's responsibilities.

Stephen Covey in *7 Habits of Highly Effective People* cites two habits that apply equally to projects: 'Habit 2: Begin with the end in mind' and 'Habit 5: Seek first to understand, then to be understood'.

Preparing the vision

There are many approaches to strategic planning and visioning. A typical approach is shown below.

TABLE 7.3 Preparing the vision

Situation–Target–Proposal	See–Think–Draw	Draw–See–Think–Plan
• **Situation** – evaluate the current situation/project/change and how it came about • **Target** – define goals and/or objectives • **Path/Proposal** – map a possible route to the goals/objectives	• **See** – what is today's situation? • **Think** – define goals/objectives • **Draw** – map a route to achieving the goals/objectives	• **Draw** – what is the ideal image or the desired end state? • **See** – what is today's situation? What is the gap from ideal and why? • **Think** – what specific actions must be taken to close the gap between today's situation and the ideal state? • **Plan** – what resources are required to execute the activities?

When draw is mentioned in the above process it is often a huge benefit to the project team to actually draw an image of what the project goals, objectives, outcomes can look like. It will also benefit if this is done as pictorially as possible, utilizing a large blank area and using coloured paper, newspaper/magazine clippings, coloured Post-its and stickers and anything that will provide a long-lasting image. Remember, a picture paints a thousand words.

Tools and approaches

Among the most useful tools for strategic planning is SWOT analysis (strengths, weaknesses, opportunities and threats). The main objective of this tool is to analyse internal strategic factors, strengths and weaknesses attributed to the organization, and external factors beyond the control of the organization such as opportunities and threats. This approach has already been discussed in Chapter 5, 'Risk and your project' but is equally useful in defining a vision and objectives for the project.

Other tools include:

- *Balanced scorecards*: which create a systematic framework for strategic planning.
- *Scenario planning*: the process in which managers invent and then consider, in depth, several varied scenarios of equally plausible futures with the objective to minimize surprises and unexpected leaps of understanding.
- *PEST analysis*: political, economic, social and technological.
- *STEEPLE analysis*: social, technical, economic, environmental, political, legal and ethical factors.

Motivation

The motivation of individuals within the project team plays a big part in the delivery of the project objectives. Some of the traditional theories and approaches to motivation are described below:

Motivational theories

Frederick Herzberg's motivation and hygiene factors

Frederick Herzberg first established his theories about motivation in the workplace. Herzberg's work, originally on 200 Pittsburgh engineers and accountants, has become one of the most replicated studies in the field of workplace psychology.

Herzberg was the first to show that satisfaction and dissatisfaction at work nearly always arose from different factors, and were not simply opposing reactions to the same factors, as had always previously been believed.

He showed that certain factors truly motivate ('motivators'), whereas others tended to lead to dissatisfaction ('hygiene factors').

According to Herzberg, man has two sets of needs: one as an animal to avoid pain, and two as a human being to grow psychologically.

He illustrated this also through a Biblical example: Adam after his expulsion from Eden having the need for food, warmth, shelter, safety, etc: the 'hygiene' needs; and Abraham, capable and achieving great things through self-development: the 'motivational' needs. Certain parallels can clearly be seen with Maslow's hierarchy theory which we cover later.

Herzberg's research proved that people will strive to achieve hygiene needs because they are unhappy without them, but once satisfied the effect soon wears off – satisfaction is temporary. Examples of hygiene needs in the workplace are policy, relationship with supervisor, work conditions, salary, status, security, relationship with subordinates, personal life.

FIGURE 7.10   Herzberg's motivators and hygiene factors

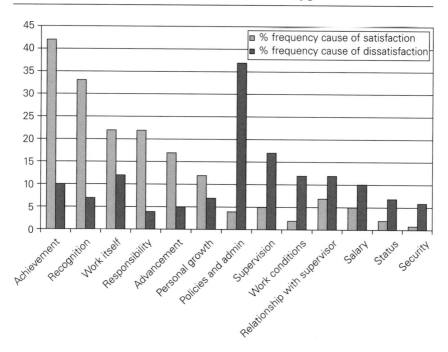

True motivators were found to be other completely different factors: achievement, recognition, work itself, responsibility, advancement, and personal growth as shown in the graph.

People commonly argue that money is a primary motivator. It's not. Surveys repeatedly show that other factors motivate more.

FIGURE 7.11   Development Dimensions international survey results

A survey by Development Dimensions International published in the UK *Times* newspaper in 2010 interviewed 1,000 staff from companies employing more than 500 workers, and found many to be bored, lacking commitment and looking for a new job. Pay actually came fifth in the reasons people gave for leaving their jobs. The main reasons were lack of stimulus and no opportunity for advancement – classic Herzberg motivators – 43% left for better promotion chances; 28% for more challenging work; 23% for a more exciting place to work; and 21% for more varied work.

Abraham Maslow's hierarchy of needs motivational model

Abraham Maslow developed the hierarchy of needs model in 1940s–1950s USA. Maslow's hierarchy of needs remains valid today for understanding human motivation and for management training.

The model holds that each of us is motivated by needs. Our most basic needs are inborn, having evolved over tens of thousands of years. Maslow's hierarchy of needs helps to explain how these needs motivate us all.

Maslow's hierarchy of needs states that we must satisfy each need in turn, starting with the first and lowest, which deals with the most obvious needs for survival itself.

Only when the lower-order needs of physical and emotional well-being are satisfied are we concerned with the higher-order needs of influence and personal development.

Conversely, if the things that satisfy our lower-order needs are swept away, we are no longer concerned about the maintenance of our higher-order needs.

- Biological and physiological needs: air, food, drink, shelter, warmth, sex, sleep, etc.
- Safety needs: protection from the elements, security, order, law, limits, stability, etc.
- Belongingness and love needs: work group, family, affection, relationships, etc.
- Esteem needs: self-esteem, achievement, mastery, independence, status, dominance, prestige, managerial responsibility, etc.
- Self-actualization needs: realizing personal potential, self-fulfilment, seeking personal growth and peak experiences.

FIGURE 7.12   Maslow's Hierarchy of Needs

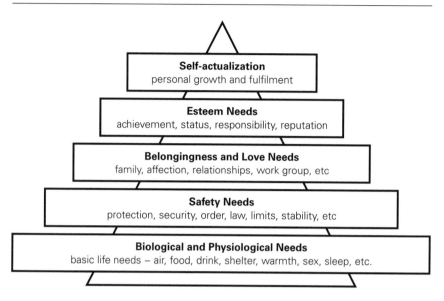

Motivation in projects

Project teams are different from normal teams, but does this mean the motivation within individuals will be different? The answer is no.

Does this mean that the above motivational theories will apply to all my team members? Again the answer is no.

Motivation should be considered as the internal drive and desire within an individual. Like a motor car, if it didn't have an alternator to continually charge its battery it would eventually stop. Motivation should be looked at in the same way, an internal charge that is continually topping up the individual's motivational battery.

One thing the two theories above commonly show is that generally people are ultimately motivated by responsibility, praise, acknowledgement, achievements, personal growth and fulfilment. However, everyone will be different.

Consider an individual within your team who has been a model team player and has delivered well above your expectations. It is decided in return for their exceptional work they should receive a promotion and they are given a senior project management role within the company's top project in West Africa. After several months within the job you find the performance of the individual has started to drop off. Why?

Maslow's theory of motivation explains that what potentially has happened is that the safety need and possibly the belonging needs have been removed, the individual is now worried about their safety, they are also separated from their friends, family, colleagues and day-to-day home activities. This would imply that because these needs are not satisfied then the higher needs of self-esteem and actualization cannot be fulfilled.

A drop off in performance may also be seen when a team member is experiencing family issues such as divorce or separation. Suddenly the belonging needs have been removed and anything above is ignored.

This shows how motivation is an individual thing and although insight can be gained from traditional motivational theories, it is the job of the project manager to work closely with every individual within their team and establish what is required to motivate that team member to achieve maximum performance.

Conflict management

> Be willing to make decisions. That's the most important quality in a good leader. Don't fall victim to what I call the 'ready–aim–aim–aim–aim–aim syndrome'. You must be willing to fire. (General George S Patton)

Conflict within projects can manifest itself in many different ways. At the highest level, disagreements can lead to the pursuit of remedies through legal channels and cost organizations large amounts of money. These normally arise as a result of contractual issues. A good project manager knows when to interdict and take action when conflict occurs.

People

At a lower level, conflict within a team may need to be dealt with by the leader or manager using softer skills and techniques. They must recognize that the pressures associated with achieving quality objectives will inevitably lead to conflict. It is people who will achieve these objectives for you, but people are complex and will require motivation and support. The detrimental aspects of conflict can be minimized, if the project manager anticipates the potential conflicts and understands their determinants.

Conflict can arise from any of the following players:

- managers;
- senior management;
- client;
- team members;
- subcontractors.

Causes of conflict

Potential causes of conflict are:

- diversity of disciplinary expertise;
- task interdependency;
- poor leadership by the project manager;

- insufficient authority given to the project manager;
- lack of communication or an understanding of objectives;
- lack of organization structures and role ambiguity;
- human emotion;
- the prospect of change.

Sources of conflict

A study by Hans J Thamhain (GEC) and David L Wilemon (Syracuse University) identified seven potential sources of conflict within projects:

- *Conflict over project priorities.* Differences of opinion over the sequence in which tasks should be undertaken. Such conflicts may not only occur between the project team and other support groups, but also within the team itself.
- *Conflict over administrative procedures.* A number of managerial and administrative-oriented conflicts may develop over how the project will be managed, for example the project manager's reporting relationships, definition of responsibilities, interface relationships, project scope, operational requirements, plan of execution, negotiated work agreements with other groups and administrative support.
- *Conflict over technical opinions and performance trade-offs.* In technology-oriented projects disagreements may arise around the staffing of the project team, with personnel from other functional and staff support areas, or from the desire to use other departments' personnel for project support, even though the personnel remain under the authority of their functional or staff superiors.
- *Conflict over manpower resources.* Conflict may arise over the staffing of the project team from personnel, under the authority of other functional support groups, or superiors.
- *Conflict over cost.* Frequently, conflict may develop over cost estimates from support areas regarding various project work breakdown packages, eg the funds allocated by the project manager to a functional support group might be perceived as insufficient for the support requested.
- *Conflict over schedules.* Disagreements may develop around the timing, sequencing and scheduling of project-related tasks.
- *Personality conflict.* Disagreements may tend to centre on interpersonal differences ('ego' centred), rather than on 'technical' issues.

In addition to this, a very common cause of conflict in a project environment can occur in the relationship between project manager and functional manager. This relationship needs to be open, communicative and focused. In a very real sense, this amounts to a relationship based upon negotiation and understanding.

The conflict cycle

Professor Morton Deutsch of Columbia University uses a clock face to describe a cycle of conflict.

FIGURE 7.13   Deutsch's conflict cycle

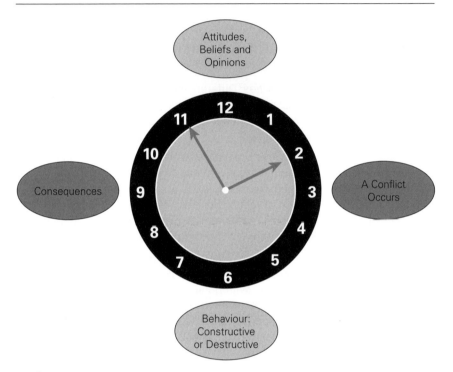

The cycle of conflict can be an unbroken loop that is fuelled by a disputant's sense of being wronged. Deutsch says: 'Conflicts occur when two or more people perceive incompatible differences between or threats to their resources, needs, or values.'

However, the conflict cycle can be broken at two key places: 12:00 (attitudes and beliefs) or 6:00 (behaviour). These places serve as 'gateways' to break destructive attitudes or behaviours. To change the conflict cycle, consider three 'challenges':

- Promote awareness of new attitudes and beliefs.
- Develop a willingness to change.
- Build new skills.

The skills required for dealing with conflict will depend on the conflict-handling mode that is most appropriate for the situation.

Dealing with conflict

Considering the clock face, ideally we should deal with conflict at 12:00, ie by understanding attitudes and beliefs. This is in effect trying to understand the other party's point of view and coming to resolution before a conflict has effectively started. One tool that can help us understand the source of the conflict is the PIN model.

The PIN model

A good decision regarding conflict means a 'win–win' response, where both disputants feel that their interests have been met. By using the PIN model the focus will be on the root of the conflict and not just the conflict statement.

- P: position: What we want.
- I: interest: Why we want it.
- N: needs: What we must have.

The conflict usually arises because of two different positions. If each party is fixated on their own position the conflict will not be resolved. It is therefore the intention of the PIN model to help parties drive below each position and find out what is driving each position or stance.

This can only be achieved through wanting to resolve the conflict, by allocating time to resolve the conflict, by establishing trust between the parties and being open to listening to each other's interest and needs.

By using the PIN model and asking the appropriate questions to establish each party's interests and needs the final position may be adjusted to suit the common interests and needs of each party.

Defining basic needs

The problem-solving strategies of conflict management address needs, and create opportunities for those needs to be satisfied. When individuals choose to continue the conflict, no one's basic needs are fulfilled. Basic psychological needs are the root of almost all conflict. The impulse to meet these needs during a conflict is so strong that we can act irrationally, even violently, if they are not satisfied.

Differing perceptions?

Discuss them and make them explicit; do not lay blame.
Consider:

Your department is totally unreliable, every time you process my expenses you do a lousy job.

Or:

> This month's expense claim is incorrect and overdue by five days. This has happened each month for three months. Can we discuss the situation and see what the likely solutions are?

Involve them in the process of reaching a conclusion, explain your position, get their commitment and involvement in the solution.

Conflict resolution approaches

If we cannot deal with our conflict at 12:00 then it may be necessary to try and break the cycle at 6:00, ie via behaviours.

The following diagram shows various options project managers have for dealing with the challenge of conflict management.

To reach a resolution that is amenable to both parties a balance of assertiveness and cooperation is required.

FIGURE 7.14   Conflict management options

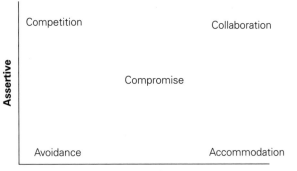

Avoidance

When a leader employs this option, they are ignoring the conflict, letting it be. For whatever reason, the leader may feel that the conflict is not worth the effort to resolve. This could be complete avoidance (never planning to come back to the conflict) or it could be avoiding the conflict at the present time and coming back to it later, when conditions are more favourable. Avoiding conflict does not deal with the issues at hand.

Accommodation

Accommodation is agreement through yielding or conforming to the positions of others; cooperation in an effort to create harmony, even at the expense of your own ideas and values; agreement in the name of peace and tranquillity, knowing full well that you don't entirely buy into it. Accommodators may not always be famous for their creativity, but can often be relied upon for social tact and diplomacy.

Compromise

Compromise involves a search for a solution which is mutually acceptable. Compromise involves two or more parties coming together and 'meeting in the middle'. With compromise, there will be give and take to get to the middle ground. 'Everybody wins something, but does not get everything.' People who compromise settle for the best they can get, as opposed to reaching a decision that everyone wants. Compromise may be one of the best ways of dealing with conflict when time is short, or when total agreement is impossible.

Competition

This is the offensive, aggressive approach to conflict resolution. It is especially attractive to those in power and authority who like to 'get things done' and 'win'. One of the criticisms of competition is that it takes advantage of the opposition's weakness, by resorting to various strategies and tactics which have a disarming nature. In a competitive situation, there is little listening, little information sharing, and little interpersonal reasoning. Leaders who fall into this area often make decisions without input from others, if any. Competitive leadership is often viewed as inappropriate and destructive by group members.

Collaboration

Collaboration is a total-membership approach to conflict resolution. In the collaborative model, the group:

- accepts the fact that there is conflict;
- takes time for sharing of values, needs, interests and resources;
- discovers many possible solutions and weighs the consequences of each;
- selects the alternative that best meets the needs and concerns of each member;
- forms a team plan, implements and evaluates the outcomes. Collaboration takes more time and requires higher levels of commitment than other leadership approaches to disagreement.

Therefore, it is often reserved for those issues of greatest importance to the membership.

Collaboration is the vehicle which:

- generates the most creative solutions;
- gets the greatest membership support;
- produces the greatest amount of personal growth.

The above list is designed to be helpful in describing different styles of leadership which can be used in the area of conflict management. There is no single best approach that will help a project manager deal with every conflict situation. It is up to each project manager to develop a situational style which incorporates many different ways of dealing with conflict. Effective project leadership is leadership which is adaptive. If leaders are able to adapt to varying conflict situations and manage them accordingly, they will be highly acclaimed!

Conflict resolution summary

- Address the substance of the conflict.
- Address the procedures for dealing with the conflict (policies, intervention strategies, etc).
- Separate the relationship that people have with the conflict, from the substance of the conflict.
- Discuss everyone's perceptions of the conflict.
- Be sensitive to the emotions which may be stirred as a result of the conflict.
- Address the emotions and acknowledge them as legitimate.
- Listen actively – listen to what is being said before developing a response.
- Focus on interests, not positions.
- Look for compatible interests and points of agreement.
- Be hard on the conflict, soft on the people.
- Brainstorm your options to solve the conflict.
- Look for mutual gain.
- Reason and be open to reason.
- Use equity and fairness in your standards and procedures.
- Check to see if all parties are comfortable with the outcomes.

CASE STUDY   Leadership at Southwest Airlines (USA)

People are at the heart of Southwest Airlines. Companies come from all over the world to find out what makes their people so special, capable of delivering service levels that are widely said to be the best in the business. It is now acknowledged that treating your people right leads to your people treating each other and your customers right. Other organizations are beginning to learn this. Southwest have known and lived it ever since they started – when the plans for the company were drawn up on a napkin over 30 years ago.

Herb Kelleher, the president, sets the tone for the Southwest culture in that, for Herb, not to have fun at work is almost a sin. Life is simply too short, he says. A small example: if there is a flight delay, the Southwest people at the departure gate have been known to open a locker, pull out a handful of pipe cleaners and then hold a competition between the passengers to see who can make the funniest pair of glasses out of the cleaners. Herb is often amongst them, helping passengers enjoy the time they spend with Southwest.

But to put into practice the 'work is fun' philosophy you cannot rely on just one person to drive it. When you are a three-plane operation with 30 employees, the inspiration and leadership of the boss's personality are there for all to see every day. When you have grown from that to run a fleet of 284 planes with 27,000 employees, flying over 50 million customers a year, generating a profit of over \$318 million, then the philosophy needs to run through the whole organization. So where do you start?

As with many organizations, the people policy starts with the mission statement which is:

> Southwest Airlines is dedicated to the highest quality of customer service delivered with a sense of warmth, friendliness, individual pride and company spirit.
>
> We are committed to provide our employees a stable work environment with equal opportunity for learning and personal growth.
>
> Creativity and innovation are encouraged for improving the effectiveness of Southwest Airlines.
>
> Above all, employees will provide the same concern, respect and caring attitude within the organization that they are expected to share externally with every Southwest customer.
>
> The Southwest mission statement is based on unique core values. Many of these are standard and easy to recognize if you have your own value statements as an organization; apart from the fact that our values include the words love, family and fun. 'How can you talk about love in a corporate environment?' you may ask. At Southwest when you walk into the building, you see pictures on the walls of employees, their families, their children and even their pets. On birthdays, Southwest employees get a card at home from us. If there is a family tragedy, they get support from everyone in the company. In short, the Southwest secret, if you want to call it that, is that we do all the things a family does to support each other.
>
> This is emphatically not just 'feel good' stuff. Soutwest can operate in this way because the company's foundations make pragmatic business sense.

Teams and your project

Introduction

Coming together is a beginning, keeping together is progress, working together is success. **HENRY FORD**

The success of any project is hugely influenced by the project team tasked with delivering it. Even the best-planned projects may fail to meet their objectives if the project team does not perform to the best of their ability. The effective development and integration of the project team is essential in the successes of a project as it is the project team who will be responsible for delivery of the scope throughout the project life cycle.

It is therefore essential to understand the processes required to organize, manage and develop the project team.

It is useful to remember that the project team does not necessarily only consist of the immediate team members but also project stakeholders such as customers, partners and sponsors.

This chapter explores the mechanics and phases of team development, highlights some of the challenges to expect throughout the project life cycle and also describes some useful tools for the development of a strong integrated team. Although leadership is an essential element in the development of a successful team, this chapter will emphasize the technical aspects of leadership and team development with the soft skills being covered in more detail in Chapter 7 'Project leadership'.

In this chapter we will cover:

- team requirements – determining the team requirements for the project;
- team development – developing a group of people into a team;
- team management – managing your team for maximum effectiveness.

Team requirements

Before a team can be developed it is essential to establish the team requirements for the project. Like many of the areas already discussed, this is part of the planning process, where not only do we need to plan the cost, time and quality aspects of the project we need to plan what resources including people are required to achieve the project outcomes.

Like many planning activities this is an iterative process, where as part of the scheduling process you may estimate the requirement for five specialist resources to work on a task at a cost of £1,000 per day for a four-week period between March and April. However, when you research the availability within your organization or the open market you find only two can be found at a cost of £2,000 per day and they are not available until May. This will then potentially affect the cost and timing of the task they are assigned to and in turn the overall project.

FIGURE 8.1 The balancing act

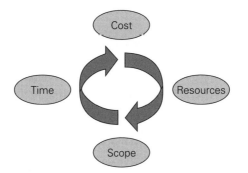

This balance of cost, time, quality and resources can be a constant headache in the planning process.

The project management team

The first step in defining the project team requirement is to establish the project management team. This is often a subset of the overall project team and will be responsible for the project management and leadership activities such as start-up, planning, executing, monitoring, controlling and closing the various project phases. This is also sometimes referred to as the executive or leadership team. By establishing this group early in the project it will assist with the planning process and help establish a context for the project.

The project management team needs to clearly understand the requirements and deliverables of the project as well as being aware of the organization's overall strategy, objectives and drivers. It is also essential for the PMT to understand the organization's professional and ethical requirements and subscribe to them and ensure that the project complies with them.

Human resource plan

The key to establishing and acquiring an effective team is by first developing a human resource plan for the project. As mentioned earlier, this is an iterative process which outlines clearly the requirements for the project. This requires a clear understanding of the personnel available inside (and potentially outside) the organization.

As a minimum the human resource plan should include the following:

- responsibility assignment matrix (RAM);
- organization chart;
- resource management plan showing how and when people are deployed;
- training plan;
- recognition and reward scheme;
- health, safety and regulations as appropriate to the project.

Responsibility assignment matrix (RAM)

The responsibility assignment matrix or RAM is key to identifying what resources will be required to executed the tasks within the project. To develop a responsibility assignment matrix or RAM, it is often useful to use the RACI process. This is a valuable tool which will help to clarify ownership to various parts of your project.

Once the project deliverables have been identified via work breakdown structure (WBS), we will need to define those actions and activities that need to be done to produce the lowest-level deliverables. This is a key planning activity and is covered in Chapter 2, 'Defining your project'.

If we look at the office relocation project we used previously, we provided an example of a project WBS by decomposing the work down to a manageable and workable level. The example we used is shown in Figure 8.2.

Note: the order of the activities doesn't need to be in any logical order at this point. However, once you have your list of activities for each deliverable, you are ready to use the RACI process to assign them to the personnel associated with the project.

Basically, RACI is a method to assign activities to resources by name or by function. RACI is an acronym that stands for four types of task assignments:

- responsible;
- accountable;
- consulted;
- informed.

FIGURE 8.2 Simulation project: WBS

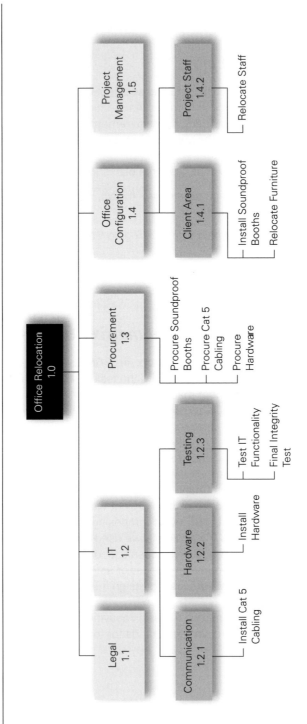

So, let's talk about the four types of assignments.

Responsible

The first type of assignment is 'R', which stands for 'responsible'. The person assigned as 'responsible' for a task is the person, or role, that is responsible for actually performing the work for the task. A few guidelines to keep in mind ... When no one is assigned as responsible for the task, chances are that it won't get done. Also, when many people are assigned to completing the work, it requires a lot of coordination and usually means further decomposition is required to make sure everyone is clear about what specifically they need to work on. Finally, if a specific person is assigned as the 'R' to multiple tasks they may become overloaded. In this case, you may want to see if someone else can fill in as the 'R' on some of the tasks.

Accountable

The second type of assignment is 'A', which stands for 'accountable'. This is the person who is held accountable for the task getting completed. One guideline to keep in mind for the person assigned as 'accountable' is to ensure only one person is assigned as accountable for each task being performed. If you end up trying to assign multiple people to a particular task you will end up with a lot of finger pointing and confusion when issues occur.

Consulted

The next type is 'consulted' – the 'C'. These are the people involved and consulted prior to a task being performed. Essentially, their input is sought after and factored in prior to action taking place. As the number of people consulted increases, the speed with which action can be taken decreases. Conversely, too few and improper decisions and actions may be made without those whose buy-in is required being assigned as a 'C'.

Informed

Finally, 'I' signifies those that need to be informed on the status and completion of a task. If necessary parties aren't informed, then confusion and delays can arise from other resources wondering whether preceding dependent tasks are completed. However, if there are people that are informed that don't need to be, you may be wasting their time with e-mails or status reports on tasks.

So, those are the four types of resource assignments. It should be noted that you may have resources with multiple assignments on a task. For example, you may have the person assigned as accountable for the task completion also responsible for doing the work.

An example of a RACI chart for the simulation project can be seen overleaf.

TABLE 8.1 Simulation project: RACI chart

Task	R	A	C	I
Install Hardware	IT	PM	CM	PL
Install CAT 5 Cabling	CM	PM	BS	PI
Relocate Furniture	BM	PM	OS	ST
Procure Hardware	BY	SM	PM	IT

IT – IT Manager
CM – Communications Manager
PL – Planner
ST – Staff
SM – Supply Chain Manager

PM – Project Manager
BM – Building Services Manager
OS – Office Services
BY – Buyer

This process should be applied to all the work that needs to be delivered within the project to ensure each piece of work is 'owned' with appropriate consultation and information in place.

The RACI diagram can also be used higher up in the WBS structure if a full decomposition has not been conducted, eg in the above example it would be perfectly acceptable to assign 1.2.3 Testing and all the tasks below it to appropriate parties.

Project organizational chart

A project organizational chart is a detailed and document-based graphical representation of the team to outline specific roles, duties and responsibilities of the team members and other stakeholders participating in the project, and to formally constitute how exactly they are expected to collaborate with each other throughout the course of the project implementation process. It is also regarded as a mechanism of managing team development processes through designing training programmes based on the group relationships established by the chart.

The project manager usually uses the organizational chart to keep track of the processes associated with team management, and to record particular relationships between group members during the course of the project life cycle. Team members can use the chart to clarify what roles and responsibilities they have been assigned to, who will share those roles, and who will manage and lead their efforts.

The following is a checklist of the key tasks for creating a project team organizational chart:

- *Make a project team list.* Assemble a list of all the personnel you require to participate in the project. This should be available from the human resource plan produced as part of your scheduling process. At this point in time if you do not have names you should use positions or job descriptions for the project.

- *Reassess stakeholders.* Once your team is formed, you now need to identify the stakeholders or those people/organizations having a direct interest in or affected by your project. Typical examples are the sponsor and the customer. Note that although some stakeholders are not participants in the team, they're added to the project team organizational plan because they influence decisions of the team.

- *Expand on job descriptions and responsibilities.* Build detailed job descriptions and responsibilities for each role on your list. This is important in clarifying the boundaries between roles and also establishing specific objectives.

- *Build the chart.* Finally, use all the data to create the chart and display relationships between the team and stakeholders on it. The relationships will show who is reporting to whom and what supervisory mechanism is used for leading teamwork.

An example organizational chart (Figure 8.3) is shown on the following page.

Resource management plan

The resource management plan, which is often represented as a histogram, is an output from the scheduling process, which typically indicates which resources are required and when. It may be used to establish when individuals or teams require to be mobilized or when tasks need to be moved to allow for availability issues or to smooth out peaks and troughs.

Consider the histogram in Figure 8.4. It indicates when and how much of an individual resource is required. It shows a requirement for a total of 144 man days of labour over a 16-day period with a maximum of 16 and minimum of 1.

FIGURE 8.3 Simulation project: organizational chart

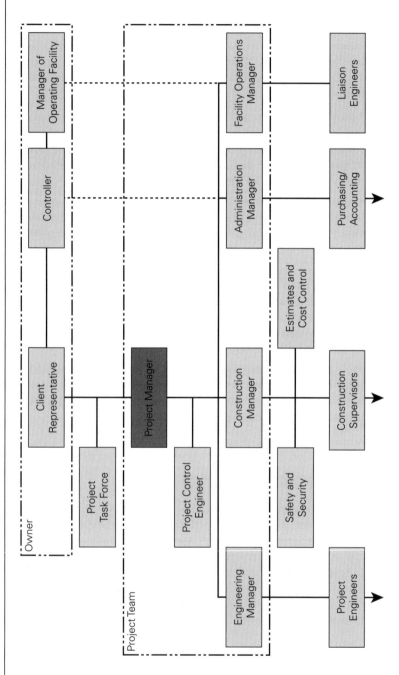

FIGURE 8.4 Original resource requirements histogram

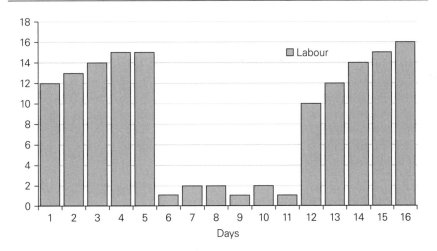

Although this indicates what resources are required to complete the work it may not be the most efficient use of the personnel involved. In the example above a team of approximately 14 labourers would need to be assembled for five days, reallocated elsewhere for six days then mobilized again for five.

It would be more efficient and potentially more cost effective if the work was carried out in the manner depicted by the histogram below, where a team could be mobilized for the early part of the work and then disbanded, leaving two labour resources to complete the last six days.

FIGURE 8.5 Revised resource requirements histogram

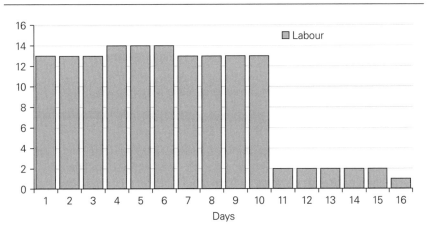

This again indicates the iterative planning process required to establish an efficient relationship between the project cost, schedule, scope and resources.

Training plan

In addition to the requirements highlighted above it is important at this point in the team development cycle to start considering the training requirements for the project team members to ensure they are competent in the delivery of all their responsibilities. This may include organization-specific training on software or systems, management or leadership training, safety or HSE training or specific technical training. This should be established as early as possible and scheduled into the resource management plan.

Recognition and reward scheme

As part of the motivation of the team a recognition and reward scheme should be established in the team requirement phase as this may also impact on other areas of the project such as cost and time.

The motivation of the team and its individuals is very important and is covered in more detail in the team development and team management areas of this chapter and is very specific to each individual team member. However, establishing an outline of the recognition and reward scheme will help to reinforce the importance of the key project deliverables and focus the team on the important aspects of the project.

The following are some examples of where project rewards and incentives could be focused:

- safety – delivery of an agreed number of work hours without a safety incident;
- timing – meeting established and agreed milestones in a timely manner;
- costs – bringing project deliverables in with the costs defined;
- quality – delivering the project within an agreed amount of non-conformance;
- progress/earned value – meeting established progress KPIs and measures;
- Team member of the month.

The delivery of effective awards and incentives can be very difficult to establish and will need quote a lot of working through. For example, if a financial reward is promised to the team for a 100 per cent safety record, safety incidents may be hidden from view so the award is granted. This could be rectified by establishing a reward for the reporting of safety incidents; the danger then is people report non-existent incidents in order to gain the reward.

Recognition and rewards should be established to help the team focus on the project objectives and deliverables but introduced with care to ensure they don't do the opposite and interfere with the effective delivery of the objectives.

Team requirement: checklist

The main deliverable and outputs from defining the team requirements will be:

- *The human resource plan*, which will define a list of roles and responsibilities required for the project. It will clarify the authority levels, responsibilities, competencies and boundaries. It will in turn contain:
- *A project organization chart* showing the team roles and the reporting structure.
- *The resource management plan*, which describes how human resource requirements will be met; are suitable skills available or will they need to be contracted from elsewhere? What is the location of the work and what challenges will that bring?
- *Training programmes*, which will be considered for staff to suit the particular skills that need to be developed to execute the project.
- *Recognition and reward schemes*: what and how the team and individuals will be recognized and rewarded for their achievements.

Team development

It should first be noted that bringing a group of people together does not necessarily constitute a team, especially not an effective working team. One of the biggest mistakes made by project managers is not recognizing this as a fact and then expecting their project team to hit the ground running from day one.

Think back to any group of individuals you met for the first time, or even people you now consider your friends; how did you react and behave when you first met? Whatever way it was it can be guaranteed that the dynamics of the group and the behaviours of the individuals changed over time.

The key to successful team development is recognizing the dynamics, behaviours, attitudes, views, communication and performance of the project team will change as the team matures. It is the project manager's responsibility to manage the team's development to ensure a cohesive integrated team is founded.

Team growth

In 1965 Dr Bruce Tuckman published his team growth model which indicated the potential stages a team may go through from commencement to conclusion. His initial stages consisted of forming, storming, norming, performing. However, he then later added a fifth stage, adjourning. Although established more than 40 years ago his theory and observation still hold good in today's project environment.

Tuckman's model explains that as the team develops maturity and ability, relationships establish, behaviours and attitudes change and the whole dynamic of the team evolves. The diagram here shows the initial four stages of Dr Tuckman's model.

FIGURE 8.6   The Tuckman model

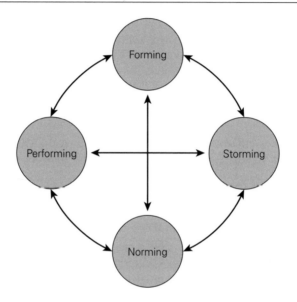

Moving through the model

Teams may develop very quickly and move quite easily to the performing stages; equally, teams may (and often do) get stuck in the storming stage. It is important to recognize what stage your team is in and what needs to be done to move it through to performing.

It is also important to note that a team may slip back to a previous stage, due to a change in the team's dynamic or goals, eg a team may move back to forming when a new member joins or a new leader is appointed, or a team may move back to storming if a project goal has been changed or has failed to be achieved.

A summary of the expectations and leadership commitment for each of the stages can be seen in the following summary.

FIGURE 8.7   Tuckman model stages

STAGE 1 - FORMING

People are cautious. They are making a transition from individual to team member status.

Characteristics may be:
- Slow progress on work
- Suspicion, fear, or anxiety about the job ahead
- Excitement, anticipation, and optimism
- Tentative attachment to the team
- Attempts to define the task and how it will be accomplished
- Long discussions of the issues, impatience from some members

Leading a team through Stage 1 (Forming)
- Leader should build trust and confidence
- Help people to get to know each other
- Provide a clear direction and purpose
- Involve the members in plans, agreeing roles and team values
- Provide enough information to get started

Forming

Summary
High dependence on leader for guidance and direction. Little agreement on team aims other than received from leader. Individual roles and responsibilities are unclear. Leader must be prepared to answer lots of questions about the team's purpose, objectives and external relationships.
Processes are often ignored. Members test tolerance of system and leader.
Leader needs to provide direction and clarify goals, roles and objectives.

STAGE 2 - FORMING

People are impatient at lack of progress, but still too inexperienced to know much about the right approach or right decision.

Characteristics may be:
- Resistant to working together, not wanting to collaborate
- Resistant and feeling uncomfortable towards new working methods
- Arguing over minor issues and agreeing on major issues
- Defensive and competitive
- Questioning the team sponsor and their recruitment of members
- Concerned about excessive volume of work, unrealistic goals

Leading a team through Stage 2 (Storming)
- Leader needs to build self-direction
- Resolve any issues of power and authority
- Develop agreements about how and who will make decisins
- Allow team to be more independent, individuals to take responsibility

Storming

Summary
Decisions don't come easily within group. Team members vie for position as they attempt to establish themselves in relation to other team members and the leader, who might receive challenges from team members. Clarity of purpose increases but plenty of uncertainties persist. Cliques and factions form and there may be power struggles. The team needs to be focused on its goals to avoid becoming distracted by relationships and emotional issues. Compromises may be required to enable progress. Leader needs to coach and deal with any conflicts that may arise.

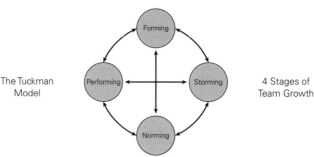

The Tuckman Model

4 Stages of Team Growth

STAGE 4 - PERFORMING

People have discovered and accepted each other's strengths and weaknesses. They are performing together.

Characteristics may include:
- Satisfaction at team's progress
- Close attachment to the team
- Understanding of group processes
- Constructive self change
- Ability to resolve group problems

Performing

Leading a team through Stage 4 (Performing)
- The leader should continue to build and encourage openness
- Ensure methods and procedures support co-operation
- Help the team understand how to manage change.
- Represent and be an advocate for the team to others.
- Monitor progress and celebrate successes and achievements.

Summary
The team is more strategically aware; the team knows clearly why it is doing what it is doing. The team has a shared vision and is able to stand on its own feet with no interference or participation from the leader. There is a focus on over-achieving goals, and the team makes most of the decisions against criteria agreed with the leader. The team has a high degree of autonomy. Disagreements occur but now they are resolved within the team positively and necessary changes to processes and structure are made by the team. The team is able to work towards achieving the goal, and also to attend to relationship, style and process issues along the way. Team members look after each other.

STAGE 3 - NORMING

People are getting used to working together. They are helping each other and beginning to understand each other.

Characteristics may be:
- A sense of cohesion, team spirit
- Acceptance of the team and being part of it
- Relief that things are working out
- More friendly and open discussion
- Confiding in each other, discussing problems
- Constructively giving feedback
- Maintaining the ground rules etc. (the "Norms")
- Significant progress is made

Norming

Leading a team through Stage 3 (Norming)
- Leader needs to build co-operation
- Fully use the member's skills, knowledge and experience
- Encourage and acknowledge member's respect for each other
- Encourage members to work collaboratively

Summary
Agreement and consensus is largely formed among team, who respond well to facilitation by leader. Roles and responsibilities are clear and accepted. Big decisions are made by group agreement. Smaller decisions may be delegated to individuals or small teams within group. Commitment and unity is strong. The team may engage in fun and social activities. The team discusses and develops its processes and working style. There is general respect for the leader and some of leadership is more shared by the team. Leader facilitates and enables team decisons.

Developing the project team

The key objective in this process is to consider the competencies of the team and to develop and improve the skills to enhance project performance. In the first case the project manager must acquire suitable skills to firstly identify the skills required, build the project team by motivating the team members by providing leadership and inspiration in order to achieve high performance in order to achieve the project's objectives.

Teamwork and strong open communication are critical for project success and the project manager must create a suitable environment for this to develop. Conflicts need to be managed in a constructive manner which will encourage collaboration, enhance problem solving and ensure good decisions are taken in a timely fashion.

Cultural and language barriers need to be accepted and team members need to respect each other to develop the trust required to deliver the project.

The project manager must seek suitable resources from stakeholders to assist with the development of their team.

Develop the project team – tools and techniques

Good *interpersonal skills* are key to successful team development. They are sometimes known as 'soft skills' and the project manager and the team members in general need to work together to recognize each other's strengths and weaknesses. This will engender good team spirit and cooperation. The project manager needs to be a good facilitator to develop the valuable assets that are the team members.

Focused *training* is important and this should be based on delivering the technical skills required. This is often achieved by coaching and mentoring and will also be the outcome of performance appraisals.

Formal and informal *team-building activities* will play a part in bonding the team members and are particularly valuable when the team operates from disparate and remote locations.

Successful teams can:

- coordinate individual effort, to tackle complex tasks;
- utilize the expertise and knowledge of everyone involved, which might otherwise remain untapped;
- improve and sustain motivation and confidence, so team members feel supported and involved;
- encourage synergy of ideas to solve problems and spark ideas;
- help improve communication;
- raise the level of individual and collective empowerment;
- support initiatives and change.

A simple 'Team health check' is provided at the end of the chapter to gauge whether a team is performing or in one of the other three stages.

Develop project team – outputs

The key output here is having a robust and reliable system for team performance assessments.

Accurate measurement of the team's performance is important for two reasons:

- to measure the effectiveness of team-building strategies, training and other investments;
- to measure technical success against agreed project objectives. High-performing teams are characterized by task-oriented and results-oriented outcomes.

Further specific and focused training and coaching are a likely outcome from performance assessments.

Managing the project team

This process revolves around monitoring team member performance, motivating and leading the team and resolving issues.

Conflict is inevitable in a project environment and when effectively managed results in greater productivity and improved decision making. Some techniques for managing conflict within a team are discussed in the 'Leadership' chapter of this book.

Interpersonal skills

As discussed under 'Develop the project team – tools and techniques', interpersonal skills have a large part to play in the successful management of a project team. Project managers require strong *leadership and influencing skills* which can support the need to *negotiate* on a variety of issues and with a variety of people and organizations.

It is absolutely paramount to the success of any work that the manager is able to lead the team within a relatively unstructured environment. This will involve dealing with managers and personnel across a wide range of functional positions, often with little formal authority.

Harold Kerzner, a well-known project management guru, suggests that an effective management style may be as follows:

- clear project leadership and direction;
- assistance in problem solving;
- facilitating the integration of new members into the team;
- ability to handle interpersonal conflict;

- facilitating group discussions;
- capability to plan and elicit commitments;
- ability to communicate clearly;
- presentation of the team to higher management;
- ability to balance technical solutions against economic and human factors.

What is expected of a project manager?

In addition to dealing with the team and the objectives and deliverables of the project, the manager also has to communicate and report to his line management. Regardless of the project and the problems that may arise, line management expect the project manager to show all of the traits listed below:

- Precisely extract the relevant fact about the project.
- Highlight any problems that are exceptional to the objectives of the project.
- Filter out unimportant and irrelevant information.
- Be enthusiastic and confident in leading the project and the team.

This can be made quite difficult due to the fact that the information received on projects can be misleading, ambiguous and often deceptive. It is therefore necessary to use the team and communication to improve the quality of information reported.

Team chemistry

As discussed, even the best-defined, appraised and planned jobs can fail to deliver on their objectives. One of the key reasons for this is that the chemistry amongst the team is just not right, resulting in familiar situations such as:

- conflict between individuals;
- low morale, leading to poor productivity and quality;
- lack of motivation of individuals;
- high turnover of team members;
- lack of communication and cooperation between groups.

Problems like these impact directly upon the key project objectives of:

- *time*: delay in work due to lack of cooperation and poor motivation;
- *cost*: duplication of effort; bringing in replacement team members;
- *quality*: lack of responsibility; people in the wrong role being careless;
- *safety*: not paying attention to problems that affect the whole project and the whole team.

Traditionally, we examine three main areas when selecting individuals for a particular role. These are generally based on either a CV or recommendations. However, we tend to judge a person's ability to perform within a team on their qualifications (academic qualifications, professional body accreditation), experience (who they have worked with before, what they achieved) or behaviour (often based on a short interview and references). How an individual behaves or interacts within a team is generally more important than the qualification or experience they have gained, but it is the most difficult to measure.

FIGURE 8.8   Team member suitability

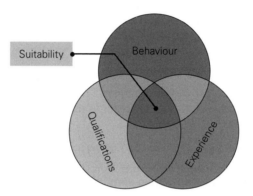

The effective performance of a team is dependent on the way the team is able to interact, and draw on the strengths of its members.

People working within a group or team bring to the group two key things. The first is their competency, specialist knowledge, qualifications, experience, etc, which are typically the reasons why they have been hired. These might include: computer skills, joinery, understanding of production techniques, typing proficiency, knowledge of health and safety, and an almost infinite array of other things. This is often called 'task' focus. The second is the way they work with and contribute to a group, thereby enhancing the effectiveness of the group. This is often called 'team' focus.

Obviously the task focus is concerned with getting the job done. Less obviously, the team focus is concerned with how the job gets done.

Team behaviour

In the early 1980s an Englishman called Meredith Belbin observed that some companies were employing the most elite personnel they could find in their field, yet when these people were formed into teams, some teams performed significantly better than others. This led him to research why this was the case; the results of his work are now applied worldwide, in organizations large and small to help in the selection and managing of project teams.

The nine Belbin team roles indicate how an individual operates within the team and concerns their tendency to behave, contribute to the team or relate to others in a particular way.

Belbin's research showed that a balanced team – one with the greatest chance of developing fully effective working arrangements – would contain a balance of team roles. Further, every team goes through phases of its activities, during which some team roles are better able to contribute than others.

Belbin's model allows a group to analyse its collective strengths and weaknesses in team-role terms and objectively plan to capitalize on those strengths and minimize the negative impact of its weaknesses. Moreover, the process offers tools to enable a team to be structured for maximum team-role effectiveness in advance of starting work where, for example, a new working group, project team or similar unit is to be created.

Belbin team roles

Belbin developed his work over a number of years, which resulted in his method of analysing team behaviour based upon nine unique roles. There are a number of factors, which set the Belbin profiles apart from other similar behaviour schemes:

- It is not hierarchical, ie none of the nine roles is any better than the others, in a general sense.
- It recognizes that people are a combination of several key role types.
- It recognizes that each role not only brings with it a particular strength, but also a certain weakness.

Described below are each of the team roles in Belbin's scheme. The key features of each role are taken from Belbin's publication *Team Roles at Work* (R Meredith Belbin, 1993 Butterworth Heineman).

The point of the separate team roles is to show that, while individuals may be technically suitable for a particular function in a team, they present a behavioural problem in that they are unsuited to the nature of the role. Or from an alternative viewpoint, an individual may have a particular behavioural role which makes them suited for a role which they might not otherwise be considered for.

FIGURE 8.9   Belbin team roles

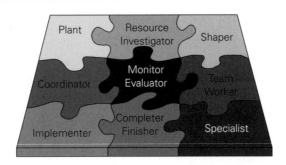

FIGURE 8.10   Belbin team role features and suitability

Role	Key features	Suitable function in a team
Plant	• Creative • Imaginative • Unorthodox	• problem solving • innovation • lateral thinking • generation of new ideas
Resource Investigator	• Extroverted • Enthusiastic • Good communicator	• developing contacts • exploring opportunities • negotiating • making links outside the team
Co-ordinator	• Delegates readily • Clarifies goals • Promotes decision making • Strong sense of objectives	• leading through empowerment • chairing meetings
Shaper	• Challenging • Dynamic • Thrives on pressure	• leading in difficult situations • taking difficult decisions
Monitor Evaluator	• Sober • Strategic • Sees all options • Judges accurately	• when enthusiasm needs to be countered with reason • problem identification
Team Worker	• Co-operative, Mikl • Perceptive and diplomatic • Averts friction	• promoting team spirit • buildling relationships with peers
Implementer	• Disciplined • Reliable • Efficient	• turning ideas into practical action • following procedures
Completer Finisher	• Painstaking, conscientious • Great attention to detail • Delivers on time • Searches out error and omissions	• where perfection is required • where errors or omissions cannot be tolerated
Specialist	• Single minded • Dedicated • Provides skills/knowledge in rare supply	• source of accurate up to date information • keeping up to date with new developments

It is rare for a person to exhibit only one of these behaviours. Most people tend to exhibit two or three of these roles as their strongest behaviours. Similarly, most people find there are two or three of these roles which clearly they are not.

With a Belbin profile of a team member, showing their strongest and weakest roles, it should be possible to ensure that people are behaviourally suited to their role eg someone with Shaper or Coordinator profiles would be suited to managing or leading people. A Plant, on the other hand, would lose motivation in a routine role, one which requires closely following procedures or instructions.

Role weaknesses

As with most advantages, there come disadvantages. What makes someone strong in a particular behavioural role generally results in them having a counteracting weakness, which Belbin calls an *allowable weakness*. The weakness is considered to be allowable, as attempting to change this person's weakness generally results in either a lack of success or a hindrance to the strength of the role.

For example, an allowable weakness of a Plant type is that they tend to neglect practical matters. By trying to force a Plant to work to a rigid schedule you will prohibit their ability to be creative.

Allowable weaknesses are also important to understand in each role, as it is generally these features which give rise to conflicts between individuals, as they fail to appreciate and live with these weaknesses.

Table 8.2, derived from Belbin's *Team Roles at Work* publication, describes the allowable weakness of each role type.

Some project managers are able to influence the choices of their project team members. In such a case, being aware of an individual's team role behaviour can help in deciding how appropriate an individual may be for a role, regardless of their technical abilities or experience. Just as importantly, such profiles will aid the project manager in looking at how the team members will interact, pinpointing possible conflicts, or potentially excellent working sub groups.

When the project manager is not given any choice in the formation of the project team, these team role profiles are equally, if not more, important, as they will help the project manager make the most of the team provided, by appreciating people's actions and being prepared for possible conflict between team members.

Certain combinations of people, exhibiting different team behaviours, will be successful while others will not.

Below are some examples of team interrelationships, which can work well:

Situation 1 – Good relationship: a Monitor Evaluator team member
  working with a Coordinator project manager.
  This can work well, as the Coordinator is able to recognize that
  the Monitor Evaluator has a crucial role to play in identifying potential
  problems in the project. While other team members may view the
  Monitor Evaluator as a bottleneck to action, the Coordinator will
  appreciate the level-headedness that the Monitor Evaluator can
  bring.

TABLE 8.2   Belbin role weaknesses

Team Role	Allowable Weakness	Unallowable Weakness
Plant	• Preoccupation with ideas. • Neglects practical matters. • Too preoccupied to communicate effectively.	• Won't cooperate. • Doesn't want to get involved with the team. • Ignores crucial matters.
Resource Investigator	• Loss of enthusiasm once initial excitement has passed. • Over excitement.	• Neglects to follow up. • Moves off to another job before completing responsibilities.
Coordinator	• An inclination to be lazy if someone else can be found to do the work. • Can be seen to be manipulative.	• Takes credit for others' efforts.
Shaper	• A proneness to frustration and irritation. • Can offend people's feelings.	• Communication breakdown. • Doesn't involve the team.
Monitor Evaluator	• Scepticism with logic. • Lacks drive and ability to inspire others.	• Cynical. • Obstructs for the sake of it.
Team Worker	• Indecision on crucial issues. • Can't say no.	• Lack of productivity due to accepting too much work. • Missing deadlines.
Implementer	• Adherence to the orthodox and proven. • Slow to respond to new possibilities.	• Obstructs change.
Completer-Finisher	• Perfectionism. • Inclined to work unduly. • Reluctant to delegate.	• Obsession with an idea or job.
Specialist	• Acquiring knowledge for its own sake. • Dwells on technicalities. • Contributes on a narrow front.	• Takes no interest in anything outside their field.

Situation 2 – Good relationship: an Implementer team member working with a Shaper project manager.

This can work well as the Shaper will be confident in the knowledge that whatever the Implementer has been tasked with will be carried out in accordance with the exact instructions. Similarly, the Implementer will feel comfortable that his task is clearly defined.

Situation 3 – Good relationship: a Team Worker team member working with another Team Worker.

This can work well as the two people understand each other well, will enjoy working with someone with a similar outlook on life and will attempt to encourage others in the team to interact more.

Situation 4 – Poor relationship: a Completer Finisher team member working with a Completer Finisher project manager.

This particular relationship can pose a real risk to the project's completion, in that both parties strive for perfection in their work, so even though the project manager may recognize the role type of the team member, there is a sort of 'positive feedback' loop set up where the desire for perfection goes out of control and work is never completed on time.

Situation 5 – Poor relationship: a team predominantly comprising Shapers.

The key problem here is self-evident, in that there are 'two many cooks', as each person wants to make their own mark and achieve their own objectives, above all else.

It is important to point out that it is possible for some of the seemingly incompatible relationships to work effectively. Often this is because the individuals involved, consciously or otherwise, understand the nature of each other's behaviours and make allowances or work around the potential for conflict.

Advantages and disadvantages of team working

Whilst most projects rely heavily on the use of teams, a project manager should be aware of the advantages and disadvantages of team working – and be sensitive to some disadvantages emerging, even in the most apparently cohesive teams.

Advantages:

- Improves quality, productivity and efficiency.
- Encourages innovation.
- Improves employee motivation and job satisfaction – can be a rewarding experience.

Disadvantages:

- Could lead to a lack of cooperation with, or opposition to, non-members.
- Difficult to change attitudes and behaviour of a team that is fully developed and has an established culture.
- Some people might find teamwork contrary to their normal 'style'. This could lead to embarrassment and marginalization of some members of the team.

Types of team

There is a variety of team types, each of which can vary over several dimensions, such as function, purpose, time duration, and leadership. The choice of team type depends on the nature of the organization, the task to be performed, and work force expertise. Team type dimensions are as follows.

Functionality

- Functional teams: Team members are from the same work unit.
- Cross-functional teams: Team members come together from different and varied work areas to resolve mutual problems.

Purpose

- Problem-solving teams: Team members are focused on specific issues to develop and implement solutions.
- Developmental teams: Team members concentrate on developing new products or systems.

Duration

- Time limited: The team is created for a specific purpose and is dissolved when the task has been completed.
- Permanent: 'Standing' team is a permanent part of the work unit or the organization.

For further information on team types within a project environment please see DLU Organization Structure, Organizational Roles.

Things to consider

Give the team time to develop

Remember a group of people does not necessarily constitute a performing team; take time to build the team remembering the Tuckman model of team growth stages. One of the biggest failings in project teams is assuming the team will hit the ground running and start performing from day one. Allow the team time to get to know each other, take time to clarify the project goals, the individuals' roles and responsibilities, set some ground rules for the project, and clarify communication channels. This does not always need to be done in a formal manner; think about running a fun workshop where people can get to meet each other socially but also set some project-related outcomes.

The continuous planning cycle

The accurate structuring of a project team will only come about after several iterations through the planning process. This will involve defining and redefining the scope, changing and modifying the schedule, assessing and reassessing resource requirements. Basically it is a continuous process of reviewing and modifying to ensure a realistic and achievable plan. Even after several iterations and a finalized team, sickness, absences, poor productivity, delays etc will require revisiting the planning process.

Different is not wrong, it's just different

By nature, as individuals we are attracted to certain personalities; there are people we will immediately make a connection with because they have similar interests, common values and culture or similar personalities. The opposite can be said for people that don't appeal to us in some of these areas, eg someone who has a brash outgoing nature may irritate us in meetings, someone who is very technical and talks with a huge amount of detail may frustrate us as we want them to be succinct. What we need to remember is we need diversity in our teams; if everyone had the same skill sets and personalities they may all get on together well but it would not be a well-rounded team. Remember for each weakness we see in someone there will be a strength, so try and recognize the strengths within each team member and utilize them effectively.

Team communications

As we have already discussed, communication is vitally important in all aspects of project management but especially in effective managing and leading of a team. In this chapter we looked more at the formal methods of communication by utilization of documents such as the RAM and organizational chart. These should not be overlooked in terms of importance as they provide the team with a tangible and definite structure for the project. By backing up these documents with good communication and leadership along with defined roles and responsibilities it should instil confidence in the team members in what they should be doing, what they are responsible for and who they are responsible to. This in turn will contribute greatly to the motivation and commitment of the team members.

Conclusion

We have learned in this chapter that the project team is one of the vital elements in ensuring project success and that developing the team is not something done in isolation but requires continuous planning involving scope, cost, quality and time. We hopefully have also clarified the need for some formal team documents to assist in the clarification of roles, responsibilities and work allocation. One of the key messages highlighted in this chapter is the fact that teams are made up of a wide range of skills and personalities and it is the project manager's job to recognize the strengths within the team, allocate work appropriately and develop the team into one cohesive integrated unit.

CASE STUDY   W L Gore

Background

W L Gore & Associates, Inc is a global, privately held company headquartered in Newark, Delaware. It employs approximately 8,000 employees (called associates) in more than 45 locations worldwide. Founded by a husband-and-wife team in 1958, its manufacturing operations are clustered in the USA, Germany, Japan, China and Scotland. There are three sites in Scotland, two in Livingston and one in Dundee, employing approximately 450 people. Gore produces proprietary technologies with versatile polymer polytetrafluoroethylene (PTFE) used in products in the healthcare and leisure industries. It is especially known for products like GORE-TEX® and Elixir guitar strings. Gore is known not just for its innovative products, but also for its innovative business style (Gore's written business objective is 'To make money and have fun'). Gore strives to create a unique corporate culture. Quite simply, the culture is driven, according to co-founder Bill Gore, from the need to 'foster the creativity and initiative that contribute to technical development'.

The 1969 discovery of a remarkably versatile new polymer (by Bill and Vieve's son, Bob Gore) led the enterprise into myriad new applications in medical, fabric and industrial markets. As the company that invented this new polymer, expanded polytetrafluoroethylene (or ePTFE), and introduced it in the marketplace, Gore is committed to remaining a leader in fluoropolymers.

The depth of Gore's technical know-how has contributed to a wide range of processes and creative, reliable technologies that continue to solve problems and change outcomes for people around the world.

Interesting facts

- In 2011, for the 14th consecutive year, W L Gore & Associates, Inc earned a position on *Fortune*'s annual list of the US '100 Best Companies to Work For'.

- For four years, Gore has been named by the *Sunday Times* as the 'Best Company to Work for' in the UK.

Team health check

FIGURE 8.11 WL Gore team health check

Characteristic	Unhealthy Conditions in a Team (Any Stage)	Healthy/Performing Team (Stage 4)	Scale
Climate	Unhealthy personality conflicts. Misuse of positions.	Clear roles. Expectations are understood and accepted. High trust, people enjoy working within the team.	1......2......3......4......5......6......7......8......9
Goal Setting	No mechanisms or systems for goal setting.	Balance of goal between task, individual and team.	1......2......3......4......5......6......7......8......9
Communication	Critical information is withheld.	Information freely available. There is openness and trust. Feedback operates.	1......2......3......4......5......6......7......8......9
Decision making	Haphazard and changing. People are not committed to them.	Involvement in the decision making process. Commitment and support of decisions.	1......2......3......4......5......6......7......8......9
Handling conflict	Conflict exists and damages relationships. People not working together.	Differences are welcomed and resolved openly.	1......2......3......4......5......6......7......8......9
Subgroups	Groups form from common interests and friendships. Cliques form.	Groups used effectively to enhance task. Form when need arises, giving flexibility.	
Relationships	Destructive, competitive and critical. People interested in protecting self.	High collaboration. Win win relationships.	1......2......3......4......5......6......7......8......9
Resources	Not aware of team resources.	Team members know what each can do. They combine resources and work synergistically.	1......2......3......4......5......6......7......8......9
Monitoring	The team deteriorates over time. Differences become more pronounced.	A process for monitoring progress and success is in place. Team improves over time.	1......2......3......4......5......6......7......8......9

- Gore Germany ranked second in the '50 Best Places to Work in Germany 2007' among mid-sized companies.
- Gore Italy ranked number 12 among the '35 Best Places to Work in Italy'.
- More than 25 million Gore medical implants have helped patients around the world live longer, healthier lives.
- Gore has been granted more than 2,000 patents worldwide in a wide range of fields, including electronics, medical devices and polymer processing.
- Virtually all of Gore's thousands of products are based on just one material, a versatile polymer called ePTFE (expanded polytetrafluoroethylene), which the company engineers to perform a wide variety of functions.

Today, with more than $3 billion in annual sales and more than 9,500 employees (called associates) worldwide, the company is owned by members of the Gore family and associates. Gore prefers this private ownership and believes this reinforces a key element of its culture to 'take a long-term view' when assessing business situations.

The organizational culture is founded on a team-based environment where teams are organized around opportunities and leaders emerge. Teams are fluid and comprise followers and leaders. Employees, known as associates, have no defined job titles, only general task/responsibility areas. Leaders emerge naturally by demonstrating special knowledge, a skill and/or experience that will move the business objective forward. Leaders are defined not by organizational status but by 'followership' because of 'personal influence, not power'. The roles of leaders and followers are interchangeable by work projects.

Enabling this corporate culture of teamwork is a commitment to four basic principles, as promoted by Bill Gore, that drive the organization's activities:

- fairness to each other and everyone with whom they come into contact;
- freedom to encourage, help and allow other associates grow in knowledge, skill and scope of responsibility;
- the ability to make one's own commitments and keep them;
- consultation with other associates before undertaking actions that could affect the reputation of the company by hitting it 'below the waterline'.

It is the corporate culture based on these four fundamental principles that integrates and enables work–life balance at W L Gore. Gore operates fairly and associates are not managed but instead manage themselves by being fair, meeting commitments and consulting others as appropriate. Consequently there are very few company policies, procedures or rules; practices develop naturally and do not need to be framed in policies. There are no policies and procedures, therefore, that explicitly relate to work–life balance. However, the company's approach to work–life balance can be seen in its approach to working hours. There are no set working hours; people make commitments ... they are never imposed and people keep to their commitments. Personal and family responsibilities are okay – people have no need to explain if they are not going to be at work, but tend to anyway because they are fair to each other. When commitments require staffing for specific hours, the team in that area decide individuals' hours of work. Some people choose to work from home, and office attendance is recorded only for fire safety.

With innovation and diversity at the heart of its business, Gore adopts an equally original approach to company culture. There are no directors, line managers, operatives or secretaries. Everyone who works at the three sites in Scotland is an 'associate' and are all accountable to each other, even to the extent that team mates influence each other's pay.

FIGURE 8.12   WL Gore high scoring

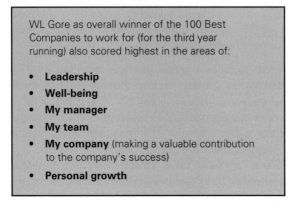

WL Gore as overall winner of the 100 Best Companies to work for (for the third year running) also scored highest in the areas of:

- **Leadership**
- **Well-being**
- **My manager**
- **My team**
- **My company** (making a valuable contribution to the company's success)
- **Personal growth**

'You've got to be a team player at Gore,' says lab engineer Dave Thompson. 'Your team rates your contribution on a scale of 1–6, and that's one of the things salaries are based on.' Staff turnover at Gore is less than 5 per cent.

Outcomes

It is widely believed that Gore's corporate culture which encourages a healthy work–life balance directly contributes to the award-winning success the company has long enjoyed. The culture and principles drive very high performance from individuals and teams, who are empowered and results oriented with a strong 'can do' attitude.

Gore's approach to work–life balance contributes to its repeatedly being included in *Fortune* magazine's best companies list.

Learning points

When they are part of a clearly understood management style, work–life balance arrangements can work without being supported by formal policies and procedures. Work–life balance can be an integral part of a holistic management approach.

Organizations should focus on life issues for employees/associates and actively work on these as well as work development to ensure the balancing of work and life.

Good leadership and mentorship are important to encourage employees to balance work and their personal life.

GLOSSARY OF TERMS

AACE The Association for the Advancement of Cost Engineering (**www.aacei.org**).

Acceptance The process of accepting a product or deliverable.

Acceptance criteria Performance requirements necessary before project deliverables are accepted.

Acceptance test A predefined test to assess the compliance of the deliverable(s) with the acceptance criteria.

Accounts variance (AV) This gives an indication of the status of project cash flow and is calculated by subtracting AC from PV.

Accrued costs These are project costs for which payment is due but has not been made.

Activity A defined task, usually the lowest unit for planning purposes.

Activity ID A unique code identifying each activity in a project.

Activity sequencing The process of putting activities in time order allowing for constraints in order to build a precedence network.

Actual cost (AC) or **actual cost of work performed (ACWP)** The cost incurred and recorded for the work performed in a given period.

Actual dates The dates that activities started and finished as opposed to planned dates.

Actual finish The specific date on which an activity was completed.

Actual start The specific date on which an activity was started.

Advance payment This is where the client or customer will pay for all or some of the project in advance of it being undertaken.

Analogous estimating The information that we use to estimate based on similar projects in the past. It is a form of expert judgement.

APM The Association for Project Management is the UK Association of the IPMA (see IPMA) – see **www.apm.org.uk** for more information.

Approval The formal acceptance of a deliverable as being fit for purpose.

Approval to proceed Approval to move to the next stage (or first stage) of the project.

Assumptions Any assumption made and additional information.

Audit A retrospective examination of the project or function to measure conformance with predetermined standards.

Authorization A decision that typically triggers the funding needed to carry on the project.

Backward pass The second 'pass' used in CPM process to calculate the latest start and finish dates.

Balanced matrix An organizational structure where functions and projects have the same priority.

Bar chart A chart which represents activities and their durations by lines drawn against a common timescale. Often referred to as a Gantt chart although this is a specific type of bar chart.

Baseline The 'frozen' plan against which progress can be measured.

Baseline cost   The amount an activity was planned to cost when the schedule was baselined.

Baseline dates   The planned start and finish dates for activities.

Baseline schedule   The baseline schedule is a fixed project schedule that project performance is measured against.

Benefits   These are specific measures against which project success can be measured.

Benefits framework   This details the expected benefits of the project.

Benefits management   The process for planning, managing, delivering and measuring the project's benefits.

Benefits management plan   This plan specifies who is responsible and how achievement of the benefits is to be measured, managed and monitored.

Body of knowledge   The term is used by both the PMI and the APM to describe their view of best practice project management.

Bottom-up estimating   This involves breaking the work into more detail in order to create an estimate that stands scrutiny. This involves using the WBS down to a level where resources can confidently be applied.

Budget   The planned cost for an activity or project.

Budgetary control   This is the system of creating budgets, monitoring progress and taking appropriate action to achieve budgeted performance.

Budget cost   The cost expected at the beginning of a project.

Budget at completion (BAC)   The total cost of the project at completion.

Budgeted cost of work performed (BCWP)   See **earned value** (EV).

Budgeted cost of work scheduled (BCWS)   See **planned value** (PV).

Budget element   This defines the people, materials or other elements needed to do the work and can be validated against a **resource breakdown structure** (RBS).

Budget estimate   An approximate estimate prepared in the early stages of a project.

Budgeting   The time-phased definition of financial requirements.

Business case   The information needed for authorization of the project.

Calendars   A project calendar lists time intervals in which activities or resources can or cannot be scheduled. Most software supports the use of different calendars for different resources to cope with different requirements such as shift work.

Capital cost   This is the cost in a balance sheet of acquiring an asset required for the project.

Capital employed   This is the amount of investment in a project.

Cash flow   This reflects the cash receipts and payments in a specified period.

Change log   A formal record of any proposed, authorized or rejected project changes.

Change management   The process through which changes to the project plan are approved or rejected.

Change control   The process through which potential changes are recorded, evaluated, authorized and managed.

Change control board   A group authorized for approving or rejecting changes to the project baselines.

Change request   A request for the approval of changes to the project scope which typically demonstrates the impact on costs, time, quality and risk.

Client   The person or organization that has commissioned the project.

Close-out   The project phase where final project closure activities take place.

Closure   The formal point of a project.

Commissioning manager   The person responsible for taking the project from completion through to operational use.

Committed costs   These are costs that are committed even if delivery has not taken place.

Communication   The transfer of information so that the recipient understands the sender.

Completion date   The date calculated when the project should finish.

Compound risk   A risk made up of a number of interrelated risks.

Configuration   The functional and physical characteristics of a product or deliverable.

Conflict management   The ability to manage conflict effectively.

Constraints   Any constraint affecting the activity's progress.

Consumable resource   A type of resource that is exhausted when used. For example, bricks in a construction project.

Contingency   The planned amount of time, cost or resource available to cope with unforeseen events.

Contingency plan   A document describing the planned use of contingency to mitigate certain events should they occur.

Contract   A binding agreement in which the contractor and the client agree what is to be provided and what is to be paid, plus any other terms they wish to agree.

Contract close-out   The formal 'settlement' of a contract.

Contractor   A person or organization that is contracted by agreement to supply goods or services to the project.

Contract target cost   The negotiated costs for the original defined contract and all contractual changes excluding the estimated cost of any authorized changes.

Contract target price   The agreed estimated cost plus an allowance for profit.

Coordinated matrix   This is an organizational structure where the project leader reports to the functional manager and doesn't have authority over team members from other departments.

Cost account   A cost account defines what work is to be performed, who will perform it and who is to pay for it.

Cost–benefit analysis (CBA)   This is an analysis of the costs of undertaking a project and the predicted benefits.

Cost breakdown structure (CBS)   A hierarchical structure that allows a project to be divided by levels into discrete cost elements for programming, cost planning and control purposes.

Cost budgeting   This involves allocating cost estimates to project components.

Cost centre   This is the element of the organization against which costs may be grouped.

Cost code   This is the unique identity for a specified element of work.

Cost curve   This is a graph plotted against a horizontal time scale and a cumulative cost vertical scale.

Cost element   These are unit of costs to perform a task or to acquire an item.

Cost estimating   This is the process of predicting the costs of a project.

Cost incurred   These are the costs identified by the use of an accrued method of accounting or costs actually paid.

Cost management   This is the financial control of the project through evaluating, estimating, budgeting, monitoring, analysing, forecasting and reporting cost information.

Cost overrun   This is the amount by which a contractor exceeds the estimated costs.

Cost performance index (CPI)   This value gives an indication of how well the budget is being managed in terms of the work.

Cost performance report   This is a regular cost report showing cost and schedule status information.

Cost plan   This is a budget which shows the amounts and expected dates of incurring costs.

Cost–time resource sheet (CTR)   This is a document describing each major element in the WBS, including a statement of work (SOW), resources required, duration, timing and a cost estimate.

Cost variance (CV)   The difference (positive or negative) between the actual expenditure and the planned/budgeted expenditure.

Critical activity   An activity that has zero or negative float.

Criticality index   Used in risk analysis, the criticality index represents the percentage of simulation trails that resulted in the activity being placed on the critical path.

Critical path   The sequence of activities through a project network which, if they 'slip', will affect the project end date. These are typically identified by a zero or negative float.

Critical path analysis   A procedure for calculating the critical path and floats in a network.

Critical path method   A technique which defines all the project's critical activities that must be completed on time. The start and finish dates of activities in the project are calculated in two passes. The 'forward pass' calculates early start and finish dates from the earliest start date forward. The 'backward pass' calculates the late start and finish activities from the latest finish date backwards. The difference between the pairs of start and finish dates for each task is the float for the task. By experimenting with different logical sequences and/or durations the optimal project schedule can be determined.

Critical success factor   A factor considered to be most important for project success.

Customer   The people who receive and pay for the benefits of the project.

Cut-off date   This is the ending date of a reporting period.

Decision tree analysis   These are structured and hierarchical (drawn horizontally) methods of graphically showing a number of decision paths and subsequent 'branches' of decisions to help analyse options.

Deliverables   These are the 'end products' of a project.

Delphi technique   This is an estimating process where a consensus view is reached by consultation with experts.

Dependency   This describes the relationship between activities – typically which one has to finish before another can start.

Dependency dates   Any dates that determine either start dates or completed dates.

Discounted cash flow (DCF)   This is the comparison of future 'income' over the life of a project or operation against its costs but using their value today for a more meaningful analysis.

Discretionary dependencies   These involve sequencing that is done because it is customary or the preferred method but could be done another way.

Duration   The length of time allocated to complete an activity.

Early dates   Calculated in the forward pass of time analysis, early dates are the earliest dates on which an activity can start and finish.

Early finish (EF)   The earliest date an activity is likely to finish following CPA.

Early start (ES)   The earliest date an activity is likely to start following CPA.

Earned value (EV) or **budget cost of work performed (BCWP)**   The sum of the budgets for completed work packages and completed portions of open work packages.

Earned value analysis (EVA) and **earned value management (EVM)**   A method of performance measurement which integrates scope, cost (or resource) and schedule measures to accurately assess project performance.

Elapsed time   This is the number of working days that are needed to complete an activity.

Estimate at completion (EAC)   This is a value expressed in either money or hours to represent the projected final costs of work when completed based on current performance.

Estimate to complete (ETC)   This is a value expressed in either money or hours to represent the cost of the work required to complete a task.

Exception report   This is a report drawing attention to instances where planned and actual results are, or are likely to be, significantly different.

Exceptions   These are occurrences that cause a deviation from a plan, such as issues, change requests and risks.

Execution phase   This is the phase of a project where the work takes place.

External constraint   A constraint from outside the project network.

External dependencies   These exist where there is a relationship between project activities and events outside the boundaries of the project, normally outside the project team's control.

Fast tracking   The process of reducing the number of sequential relationships and replacing them with more effective relationships to shorten the overall project duration.

Finish date   The actual or estimated date of an activity's completion.

Finish-to-finish lag   The finish-to-finish lag is the minimum amount of time that must pass between the finish of one activity and the finish of its successors.

Finish-to-start lag   The finish-to-start lag is the minimum amount of time that must pass between the finish of one activity and the start of its successors. The default finish-to-start lag is zero.

Free float   This is the amount of time a task can be delayed without affecting the succeeding tasks.

Forecast at completion (FAC)   The scheduled cost of a task.

Forward pass   This is the first analysis of a project network which calculates the earliest start and finish times.

Functional manager   The person responsible for supplying the workforce for the project (in a matrix structure).

Functional matrix   This is a management structure where the project has a team leader in each functional department and the products are passed from one team to the next.

Functional organization   This is a management structure where specific functions are grouped into specialist departments that provide a dedicated service to the whole of the organization.

Gantt chart   A particular type of bar chart showing planned activity against time. Activities are listed with other tabular information on the left side with time intervals over the bars. Activity durations are shown in the form of horizontal bars.

Histogram   A graphic of planned and/or actual resource usage over a period of time. It is shown in the form of a vertical bar chart, the height of each bar representing the quantity of resource usage in a given time unit.

ICB   The IPMA's International Competence Baseline.

Impact   This is an assessment of the adverse effects of a risk occurring.

Incurred costs   These are the actual and committed costs, whether paid or not.

Internal rate of return (IRR)   This is the discount rate at which the net present value of a future cash flow is zero.

IPMA   The International Project Management Association – visit **www.ipma.ch** for more information on this professional body.

Key performance indicators (KPIs)   Measurable indicators that are used to report progress and usually reflect the critical success factors of the project.

Lag   The minimum necessary lapse of time between the finish of one activity and the finish of an overlapping activity.

Late dates   These dates are calculated during the backward pass of network analysis and are the latest dates by which an activity can be allowed to start or finish.

Latest finish time   The latest possible time by which an activity has to finish within the logical constraints of the network, without affecting the total project duration.

Latest start time   The latest possible time by which an activity has to start within the logical constraints of the network, without affecting the total project duration.

Lead   The minimum necessary lapse of time between the start of one activity and the start of an overlapping activity.

Mandatory dependencies   Also known as 'hard logic', they involve physical restrictions that cannot be avoided.

Master network   This is a network which shows the complete project, where more detailed networks can be derived from.

Master schedule   This is the high-level summary project schedule that identifies major activities and milestones.

Matrix organization   This is an organizational structure where the project manager and the functional managers share the responsibility of assigning priorities and for directing the work.

Mid-stage assessment   This is an assessment in the middle of a project to ensure the project is on track and discuss any options.

Milestone   This is a key event usually identified for reporting purposes.

Milestone payment   These are made on the successful achievement of agreed project milestones, which can be on an agreed value or as a percentage of the phase or project.

Milestone plan   This is a plan containing only milestones which highlight the key points of the project.

Milestone schedule   This is a schedule that identifies the major milestones.

Mitigation   This is the process of reducing a risk by lowering its chances of occurring or by reducing its effect if it occurs.

Monte Carlo simulation   This is a technique used to estimate the likely range of outcomes from a complex process by simulating the process under randomly selected conditions a large number of times.

Net present value (NPV)   This is the total future net cash flows discounted back to a common base date.

Network   This is a graphical presentation of the project 'logic', often referred to as a precedence network, flowchart, PERT chart, logic drawing or logic diagram.

Network analysis   This is a method for calculating a project's critical path, activity times and floats.

Network logic   This represents the activity dependencies that make up a project network.

OGC   The UK's Office of Government and Commerce which provides extensive project, programme and portfolio management guidance; see **www.ogc.gov.uk** for more information.

Opportunity   This is the opposite of a risk in project management.

Organizational breakdown structure (OBS)   A hierarchical structure that allows a project's organization to be divided by levels into discrete groups for programming, cost planning and control purposes.

Originator   The person who suggested the project.

Parallel activities   These are two or more activities than can be worked on at the same time.

Payment on completion   This is where payment is made on delivery of the end product or service.

PEP   Project execution plan. Sometimes also known as the project initiation document (PID) or project management plan (PMP). This contains all plans relevant to the project.

Percent complete (PC)   This is a measure of the completion status of a partially completed activity.

Performance measurement baseline   The PMB is the time-phased budget plan against which contract performance is measured. It is formed by the budgets assigned to scheduled cost accounts and undistributed budgets. It equals the total allocated budget less management reserve.

PID   Project initiation document. Sometimes also known as the project management plan (PMP) or project execution plan (PEP). This contains all plans relevant to the project.

Planned value (PV) or **budget cost of work scheduled (BCWS)**   The planned cost of a defined scope of work that is scheduled to be done during a given period. Specifically BCWS is the sum of all budgets for all packages of work and in total forms the PMB.

Planning   This is the process of identifying the means, resources and actions necessary to accomplish an objective.

Planning stage   This is the stage prior to execution when the project management plan (PMP) is developed.

PMI   The Project Management Institute – visit **www.pmi.org** for more information on this professional body.

PMP   Project management plan. Sometimes also known as the project initiation document (PID) or project execution plan (PEP). This contains all plans relevant to the project.

Post-implementation review   This is a review after a project has met its objectives to confirm that it met the objectives and satisfies the business plan.

Post-project appraisal   This is an evaluation that provides feedback in order to learn for the future – often referred to as a lesson learned report.

Precedence network   A graphical network in which a sequence of activities is described with the constraints (or logic) that applies to them.

Predecessor   This is an activity that must be completed (or be partially completed) before another activity can begin.

PRINCE2   The 'PRojects IN a Controlled Environment' methodology owned by the APM Group – see **www.prince2.com** for more information on this professional body.

Probabilistic network   This is a network containing alternative paths with which probabilities are associated.

Product breakdown structure (PBS)   A hierarchical structure that allows a project to be divided by levels into discrete groups based on products (deliverables) for programming, cost planning and control purposes.

Programme evaluation and review technique (PERT)   This is a project management technique for determining how much time a project needs before it is completed.

Project   There are many definitions but a common one is a 'unique set of coordinated activities, with definite starting and finishing points, undertaken by an individual or organization to meet specific objectives within defined time, cost and performance parameters'.

Project appraisal   This describes methods of calculating the viability of a project.

Project base date   This is the date used for the start of a project calendar.

Project board   The project board is the body to which the project manager is accountable for achieving the project objectives.

Project brief   This is a statement that describes the purpose, cost, time and objectives of a project.

Project calendar   This is a calendar that defines project working and non-working periods.

Project champion   The person who makes the project happen. Often a person with influence in high places.

Project closure   This is the formal termination of a project at any point during the project life cycle.

Project initiation document (PID)   This is a document approved by the project board that defines the terms of reference for the project – often also known as a project execution plan (PEP) or a project management plan (PMP).

Project life cycle   All phases or stages between a project's conception and its termination. Note: The project life cycle may include the operation and disposal of project deliverables. This is usually known as an 'extended life cycle'.

Project life cycle cost   Cumulative cost of a project over its whole life cycle.

Project log   This is a project diary recording significant occurrences throughout the project.

Project management   There are many definitions of project management but a common one is the 'planning, monitoring and control of all aspects of a project and the motivation of all those involved in it to achieve the project objectives on time and to the specified cost, quality and performance'.

Project management plan (PMP)   This is a plan for carrying out a project to meet specific objectives and is also often known as a project execution plan (PEP) or project initiation document (PID).

Project manager   The person with the authority, accountability and responsibility for managing a project to completion, achieving specific objectives within cost, time and quality parameters .

Project matrix   This is an organizational structure that is project based in which the functional structures are duplicated in each project.

Project monitoring   This is the comparison of current project status with what was planned to be done to identify and report any deviations.

Project schedule   The planned dates for starting and completing activities and the project as a whole.

Project scope statement   This details the constraints and assumptions that need to be considered when estimating activity durations.

Project sponsor   The person within the organization who acts as custodian of the project's objectives. Also the person who will authorize expenditure.

Project success/failure criteria   These are the criteria by which the success or failure of a project may be judged.

Project support office   Describes the centralized approach to project support functions such as planning, cost management, estimating, documentation control and procurement.

Project team   The team members who plan, organize, implement and control the work of the contractor (if they are different) to deliver the project within the constraints of cost, time and quality and to meet the stated objectives.

Published estimating data   Where standard units of cost, time or resources can be applied using recorded industry norms.

Qualitative risk analysis   This involves analysing the types of risk that may occur in a project based on the expertise, experience and knowledge of the team members taking part.

Quality assurance   The process of evaluating overall project performance on a regular basis to provide confidence that the project will satisfy the relevant quality standards.

Quality assurance plan   This is a plan that guarantees a quality approach and conformance to all customer requirements for all activities in a project.

Quality audit   This is an official examination to determine whether practices conform to specified standards or a critical analysis of whether a deliverable meets quality criteria.

Quality control   This is the process of monitoring specific project results to see if they comply with agreed standards and identifying ways to eliminate causes of unsatisfactory performance.

Quality criteria   The characteristics of a product or service that determine whether it meets the requirements.

Quality plan A component of the PMP (or PID or PEP) that describes quality management and quality assurance strategies for the project.

Quality planning This is the process of determining which quality standards are necessary and how to apply them.

Quality review A review of a product against an established set of quality criteria.

Quantitative risk analysis This involves analysing the types of risk that may occur in a project based on statistical evidence of previous similar projects and other methods.

Recurring costs These are expenditures for specific tasks that will occur on a repetitive basis.

Remaining duration (RDU) This represents the time needed to complete the remainder of an activity or project.

Request for change This is a proposal by the project manager for a change to the project as a result of a project issue report.

Requirements These are the negotiated measurables required by the customer.

Requirements definition This is the statement of the needs that a project has to satisfy.

Requirements management The set of activities encompassing the collection, control, analysis and documentation of a project.

Resource The people, equipment, facilities, finances or any other variable needed to perform the work of a project.

Resource aggregation The total of the requirements for each resource required against each time period.

Resource analysis The process of analysing and optimizing the use of resources on a project.

Resource assignment The activity linked to the resource required to achieve it.

Resource availability The availability of a resource at any one time.

Resource breakdown structure (RBS) A hierarchical structure of the identified resources by resource category and resource type.

Resource calendar A calendar that defines the working and non-working hours for a specific resource.

Resource compression This method utilizes float within a project, increasing or decreasing the resources required for specific activities so that peaks and troughs in resource usage can be smoothed out.

Resource constraint This describes any limitation of the availability of a resource.

Resource-driven task durations Task durations that are driven by the need for scarce resources.

Resource histogram A graphical view of project data in which resource requirements, usage and availability are shown using vertical bars against a horizontal time scale.

Resource level A specified level of resource required by an activity per time unit.

Resource levelling See **resource-limited scheduling**.

Resource-limited scheduling The process of scheduling activities so that predetermined resource levels are never exceeded.

Resource optimization Optimizing the use of resources using resource levelling or resource smoothing.

Resource planning Evaluating what resources are needed to complete a project and determining the quantity needed.

Resource requirement The requirement for a particular resource by a particular activity.

Resource scheduling The process of calculating dates on which activities should be performed to smooth out resource demand.

Resource smoothing The process of scheduling activities, within the limits of their float, so that fluctuations in individual resource requirements are minimized.

Responsibility assignment matrix (RAM) The combination of a WBS and an OBS into a report which shows which tasks are allocated to which part of the organization ie who does what.

Retention This is where the customer or client holds back some payment for a period of time, often to ensure the correct operation of the deliverables or products.

Revenue cost These are the costs charged to the profit and loss account as incurred or accrued.

Risk The combination of the likelihood and impact of a defined threat or opportunity occurring.

Risk analysis This is the process of using available information to determine how often specified events may occur and the magnitude of their likely consequences.

Risk assessment This is the process of identifying potential risks, quantifying their likelihood of occurrence and assessing their likely impact on the project.

Risk breakdown structure (RBS) Thus is a hierarchical structure representing project risks grouped using a variety of methods.

Risk evaluation This is a process used to determine risk management priorities.

Risk event This is a discrete occurrence that affects a project.

Risk identification This is the process of determining what could be a risk.

Risk management This is the process where decisions are made to accept risks and implement actions to reduce the consequences or probability of occurrence.

Risk management plan This is a document defining how project risk analysis and management are to be implemented in a project.

Risk quantification The process of applying values to the various aspects of a risk.

Risk ranking Classifying the impact or likelihood of a risk, typically on a scale.

Risk reduction A strategy for reducing the likelihood or impact of a risk.

Risk register The formal log for recording identified risks.

Risk response A contingency plan to manage a risk if it happens.

Risk sharing Diluting a risk by sharing it with other parties.

Risk transfer Transferring the liability for the costs of a risk to another party.

Rolling wave planning A planning approach which accepts that the level of detail moves in time as the project progresses.

S-curve A graphic showing cumulative costs, labour hours or other quantities plotted against time.

Schedule This is the timetable for the project, showing tasks are planned out over a period of time.

Schedule control The process of controlling schedule changes.

Schedule dates The start and finish dates calculated using CPM.

Schedule performance index (SPI) This value gives an indication of how well the budget is being managed in terms of the costs incurred.

Schedule variance (SV) – cost   The difference between the BCWP and BCWS.

Schedule variance (SV) – time   The difference between original duration (OD) planned and actual time expended (ATE) on the work to date.

Scheduled finish   The earliest date on which an activity can finish based on the constraints.

Scheduled start   The earliest date on which an activity can start based on constraints.

Scheduling   The process of calculating when project activities will take place depending on defined durations and precedent activities.

Scope   This is the work content of a project best described by the WBS or OBS.

Scope change   Any change in scope that requires a change in cost or schedule.

Scope change control   The process of controlling changes to the scope.

Scope of work   A description of the work to be undertaken or the resources required.

Scope verification   The process of ensuring that all identified deliverables have been completed satisfactorily.

Secondary risk   A risk that may occur as a result of invoking a risk mitigation response.

Sequence   The order in which activities should occur in relation to each other.

Slippage   The amount of 'float' used by the current activity due to a delayed start or increased duration.

SMART   Specific, Measurable, Agreed, Realistic and Timebound objectives.

Stage   A natural high-level section of a project for monitoring purposes and/or connected with stage gates.

Stage gate   A specific approval stage where conditions need to be satisfied before a project can proceed to the next stage.

Stage payment   A payment made part of the way through a project or at an agreed milestone.

Stakeholder   These are people or groups of people who have a vested interest in the success of the project.

Start-to-start lag   This is the minimum amount of time that must pass between the start of one activity and the start of its successor(s).

Statement of work   A document stating the requirements for a given project task.

Status reports   These reports provide the status of an activity, work package or project and are used to control the project and to keep management informed.

Steering group   This is a body designed to monitor the project and give guidance to the project manager.

Sub project   A group of activities represented as a single activity in a higher-level plan.

Subcontractor   This is an organization that supplies goods or services to a contractor.

Success criteria   The criteria agreed for judging if the project is successful.

Success factors   The factors that will ensure achievement of success criteria.

Successor   An activity whose start or finish depends on the start or finish of a predeceeding activity.

Sunk costs   Unavoidable costs.

Suppliers   The external organizations or people that supply materials or equipment (see also **vendors**).

Target completion date   A date which is targeted as the date for completion of the activity.

Task   An activity may consist of a number of tasks which together describe the activity's scope.

Technical assurance   The process of monitoring the technical integrity of the products or deliverables.

Termination   The completion of the project either according to plan or because the project business case is no long valid and the project has been stopped.

Terms of reference   These outline a team member's responsibilities and authorities within the project.

Three-point estimating   Also known as PERT estimating, this recognizes the inherent risk of measuring activity durations and involves making optimistic, most likely and pessimistic estimates.

Time-based network   A bar chart showing logical constraints between activities.

Time-limited resource scheduling   The calculation (often by software) of scheduled dates in which resource constraints may be relaxed if necessary to avoid any delay in project completion.

Time-limited scheduling   The scheduling of activities, so that the specified project duration or any imposed dates are not exceeded.

Time now   The date used for calculating a forward analysis, typically for reporting progress.

Time recording   The recording of effort expended on each activity in order to update the plan.

Time variance (TV)   By determining the date at which the current EV value is equal to PV, it is possible to determine a variance to indicate how early or late a project is running.

Top-down estimating   This is where the total project estimate is based on historical costs and other project variables and then subdivided down to individual activities.

Total float   This is defined as the amount of time which an activity can be delayed without affecting the end of the project.

Total quality management   An integrated total management system for quality within an organization.

Users   The person or people who will use the resulting 'product' on behalf of the owner when the project is completed.

Value management   A means of improving business effectiveness that includes the use of management techniques such as value engineering and value analysis.

Variance   A discrepancy between the actual and planned performance on a project, in terms of either schedule or cost.

Variance at completion (VAC)   The difference between budget at completion (BAC) and estimate at completion (EAC).

Variation   A change in scope or timing of work which a contractor may agree to.

Variation order (VO)   A document authorizing an approved change or variation.

Vendors The external organizations or people that supply materials or equipment (see also **suppliers**).

'What if' analysis The process of evaluating alternative strategies.

'What if' simulation This is creating often multiple simulations of the project network to see its behaviour under different scenarios.

Work The total number of hours or resources estimated to complete a task.

Work breakdown code (or identifier) A code that represents the specific element in a work breakdown structure usually using a hierarchical numbering system.

Work breakdown structure (WBS) A hierarchical structure that allows a project to be divided by levels into discrete groups for programming, cost planning and control purposes.

Work package A group of related tasks that are defined at the same level within a work breakdown structure.

Work units These are the basic units of measurement for resources.

Workload This is the amount of work units assigned to a specific resource over a period of time.

Zero float This is where there is no difference between early and late dates, indicating that they are critical activities.

INDEX

NB entries in *italics* indicate a figure or table in the text

AACE (Association for the Advancement of
Cost Engineering)   215, 289
   cost estimate classification matrix   *216*
actual cost (AC)   140, 156
actual cost of work performed (ACWP)   140
Adair, John   236
AMEC   124–27, 226–32
Association for Project Management (APM)
   1, 77, 85–87, *86*, 157, 289

bar chart   98, 289
baseline   129, 236, 289
Belbin, Meredith   277
budget at completion (BAC)   156, 290
budget cost of work performed (BCWP)
   140, 290
budget cost of work scheduled (BCWS)
   140, 290, 296
business case   32–37, 290
   analysis   33
   benefits   34–35, 47–48
   composition   34
   example   35–37
   ownership   35
   purpose   32

cash flow   132–33, *132*, 290
change control   150–53
   process   *152*
   request form   *151*
change management   156, 290
change register   153
communication   240–*42*, 291
   effective   *241*
   face to face   242
   feedback   242–46
   medium   *242*
   teams and   284
   voice   242
   written word   242
communication management   43, 58
   sample plan   43
conflict   252–58, 275
   accommodation   256–57
   approaches to resolution   256–58

avoidance   256
causes   252–53
collaboration   257–58
competition   257
compromise   257
dealing with   255
differing perceptions   255–56
people   252
PIN model   255
sources   253
conflict cycle   *253*
contractors   51
control   55
cost account   131, 291
cost breakdown structure (CBS)   80–82,
   81, 291
cost reporting   130–34
cost, time, quality triangle   *6, 31*
cost variance (CV)   140
   see also variance
critical path   110–12, 292
customers   51, 292

de Mille, Cecil B   211
decision tree analysis   188–94, 292
   examples   *189, 190, 191, 192, 193*
deliverables   60, 61, 77, 262, 292
Deutsch, Professor Morton   254
distributions   199–201
   custom   200–01
   discrete   199–200
   normal   201

earned value (EV)   137, 140, 156, 157, 293
   analysis (EVA)   117, 293
   example calculation   140–43
   measurements   137
efficiency measures   144
estimate   211
estimate at completion (EAC)   144–45,
   156, 293
estimating funnel   213–14, *214*
estimating the project   211–32
   bottom-up   212
   case study   226–32

common mistakes 225
communication 223
classes of estimate 214–15
comparative (analogous) 212,
218–19
considerations 222–23
contingency and 223, 224
importance 211–14
optimism and 223
parametric (statistical modelling) 212,
219
risk and uncertainty 224
rules 224–25
skill levels 22
techniques 212
three point 213, 221–22, 301
top down 212, 219–21
evaluation 61
post-project 154–55
see also financial evaluation
executing the project 129–62
accuracy of progress measurement
156–57
baseline 129, 236, 289
benefits 138–45
case study 157–62
change control 150–53
close-out and handover 153–55
cost reporting 130–34
forecasting 144
measures 129, *130*
post-project evaluation review 154
progress reporting 134–38, *135*
simulation exercise 145–50
things to consider 155–57

feedback 242–46
acceptance 244
anger 244
denial 244
developmental 243, 244
examples 245–46
giving 243
motivational 243, 244, 246
rationalization 244
receiving 244–47
taking action 244
types 243
financial evaluation 63–68
discounting 65–68
internal rate of return (IRR) 67–68
net present value (NPV) 66–67
payback 64
return on investment (ROI) 64–65
time value of money 63

Ford, Henry 261
forecasting 133–34
functional managers 51, 293

Gantt chart 41–42, 98, 136, 294
gate procedure 13–14, *14*
glossary of terms 289–302
Gore, Bill 285
governance 23
Gumz, Joy 1

Halliburton Pipeline and Process Services
(PPS) case study 94–96
Harvey-Jones, Sir John 97
Herzberg, Frederick 248–49

International Project Management
Association (IPMA) 3, 4–5, 22,
294

Kelleher, Herb 259
Kerzner, Harold 275–76
key performance indicators (KPIs) 53,
294
see also performance measurement

leadership 233–59, 275
action-centred 236–38
case study 259
communication 240–42
conflict management 252–58
difference from management 234–35,
235
feedback 242–46
motivation 248–52
people 237
projects and 235–46
skills 240
task 237
team 237
tools 248
visionary 246–48, *247*
learning organization 129, 157

management
difference from leadership 234–35
effective 275–76
Marshall, Peter 246
Maslow, Abraham 249, 250–51
Monte Carlo simulation 194–95, 202,
295
motivation 248–52
hierarchy of needs 250, *251*
hygiene factors 249
motivators *249*

projects and   251–52
recognition/reward   270
team   270
theories   248–51
Mott MacDonald case study   203–09

net present value (NPV)   66–67, 295

objectives   29–32, 82, 270
poor   54
SMART   *31*, 39, 68, 300
organizational breakdown structure (OBS)
80, 295
organizational structures   14–23
centralized   *20*
decentralized   20
flat   *16*
hierarchical   *17–18*
matrix   *18–19*
tall   *17*
types   16–20
organizations
culture and   223
key features   15–16
originator   50
owner   50

Patton, General George S   252–58
payment methods   133
people management   240
performance management   137–38
performance measurement baseline
(PMB)   140
efficiency   144
PEST(LE) model   7–8, 248
PIN model   255
planned value (PV)   140
planning   55, 90, 97–127, 295
activity sequence   103
AMEC case study   124–27
assigning resources   115
back pass   107, 108, 289
balanced scorecards   248
bar chart   98, 289
critical path   110–12, 292
documents   *98*
float   108–10
forward pass   105–08, 293
Gantt chart   41–42, 98, 136, 294
lag   102
lead   102
level of   123
managing schedule   116–21
over-optimism   121–22
owning the plan   122

precedence network   98, 100–04, *101*
progressive elaboration   98
resource allocation   113–15
resource compression   118
resource levelling   117–19
resource planning   115–16
reverse   123
'rolling wave'   98, 299
S-curve   98, 119–21, 131, 299
scenario   248
scope management   99–103
simulation example   109–12
software   122
SWOT analysis   175–76, 248
teams and   284
things to consider   121–22
time, cost or quality   122–23
PRINCE2   3, 4, 5–6, 22, 296
product breakdown structure (PBS)   39, 77,
78, 90
programme manager   89
programmes   89
consolidations   89–93
projects and   91
project champion   50
project management
avoiding failure   53–56
benefits   22
challenges   20–21, *21*
change control   150–53
cost   6
definition   1, 3, 297
estimating   211–32
leadership and   233–59
methodology   3–6, 22–23
processes   10–11
quality   6
scope   60
ten tips for guaranteed failure   62–63
things to consider   22–23
time   6
twenty actions to ensure success
56–59
value   11–13
Project Management Institute (PMI)   3, 4,
5, 10–11, 22, 157, 296
project management plan (PMP)   38–47,
69, 77, 295, 296, 297
approvals   45
contents   39–46
estimating and   213
example   38–46
purpose   38
risk management   42–43
schedule/milestones   41–42, 60

project manager   297
  behaviours   236
  expectations of   276
  focus   *239*
  interpersonal skills   275–76
  leadership   246, 275
  responsibilities   237–38
  role   246
  'soft skills'   274
  task management   237–38
  team management   238, 274
  team members and   238
  weekly checklist   60–61
project sponsor   50, 97, 123, 297
project team   51
projects
  balancing   239–40
  breakdown structure   82–83
  business   *2*
  business case   32–37
  cancelling   69
  characteristics   1
  clarifying needs   29–30
  common reasons for failure   54–56
  common sense guidelines   83–84
  context   7–8
  costs   57
  defining   77–96
  definition   235, 296
  executing   129–62
  life cycle   4, 8–10, *8*, *9*, 22–23, 33, *236*,
      297
  motivation in   251–52
  objectives   29–32
  programme planning   87–88
  purpose   2
  risk   167
  quality plan   57
  social   *2*
  starting   29–75
  status reports   137, 300
  teams and   261–88
  things to consider   90–91
  viability check   32

RACI process   263, 265–66
  example chart   *266*
Reiss, Geoff   91
requirements management   85–86
resource management plan   267,
      269–70
responsibility assignment matrix (RAM)
      81–82, *81*, 91, 263–66, 299
  RACI process   263, 265–66

risk   163, 299
  assessment   168, 184
  cultures   164–66
  definition   164
  opportunity and   167–68
  impact   167, 178–80
  probability   167
  projects and   167
  qualitative approach   166
  quantative approach   166, 188–99
  sources of   173
  tolerances   165
  types   164
  uncertainty and   224
risk breakdown structure (RBS)   182–85,
      183, 299
risk management   42–43, 168–210, 299
  benefits   168–69
  brainstorming   174
  case study   203–08
  checklists   176, 184
  cost   169–70
  cost impact   179–80
  decision tree analysis   188–94
  definition   168
  Delphi technique   174–75
  distributions   199–201
  estimating and   224
  identification   172–78, 183–84, 299
  impact analysis   178–80
  interviews   174
  mitigation strategies   173, 185–87, *186*
  monitoring and review   187–201
  Monte Carlo simulation   194–95, 202,
      295
  nominal group technique (NGT)   174
  ownership   176, *177*
  probability analysis   180–81, *180*, 202
  process   170–72, *171*
  reviews   187, 188
  risk exposure   181–85
  SWOT analysis   175–76, *176*
  techniques   174–78
  things to consider   202
risk management plan   123
risk quantification   299
risk register   172, 176, 299
  corporate   188
  example   *178*
Robbins, Anthony   129
Rumsfeld, Donald   163

schedule variance (SV)   140
senior management   51

sponsor   50, 97, 123, 297
stakeholder grid   52
stakeholders   48–50, 267, 300
    agreement   90
    analysis   50–52, *52*
    management   52
    primary   49
    secondary   50
statement of work (SoW)   82
STEEPLE model   8, 248
Subsea 7 case study   70–75
    project management and execution plan
        (PMEP)   73–75
success criteria   29, 69, 300
suppliers/vendors   51
supporters   51

Talisman Energy case study   23–28
team management   238, 240
team roles   277–82
teams   261–88
    advantages/disadvantages   282–83
    behaviour   277–78
    Belbin roles   277–82, *279*
    case study   285–88
    checklist   271
    chemistry   276–83
    communications   284
    development   274–76, 283–84
    duration   283
    forming   272–73
    functional   283
    growth   271, 272–73
    health check   266
    human resource plan   263, 271
    importance of diversity   284
    management of   275–76
    motivation   270

norming   272–73
organization chart   266–67, *268*,
    271
outputs   275
performing   272–73
project management   262–63
project requirements   262–71
purpose   283
recognition/reward   270, 271
resource management plan   267,
    269–70
role weaknesses   280
storming   272–73
successful   274–75
'task' and 'team' focus   277
things to consider   283–84
training plan   270, 271
types   283
Thamhain, Hans J   253
Tuckman, Dr Bruce   271–73, 283

users   51, 301

variance   60, 134, 136, 301
    analysis   117
    see also cost reporting
variation at completion (VAC)   144–45
vision   246

WGSPN project management
        framework   157–62
Wilemon, David L   253
Wilson, Woodrow   233
W L Gore & Associates   285–88
work breakdown structure (WBS)   39, 77,
        78–79, *79*, 84, 87, 91–93, 99–100,
        123, 130, 302
    estimating and   221